The prophets who predicted Trump's presidency, the factors that led to his nomination, and the analysis, events and prophecies since Donald Trump took office—it's all here in Professor Beverley's comprehensive guide.

I have been close friends with Professor Beverley for twenty-five years. You can trust his research.

—Dr. Rodney Howard-Browne, Revival Ministries International, Tampa, Florida, and spiritual adviser to President Donald Trump

In *God's Man in the White House*, my longtime colleague James Beverley has catalogued, in chronological order, the most comprehensive collection of the Christian prophecies about President Trump. This more-than-useful guide also sets them in the political, social, and religious contexts of contemporary America and allows readers to make their own assessments of the prophecies and the president.

—J. Gordon Melton, Distinguished Professor of American Religious History, Baylor University, Waco, Texas

GOD'S MAN
IN THE
WHITE HOUSE

Donald Trump in Modern Christian Prophecy

JAMES A. BEVERLEY
WITH LARRY N. WILLARD

GOD'S MAN IN THE WHITE HOUSE:
DONALD TRUMP IN MODERN CHRISTIAN PROPHECY
Copyright ©2020 James A. Beverley with Larry N. Willard
All rights reserved
ISBN 978–1-988928–30–2 Soft Cover
ISBN 978–1-988928–31–9 EPUB

Published by: Castle Quay Books
Burlington, ON, Canada | Riviera Beach, FL, USA
Tel: (416) 573-3249
E-mail: info@castlequaybooks.com | www.castlequaybooks.com

Edited by Marina Hofman Willard
Book interior and cover by Burst Impressions

Library and Archives Canada Cataloguing in Publication
Title: God's man in the White House: Donald Trump in modern Christian prophecy /
authors, James A. Beverley, PhD, and, with Larry N. Willard, MDiv
Names: Beverley, James A., author. | Willard, Larry N., 1950- author.
Description: Includes index.
Identifiers: Canadiana 20200167014 | ISBN 9781988928302 (softcover)
Subjects: LCSH: Trump, Donald, 1946- | LCSH: Presidents—United States—Prophecies.
| LCSH: United
States—History—Prophecies. | LCSH: Christianity and politics—United States. | LCSH:
Prophecy—
Christianity.
Classification: LCC E912. B48 2020 | DDC 973.933—dc23

To my wonderful son Derek
My favorite partner in political conversation
With love and admiration

Contents

Prophecies, Events and Analysis

Foreword by Larry Willard

You did not have to be a prophet to predict that Donald Trump would contend for distinction as the most controversial president to hold that office in American history. From the day he emerged out of one of the most combative nominations in Republican history, and then one of the most contentious elections in American history, Donald Trump has polarized US politics like no one before him. Yet, alongside these realities, one of the most interesting side facts is that he has overwhelmingly been embraced by a significant part of the Evangelical community throughout the USA.

Trump's many prevalent and visible traits are not the usual qualities that attract Christians, especially Evangelicals, to a leader. He is somewhat an enigma, with endless adversaries always ready to broadcast and highlight his unchristian side as a brash self-promoter, a verbal brawler, a casino owner, a womanizer, and worldly focused. Yet, these are paradoxically offset by the fact that he is privately highly disciplined, sober, often generous, a clever businessman, a devoted father, and the most pro-life president ever, who, since his election, has surrounded himself with a bounty of men and women of Christian faith and has made the defense and even promotion of religion, religious issues, and traditional values a hallmark and key component of his image and presidency.

This book does not try to itemize, legitimize, analyze, litigate, or defend the many issues or contentious opinions that exist around Trump; rather, we present documentation that, even before his nomination win, a number of prophets predicted he would not just become president of the USA in 2016—uprooting corruption in American politics—but also reverse the lengthy deterioration of traditional US values.

I am aware that many publishers are averse to presenting the prophetic material referenced in these pages, mostly because of the fear that such material can be a death kiss to the credibility of a publisher. Professor

Beverley and I both realize that our intentions and integrity might be questioned by publicizing the prophecies to the public or even by simply doing a book about Donald Trump. However, as you will notice, we present the prophecies without much commentary. We are leaving it up to the readers to make their own judgments about Trump, Republicans, Democrats, the USA, and the accuracy or importance of prophecy to the saga of Donald Trump.

Our interest in the topic of Donald Trump in modern Christian prophecy arises from two factors. First, for Professor Beverley, as he notes in his introduction, his investigation of Trump prophecies arises out of four decades of study of charismatic and Pentecostal prophecy. He has lectured on prophecy-related topics all over the world, including a presentation on the Trump aspect at an international conference in Taiwan in 2018. He has also written frequently on modern Christian prophecy, including his book *Holy Laughter & The Toronto Blessing* (Zondervan, 1995). So, there is an academic angle to this current book.

There is a second and very personally compelling reason—my own interest in the Trump presidency and prophesies concerning his work in the White House, related to my own unusual experience. It was a personal encounter and is one of only two or three such incidents that I have ever experienced. The incident converted my view about Trump as it relates to his selection or at least favor by God for the job as president at this moment in history.

Before I had heard there were people of various prophetic camps making predictions about Trump's political future and identity, one evening I was sitting and thinking about how far Trump had gone in the candidacy selection of the Republican Party, with such fervent opposition from so many segments of the established party faithful and his use of such unconventional approaches. I wondered if it was good for him to win the top job. I didn't doubt his skills and acumen in business and communication, as no one becomes a billionaire without a lot of shrewdness, discipline, and savvy. I also reminded myself that he was not running for the head of a religious denomination, so maybe being a Christian was not the most important quality to meet the need for a leader of America at this time.

Then, quite suddenly, I felt compelled to look up Isaiah 45. I ignored the impulse at first, thinking it was odd and untimely, and I could not remember the topic of the chapter, so why should I look at it? But the sense that I needed to look at that chapter finally apprehended me, and I pulled out my Bible, and I looked it up. My eyes fell on the words in verse 4: "I call you by your name, I name you, though you do not know me." This is a reference to Cyrus, the king of Persia, who was chosen by God to help the Jewish people. I read the whole chapter, and the words struck me and, point after point, seemed to say, "This is why Trump will be selected." Most striking to me were these verses:

"I will go before you
and level the exalted places,
I will break in pieces the doors of bronze
and cut through the bars of iron,
I will give you the treasures of darkness
and the hoards in secret places." (45:2–3)

I wondered if all the Trump-talk about "draining the swamp" had somehow subconsciously impacted my bias and I was merely reading into these verses that Trump would be used to level the exalted ones in Washington, as a kind of Cyrus type.

Since that experience, I have followed the Trump saga closely and, like others, have been amazed at what Trump has endured. If you consider the host of opposition, as fierce and overwhelming as it has been, you might wonder what Trump is made of. The arrows came from traditional and untraditional opponents, both expected and unexpected, from anticipated opposition groups like the liberal Democratic party, the liberal establishment in government, and the liberal part of the media.

But then it grew to new unexpected opposition, including elite members of his own Republican party and elite leaders within the CIA, FBI, and DOJ. The Democratic House even took the extraordinary step of putting forward articles of impeachment against the president.

If Mr. Trump survives and endures all of this and wins another election, as some of these prophesies declare, then we might suspect we have been in the presence of real prophets.

"Only God" could do what is prophesied for Donald Trump this year and in the next term. Only God can take a Cyrus and use him to fulfill the ultimate divine will and plan.

It will not be long before we find out if the prophets are right about Trump in the looming November election. Of course, if Trump loses, that will have to count as evidence that there is something wrong in modern Christian prophecy.

As Professor Beverley notes, the prophetic element should not be the deciding factor in judgment and analysis of President Trump. First, Christian prophets can be seriously wrong, as in predictions that Romney would win in 2012. Second, the prophets sometimes disagree with each other, though on Trump there is virtual unity and commendation. Third, the more important factors for judging the president involve issues of moral character, political acumen, financial health, and social betterment. Nevertheless, the prophetic element is a significant aspect, and we trust that this vast collection is a useful resource.

We have done our part by assembling the major prophecies about Trump in the context of ongoing social and political storms and have saved our readers dozens of hours of searching through the hundreds of prophetic writings that are available. Readers will notice that we have included entries from diverse perspectives (and inclusion of any entry does not necessarily mean endorsement). To avoid endless repetition, we have not put "alleged" when referencing a prophet or prophecy.

Larry N. Willard, MDiv, is founder and publisher for Castle Quay Books Canada. He has held several major senior management positions with top 100 corporations and served for 9 years in various VP roles for Tyndale University in Toronto. Castle Quay Books titles have been nominated for over 70 publishing awards by various groups and have won 29 of those nominations.

Preface

This book identifies Christian prophecies about Trump and introduces the major prophets who have prophesied or written about him. Context for these prophesies is provided by entries referencing the most important events in American politics before and after Trump's 2016 win and opinion pieces about Trump.

Entries are listed in chronological order. Key quotations and sometimes the full text of prophecies and publications are included. (Mark Taylor, for example, gave permission to have all his prophecies printed in this guide.) When the title itself does not depict the content, a brief summary is provided.

The digital version of *God's Man in the White House* provides embedded weblinks to the prophecies, events, and articles referenced in this book.

All quotes and website information included in this book have been taken directly from the authors' work and have not been copy edited for errors, and alterations in content have not been made.

Acknowledgements

I have been working on this project on Donald Trump and prophecy since before the November 2016 victory of Trump over Hillary Clinton. I am grateful to Rebekka Paul, my administrative assistant, for her enormous help on many items and tasks. As well, thanks to Janice Van Eck and Cindy Thompson for their work on design and format issues. I am grateful to Annette Johnson for help on researching details about various prophets and leaders mentioned in this book. For computer problems, I have been rescued by Robert Weiland (former IT specialist, Tyndale) and Dave McPherson (Softec Solutions). Thanks to Brian Cogswell for help on social media.

This guide illustrates that the most important place to go for modern Christian prophecies is The Elijah List, founded and run by Steve Shultz. I am grateful to Steve for help in my continuing research on the topic of prophecy and for assistance in contacting various prophets.

I appreciate the endorsement from my friend Rodney Howard-Browne, one of the great leaders in the charismatic and Pentecostal world. As well, thanks to Gordon Melton, founder of the Institute for the Study of American Religion, for his support and endorsement. This is my fourth book with Larry Willard, my publisher and long-time friend. It is a privilege to work with him.

Further, I am grateful to a circle of family and friends who have provided love and encouragement to me in my life and work, though not necessarily agreement with the contents of this or other books I have written. Thanks to Bob Beverley (my twin brother), my son (Derek Beverley), my daughter (Andrea Beverley), my son-in-law (Julien Desrochers), my uncle (Keith Beverley), my uncle (James Beverley—my namesake), John Wilkinson, Don Wiebe, Larry Matthews, Charis Tobias, Reg Horsman, Gordon Melton, Randy McCooeye, Bruxy Cavey, Ken MacLeod, Kaarina Hsieh, Kevin Rische, Robert Spencer, John Kessler, Carol Greig, Bill

Webb, Sam Mikolaski, Gary LeBlanc, Craig Evans, Darlene Keirstead, Jill Martin-Rische, Terrance Trites, Gary Habermas, Sherrilyn Hall, Dave Collison, Sharon Geldart, John Reddy, Todd Johnson, Eileen Barker, Marta Durski, Miriam MacLeod, Wayne Hsieh, Bruce Fawcett, Bruce Preston, Mark Galli, Lorne Gillcash, Paul Standring, Nina Cavey, Stephen Stultz, Mary-Lynne Rout, Bryan Taylor, Cheryl Nickerson, Johnnie Moore, Trish Wilkinson, Tom Dikens, Jim Sutherland, Annie Bain, Craig Keener, Chad Hillier, David Sherbino, Sandra Quast, Jon Atack, Ian Scott, John Stackhouse, Brian Stiller, Cheryl Geissler, John Axler, Linda Horsman, Hye Sung Gehring, Doug Markle, Bill Rout, Jon Thompson, Rick Anderson, Jerry Reddy, Carolyn Preston, Rick Tobias, Boris Lawryshyn, Norm Keith, Jeannie Taylor, Cathy Clark, Darren Hewer, Ralston Nickerson, Linda Gillcash, Randy Campbell, Andy Bannister, Pat Markle, Steve Matthews, Drew Marshall, David Keirstead, and Massimo Introvigne for their encouragement and help in various ways.

Most important, I am grateful for the support and patience of my wife, Gloria, as she has had to listen to details about all my research over many years.

Introduction by James A. Beverley

Millions of Evangelical Christians supported Donald Trump and helped lead him to victory on November 8, 2016, in the stunning upset of Hillary Clinton. They voted for him in part because they believe Trump is God's "man for the White House." In particular, many Pentecostal and charismatic Christians supported Trump because they believed the Christian prophecies that Trump was the divine choice for president.

It is widely reported that Kim Clement, one of the most famous Christian prophets, announced Trump's presidency in 2007. Mark Taylor—firefighter turned prophet—has become famous for his 2011 announcement that Trump was to be commander in chief, though Taylor originally thought that prophecy was for the 2012 election. Other prophecies about Trump can be traced to the summer and fall of 2015, when Jeremiah Johnson, Lance Wallnau, and Lana Vawser (Australia) made known their belief that God was going to use Trump for divine purposes. (Remarkably, they came at a time when most Evangelical leaders were supporting Ted Cruz or Marco Rubio—and Donald Trump was doing very poorly in polling.) Prophecies about Trump increased with a frenzy during 2016, leading up to the November election. Prophets also issued divine warnings about Barack Obama, Clinton, and the Democrats in general.

While there has always been a prophetic dimension in church history and there are prophets in the Bible, especially the Old Testament, the current manifestation of prophets owes most to the rise of the Pentecostal and charismatic movements in the early twentieth century. In the last few decades, the prophetic element was dominant in several parts of the larger Pentecostal and charismatic world: the Kansas City Fellowship (led by MikeBickle), the Vineyard Movement (connected most famously with John Wimber, now deceased), the Holy Laughter movement (Rodney Howard-Browne), the Toronto Blessing (John and Carol Arnott), the

Pensacola Outpouring (John Kilpatrick), and through the New Apostolic Reformation (most often associated with Peter Wagner, now deceased, and Cindy Jacobs).

These movements form some of the matrix for the prophets who focus on Donald Trump. Providing important support, the prophetic angle to Trump's victory and presidency has been endorsed by leading figures in Pentecostal Christianity, including Stephen Strang, Jim Bakker, Rick Joyner, and Lou Engle.

———

In answer to the question "Is Trump God's man in the White House?" there are four main responses from Christians and from Christian prophets:

1. Most Christian prophets say yes and believe that God chose Trump to make America great again. These prophets are supported by millions of Pentecostals and charismatics who celebrate Trump's presidency, though often with concerns about various moral and spiritual aspects of his life.
2. A few Christian prophets say that Trump represents God's judgment on America and that he is part of an unfolding apocalyptic scenario, either wittingly or not. From this perspective, Trump is a sign that things will get worse as the world awaits the return of Jesus Christ.
3. Many Christians do not believe that the gift of prophecy is for today but believe Trump is God's man for other reasons, like his pro-life stance, views on immigration, and boost of the economy.
4. Christians who oppose Trump usually dismiss the prophets as deluded, lying, or gravely mistaken, at least about Trump. Disagreements over Trump's perceived moral and political failings lead these Christians to a repudiation of the prophetic angle on the president.

Whether one supports Trump or not, three facts should be noted about Christians who believe in the gift of prophecy. First, they do **not** accept everyone who claims to be a prophet. Steve Shultz, for example, does not cover every prophet named in this book in his famous Elijah List because he actually doubts some who claim to speak for God. Given this, it is not fair to lump all the prophets together.

Second, it should be remembered that Pentecostal and charismatic Christians do **not** believe that modern-day prophets are infallible. They can and do make mistakes—as in various predictions that Mitt Romney would win in 2012 and that Republicans would win both the House and the Senate in the 2018 mid-terms.

Third, while almost all contemporary Christian prophets are pro-Trump, they are **not** unaware of his past or present weaknesses. Jeremiah Johnson, for example, issued a prophetic warning in early 2018 about Trump's need for improvement in character.

———

While I leave it up to my readers to make their own judgments about Trump and prophecy, two observations are in order.

First, as Larry Willard notes and bears repeating, decisions about Trump should be based primarily on consideration of matters beyond the prophetic. We have in mind moral integrity in leadership and the best policies and actions regarding economic welfare, terrorism, foreign policy, health care, gun rights, immigration, social security, the education system, Supreme Court appointments, trade policies, the environment, and a pro-life agenda.

Second, in terms of style and emphasis, most prophets studied in this work are offering messages they believe are from God via dreams, visions, natural signs, and inspired thoughts. Other prophets focus on the interpretation of biblical material to talk about Trump's role in God's plans. (Of the latter, Jonathan Cahn, a messianic Christian rabbi in New Jersey, is a prime example.) Readers should assess both types of prophetic claims.

I realize that nothing can bridge the divide in society or the Christian church about Donald Trump, as shown recently in the impeachment battle and by the reaction to *Christianity Today* magazine's recent call for Trump to be removed from office. Regardless of how readers judge Trump and prophecy, I hope this resource is helpful in the task of ethical, political, and spiritual decision making as the November 2020 USA election approaches.

James A. Beverley
Tyndale University, Toronto, Canada
Institute for the Study of American Religion, Woodway, Texas, USA
www.jamesbeverley.com
March 5, 2020

Basic Timeline for Donald Trump and His Family 1905 to 2005

October 11, 1905: Birth of Fred Trump (Donald Trump's father)
May 10, 1912: Birth of Mary Anne MacLeod (Donald Trump's mother)
January 1936: Wedding of Trump's parents
June 14, 1946: Birth of Donald Trump
1959: Confirmation
1968: BS in economics
1971: Move to Manhattan
April 7, 1977: Marriage (Ivana)
December 31, 1977: Birth of Donald Trump Junior
1981: Death of Freddy Trump, a brother, of alcoholism
October 30, 1981: Birth of Ivanka
January 6, 1984: Birth of Eric
1987: *The Art of the Deal*
1992: Divorce from Ivana
October 13, 1993: Birth of Tiffany (daughter of Donald Trump and Marla Maples)
December 1993: Marriage (Marla)
1999: Divorce from Marla
1999: Death of Donald Trump's father
August 2000: Death of Donald Trump's mother
Late 2001/early 2002: Begins friendship with Florida pastor Paula White
2004: *The Apprentice* debuts
January 22, 2005: Marriage (Melania Knauss at church in Palm Beach, Florida)

I. Path to Presidential Run
2005 to 2014

James A. Beverley

January 22, 2005 Bill Yount
Donald Trump's Wedding May Be Prophetic to the Body of Christ!
Elijah List

Yount recounts a vision in which he sees that Trump's wedding is a prophetic sign to and about the church.

January 14, 2006 Kim Clement
Hillary Clinton to Be President in a Christian World
Orlando, Florida

And some of you said, when the Spirit said Hillary Clinton, some of you shouted out "yes." God said, I have already dealt with her heart, not to be President of this Nation but to be president in a Christian world. She will have a testimony second to none and will eventually come out with it and make declaration that Christ Jesus saved her marriage, saved her child, and saved her life. And when this happens there will be a shaking in the Democratic Party so powerful. They will say, what choice do we have? And God says, one of the Kennedy sons who has lost a limb will come into the Kingdom and break the Kennedy curse once and for all, says the Spirit of God.

March 20, 2006 Donald Trump
Birth of Barron

February 10, 2007 Kim Clement
Kim Clement on a president with "hot blood" [Scottsdale, Arizona]
HouseofDestiny.org

For God says, let Me remind you I will place at your helm a President that shall pray to Me, says the Lord. He will pray to Me. And God says, in the next two terms there will be a praying President, not a religious one, for I will fool the people, says the Lord. I will fool the people, yes I will. God says, the one that is chosen shall go in and they shall say, he has hot blood. For the Spirit God says, yes he may have hot blood, but he will bring the walls of protection on this country in a greater way and the economy of this country shall change rapidly, says the Lord of Hosts. God says, I will put at your helm for two terms a President that will pray but he will not be a praying President when he starts. I will put him in Office and then I will baptize him with the Holy Spirit and My power, says the Lord of Hosts.

April 4, 2007 Kim Clement

Kim Clement on Trump (YouTube) Redding, California
Time Magazine Has to Say What God Wants
Elijah List, April 14 report

The Spirit of God said, this is a moment of resurrection. For the Spirit of God says, honor Me with your praise and acceptance of this that I say to you. This that shall take place shall be the most unusual thing, a transfiguration, a going into the marketplace if you wish, into the news media. Where Time Magazine will have no choice but to say what I want them to say. Newsweek, what I want to say. The View, what I want to say. Trump shall become a trumpet, says the Lord! No, you didn't hear me. Trump shall become a Trumpet. Are you listening to me? I will raise up the Trump to become a trumpet and Bill Gates to open up the gate of a financial realm for the Church, says the Spirit of the Living God!

For God said, I will not forget 911. I will not forget what took place that day and I will not forget the gatekeeper that watched over New York who will once again stand and watch over this Nation, says the Spirit of God. It shall come to pass that the man that I place in the highest office shall go in whispering My name. But God said, when he enters into the office he will be shouting out by the power of the Spirit for I shall fill him with My Spirit when he goes into office and there will be a praying man in the highest seat in your land. And God says, even a greater move of the Spirit shall take place and your enemies will finally be subdued by the year 2009.

January 5, 2011 Donald Trump

Trump talks with Forbes about run for presidency

March 17, 2011 Donald Trump

Trump questions whether President Obama was born in the USA.

April 28, 2011 Mark Taylor
Commander in Chief [#1 in list of Taylor's prophecies]
Sord Rescue

Taylor admits on the *Jim Bakker Show* in 2016 that he thought this prophecy was for 2012. Taylor claims that God said His people were not ready for change in 2012 and thus the prophecy was shifted to 2016.

The Spirit of God says, I have chosen this man, Donald Trump, for such a time as this. For as Benjamin Netanyahu is to Israel, so shall this man be to the United States of America! For I will use this man to bring honor, respect and restoration to America.

America will be respected once again as the most powerful and prosperous nation on earth, (other than Israel). The dollar will be the strongest it has ever been in the history of the United States, and will once again be the currency by which all others are judged.

The Spirit of God says, the enemy will quake and shake and fear this man I have anointed. They will even quake and shake when he announces he is running for president, it will be like the shot heard across the world. The enemy will say what shall we do now? This man knows all our tricks and schemes. We have been robbing America for decades, what shall we do to stop this? The Spirit says HA! No one shall stop this that I have started! For the enemy has stolen from America for decades and it stops now! For I will use this man to reap the harvest that the United States has sown for and plunder from the enemy what he has stolen and return it 7 fold back to the United States. The enemy will say Israel, Israel, what about Israel? For Israel will be protected by America once again. The Spirit says yes! America will once again stand hand and hand with Israel, and the two shall be as one. For the ties between Israel and America will be stronger than ever, and Israel will flourish like never before.

The Spirit of God says, I will protect America and Israel, for this next president will be a man of his word, when he speaks the world will listen and know that there is something greater in him than all the others before him. This man's word is his bond and the world and America will know this and the enemy will fear this, for this man will be fearless.

The Spirit says, when the financial harvest begins so shall it parallel in the spiritual for America. The Spirit of God says, in this next election they will spend billions to keep this president in; it will be like flushing their money down the toilet. Let them waist their money, for it comes from and it is being used by evil forces at work, but they will not succeed, for this next election will be a clean sweep for the man I have chosen. They will say things about this man (the enemy), but it will not affect him, and they shall say it rolls off of him like the duck, for as the feathers of a duck protect it, so shall my feathers protect this next president. Even mainstream news media will be captivated by this man and the abilities that I have gifted him with, and they will even begin to agree with him says the Spirit of God.

May 16, 2011 Donald Trump
Trump decides he will not run for president in 2012.

July 21, 2012 Benny Hinn
The Sign Will Be Billy Graham's Death
YouTube

Hinn says God told him in 1989 that the deaths of Oral Roberts and Billy Graham "will be the key—it will be the sign of the beginning of the greatest revival on earth ... Oral is home, Billy is about to go home" (3:10).

[While Hinn does not mention Trump, he brings up a common theme in charismatic prophecy: belief that a great revival will soon be sweeping the globe.]

September 2012 Donald Trump
Trump visits Liberty University at invitation of Falwell Jr. and Johnnie Moore.

November 6, 2012 Barack Obama
Obama wins re-election.

November 2012 Jeremiah Johnson
After Obama was re-elected in 2012, Johnson had a series of dreams that warned about Obama and Hillary Clinton.

Here is an excerpt from Johnson's book *Chronicles of the Unknown Dreamer 2013*:

In the dream I found myself working in a carpet truck and pulling up to the White House in Washington D.C. I walked inside and began tearing up the carpet and crying out, "We are living in the days of King Hezekiah." The White House staff became very alarmed and gathered around me as I began to weep. Sobbing and crawling around on my hands and knees, I said to them, "Was it not in the days of King Hezekiah where he foolishly welcomed the Babylonians into his kingdom, and there was nothing in his house nor in all his dominion that Hezekiah did not show the Babylonians? Behold, President Obama has acted foolishly. He has welcomed the Muslim Brotherhood into the White House. He has welcomed assassins who have been trained to kill the patriotic spirit. President Obama has formed an unholy alliance with Hillary Clinton. They wish to welcome the Islamic regime into America. He is and will continue to appoint strategic men and women in positions of authority to pave the way for Hillary."

At this point in the dream, the White House staff had attacked me and thrown me out on the White House steps. I got into my carpet truck and drove to a meeting of church leaders who were anxiously awaiting my arrival. Everyone seemed to know I had entered the White House and prophesied to the staff. I walked into the meeting with the pastors and leaders and prophesied to them. This is what the Lord says, "The end time church must not be deceived in this hour. They must intercede that the Muslim Brotherhood be exposed. America must not make a pact with Egypt against Israel. The will on Capitol Hill is demonically influenced. EVEN NOW I AM BREATHING UPON RUBIO. I am breathing upon those who carry the patriotic spirit of America. This nation must return to Me with weeping and wailing. They must pray for deception and demonic strategy to be revealed among President Obama and Hillary Clinton." Then I awoke.

February 4, 2013 Marko Joensuu
Why did so many prophets get the US election wrong?
Mentoring Prophets

On the false prophecies that Romney would defeat Obama.

Prophetic ministry is about staying in the counsel of the Lord rather than declaring what you might have heard from the Lord in some prophetic conference at the earliest opportunity. That takes time. It doesn't fit with our busy schedules, and it definitely doesn't fit with the demand of running a profitable prophetic business. But the prophets should learn to shut up if the Lord hasn't spoken. There's only one way to get out of the bankrupt state of the Western prophetic movement. It is to stop listening to all other voices and begin to listen to God.

August 12, 2013 Patricia King
"Pitfalls of a Spiritual Experience"
Charisma

Are there dangers in the school of spiritual experience? Yes! If a person lives outside the perimeters of the Word, way or will of God in any area of his life, danger lurks.

While Patricia King does not mention Trump in this teaching, her teaching about obedience to the Bible ("the Word") is a common theme among all Christian prophets.

April 20, 2013 Kim Clement
Donald, Mr. Clark, American Flag and Election
YouTube

Kim gives a prophetic word to Mr. Clark and a man named Donald:

I feel that cancers are being broken; I feel that there are sicknesses and diseases that are being healed at this very moment right now. There is a man by the name of Mr. Clark and there is also another man by the name of Donald. You are both watching me, saying could it be that God is speaking to me? Yes, He is! Somebody, just a few minutes before you came on the show, you went out and you took the American flag and you said, "I'm proud of my nation." You raised it up, and God said, "You have been determined through your prayers to influence this nation." You're watching me; you're an influential person. The Spirit of God says, "Hear the word of the prophet to you as a king, I will open that door that you prayed about and when it comes time for the election, you will be elected."

Kim's assistant, Sunil Isaac, says later that Kim did not know it was Donald Trump. (See remarks on this and other items in Isaac's reflection on the November 2016 election.)

November 2013 Donald Trump
Trump and his wife attend birthday party for Billy Graham.

2013 Mark Taylor
Medical appointment with Dr. Don Colbert; Taylor shows his "commander-in-chief" prophecy to Dr. Colbert and his wife, Mary.

February 22, 2014 Kim Clement
Prophetic Alert
HouseofDestiny.org

One of Kim Clement's most famous prophecies speaks about a vision of a man who will become president of the United States and will be used of God to restore America and Israel. Some of the description fits Donald Trump, but some does not fit.

Hear Me, for I have found a man after My own heart. I have found a man after My own heart and he is amongst you. He is one of the brothers but singled out for Presidency of the United States of America.

I have searched for a man and a woman who would stand in the Oval Office and pray and call for the restoration of the fortunes of Zion. I have looked for a man who would pray for the restoration of the fortunes of Zion.

Watch how I change everything, for there shall be those who are in justice. There are those who are in a strong position, I'm just hearing this now, in the highest court in the land, the Supreme Court. Two shall step down for the embarrassment of what shall take place for I wish to place in the highest court in the land, righteousness.

I shouted and they all shouted. They were one; they were one; one party, one party of people. It continued until I realized that in the unity of these, amongst them stood one that God had set aside to be the leader of this nation. I said why am I hearing this so soon? Surely You would show me a little bit of it closer to the time. And the Spirit of God said to me, this man has a humble stature but he is a genius. And then I heard "gold." I wasn't sure if this was attached to his name, but He said to me, he will restore the fortunes in this nation because of his brilliance.

And the Spirit of God made me look at him, and He said, this man will throttle the enemies of Israel. This man will throttle the enemies of the West, and there are highly embarrassing moments that are about to occur for many, many politicians in this nation. There will be a shaking amongst the Democrats in the upcoming elections, but unsettling for the Republicans. Why is God doing this? For God said, I am dissatisfied with what emerges from both parties.

And then there is a nation, He showed me, He took me, itching for a new kind of war with America. They will shout, "Impeach, impeach," they say, but nay. This nation shall come very subtly but he shall not come in the time of President Obama. They shall come when this new one arises, My David that I have set aside for this nation, a man of prayer, a man of choice words, not a man who is verbose, who has verbosity, who speaks too much. They will even say, "This man is not speaking enough," but God says, I have set him aside. They will shout, "Impeach, impeach," but this shall not happen, and then, God says, highly embarrassing moments when another Snowden arises and people will become very afraid.

In this next week, this man shall begin to emerge, and in the following two weeks, which is a three-week period, he shall slowly come to the fore.

I have placed that man amongst you, a humble man. And as Samuel stood before the brothers, and they had rejected David to come because of his age, take all these little remarks I'm giving you, they are gems. The name and the word "gold," remember that. A man that is amongst them but is young. And God says, these that shall reject him shall be shocked at how he takes the giant down. Now hear me please. The giant of debt, the giants that have come, the brothers of Goliath, stand in glee watching America. "We will cripple you. You will lose your credit." But God said, watch, I said 20,000. Look not to Wall Street; however, observe.

God says, once you recognize the man that I have raised up, pray, for the enemy will do everything in his power to put a witch in the White House. Did anybody hear what He just said? For Jezebel has chased away the prophets and even Elijah. Now I have said, go back, for this shall be dismantled so that there will be no more corruption in the White House, says the Spirit.

America, freedom is yours in the Spirit! Israel, freedom to reign— America, righteous judgment and a great shaking of the Spirit in America!

March 1, 2014 Bob Jones
"Prophecy from 2006 Still Stirs"
Charisma News

Various contemporary prophets cite Jones frequently. [Jones passed away on February 14, 2014.]

October 3, 2014 Donald Trump
Trump calls into Sirius XM Radio to talk with Joel and Victoria Osteen
YouTube

II. Decision to Run
and Early Campaign
2015

March 2, 2015 Hillary Clinton
"Hillary Clinton Used Personal Email Account at State Dept., Possibly Breaking Rules"
Michael S. Schmidt at *New York Times*

March 14, 2015 Kim Clement
Prophecy of a strong figure to help America
HouseofDestiny.org and YouTube

I'm actually feeling right now that I'm standing in 2017 and I feel like it's—when are the elections for the new President? (Sunil says 2016) 2016—I'm standing, I'm feeling like I'm standing in 2017 and things have been disrupted so badly that people are confused because their plans didn't work. I'm seeing this very strong figure standing in the United States of America saying, now we've got to clean up the mess! And they have the skill and the ability to do it. And they'll say, well the pen has already signed. And I'm hearing this strong figure saying, I don't care what was signed, we will make the changes. So I want to encourage many of you that are watching that are saying we hear about judgment and we hear about fear. Fear's been brought upon our nation because of the display of ISIS, the display of the beheadings and the display of the arrogance and all of this—and yet God is doing some stuff that we don't even know about. That's what we're going to find out. And so I got caught up just into the next administration, if you wish, and I didn't see bad. I saw calmness, I saw peace—there's so much stuff that's coming to my head right now, it's amazing.

April 27, 2015 Paula White
Trump's spiritual advisor and long-time friend, Paula White, marries Jonathan Cain, a famous rock star with the group Journey.

Summer 2015 Democratic National Committee
Hackers gain access to the servers of the Democratic National Committee.

June 16, 2015 Donald Trump
Trump announces run for presidency.

Trump's most controversial statement involved immigration: "When Mexico sends its people, they're not sending their best. They're not sending you. They're not sending you. They're sending people that have lots of problems, and they're bringing those problems with us. They're bringing drugs. They're bringing crime. They're rapists. And some, I assume, are good people."

June 16, 2015 Donald Trump
"Witless Ape Rides Escalator"
Kevin Williamson at *National Review*

"Donald Trump may be the man America needs. Having been through four bankruptcies, the ridiculous buffoon with the worst taste since Caligula is uniquely positioned to lead the most indebted organization in the history of the human race. The problem with messiah complexes is that there's no way to know whether you are going to rise on the third day unless somebody crucifies you. Trump has announced, and I say we get started on that."

[This *National Review* piece is important since it indicates the animosity towards Trump at the very beginning of his run for president from consistently conservative outlets.]

June 20, 2015 Mark Taylor
American Pharaoh Article [#2 in list]
Sord Rescue

Hello brothers and sisters in the Lord I wanted to share something with you I believe will be an encouragement to the body of Christ, which the Lord led me to do back in 2011. I will keep this short. Prophet Paul Keith Davis always spoke of how the horse Secretariat represented the end time church. Well, while watching the movie (Secretariat), I kept hearing "there's another one coming, there's another one coming." I then sat down to listen and write what the Lord was saying.

I wrote a prophetic word on 7–24–11 called The Great Horse, it's a little lengthy, so I will just give you the main parts. What God was saying, is that there is another Triple Crown winner coming and it would be a sign to the church and this generation that her time to break out is here. He would break records including Secretariat's, a sign to the church it would do things never seen before.

American Pharaoh broke Secretariat's time in the last turn, quarter mile, a sign that we are in the last turn coming into the home stretch toward the finish line. Does this mean we are in the end times? Yes, does it mean we are at the end of time? NO! There is still much to be done, the end time harvest is just beginning where God will bring 1 billion souls into his kingdom before he returns. Well, it has happened, the Triple Crown, and I believe this was our sign for the American church. (American Pharaoh).

The word Pharaoh means Great House, Royal Palace. He had the number 5 which is Grace and Redemption, the winning time was 2: 26 which I believe is Rev 2: 26, (to all who are victorious, who obey me to the very end, to them I will give authority over all the nations). The jockey was from a 12-child family, and was the 12th Triple Crown win. 12 means Gods government (will be established upon the earth).

You will see a lot of the number 12 in the coming season. Donald Trump 12th candidate to enter the presidential race, hhhmmm, more on that another time.

Some of the names in American Pharaoh's bloodline- Empire Maker, Star of Goshen, Lord at War, Unbridled, Image of Reality, General, Key to the Kingdom, if these aren't prophetic signs then I don't know what is. There is an article posted on Elijahlist.com from Jonny Enlow and the revelation he got from the Triple Crown race, I encourage you to read it.

Back in 2013, I was listening to Gen. Eisenhower's D-Day speech and kept sensing something was there. I again sat down to write the speech and see what the Lord was saying. I heard him say, "I want you to re-write the speech and address it to my church," so I did just that, but didn't release it as I didn't know the timing. Then it dawned on me that the Triple Crown race was on D-Day, June 6th 2015. As I was reading the speech, I felt now was the time to release it. Below is the speech in pdf format. Feel free to share it as I hope it encourages the Body of Christ. After you read it, go to YouTube and search for Rick Pino and his sing called The Army of God, it will bless you. NOW IS THE TIME! Advance! Do not retreat. I like what Gen. Patton said, "I don't like paying for the same real-estate twice." Blessings, Mark.

July 1, 2015 Donald Trump
Trump references Kathryn Steinle in immigration debates. She was killed in a shooting at Pier 14 in San Francisco. An illegal immigrant was charged with murder but only convicted of illegal possession of a firearm.

July 7, 2015 Stephen Strang
Strang reports on founding of Charismatic Caucus.

July 10, 2015 Hillary Clinton
FBI opens criminal investigation into Hillary Clinton's use of classified material.

July 15, 2015 Jeremiah Johnson
"Prophecy about Donald Trump as Cyrus figure"
Prophetic Insight from *Charisma*

In His great wisdom throughout the course of human history, God has chosen not only to fulfill His plans and purposes through men and women who have yielded to the sound of His voice, but He has also chosen to accomplish His will through men and women who have ignored and rebelled against Him. One such man was King Cyrus mentioned in Isaiah 45.

Isaiah prophesied of Cyrus and speaks as a mouthpiece of the Lord when he declared, "I have even called you by your name [Cyrus]; I have named you, though you have not known Me. I am the Lord and there is no other; there is no God besides Me. I strengthen you, though you have not known Me, so that they may know from the rising of the sun and from the west that there is no one besides Me. I am the Lord, and there is no other" (Is. 45: 4–6).

What a powerful and profound prophetic declaration to a man who did not know or serve the Lord! Could God not use the wicked and ungodly to bring about His plans and purposes thousands of years ago and can He not still do the same thing again, especially in the midst of the crisis that we find America in today?

I was in a time of prayer several weeks ago when God began to speak to me concerning the destiny of Donald Trump in America. The Holy Spirit spoke to me and said, "Trump shall become My trumpet to the American people, for he possesses qualities that are even hard to find in My people these days. Trump does not fear man nor will he allow deception and lies to go unnoticed. I am going to use him to expose darkness and perversion in America like never before, but you must understand that he is like a bull in a china closet. Many will want to throw him away because he will disturb their sense of peace and tranquility, but you must listen through the bantering to discover the truth that I will speak through him. I will use the wealth that I have given him to expose and launch investigations searching for the truth. Just as I raised up Cyrus to fulfill My purposes and plans, so have I raised up Trump to fulfill my purposes and plans prior to the 2016 election. You must listen to the trumpet very closely for he will sound the alarm and many will be blessed because of his compassion and mercy. Though many see the outward pride and arrogance, I have given him the tender heart of a father that wants to lend a helping hand to the poor and the needy, to the foreigner and the stranger."

[This prophecy and statement was featured in *Charisma* magazine's Prophetic Insight blog on July 28th but the full text is no longer available at the *Charisma* site. The full prophecy and statement from Jeremiah is copied from other sites.]

July 18, 2015 Donald Trump
Trump appears at Leadership Summit in Ames, Iowa, hosted by The Family Leader.

Trump was applauded for several of his campaign platforms but attacked for his criticism of Sen. John McCain as a war hero. Trump's criticism of McCain was due to the latter's attack on the rally Trump held in Phoenix a week earlier.

Trump was asked at the Ames Summit whether he had ever asked God for forgiveness. Trump replied, "I am not sure I have … Now, when I take— you know, when we go in church and when I drink my little wine, which is about the only wine I drink, and have my little cracker, I guess that is a form of asking for forgiveness."

July 26, 2015 Lance Wallnau
Is Donald Trump Being Used as a Trumpet?
Facebook

"A few years ago my friend Kim Clement spoke about Donald TRUMP being a TRUMPET. Kim mentioned MAY and OCTOBER as being significant months in a MOVEMENT that NOBODY SAW COMING."

July 28, 2015 Jeremiah Johnson
Clarification of Prophecy About Trump

What the article does NOT say:
1. Donald Trump will be the next US President.
2. Donald Trump will be the GOP nominee.
3. That I (Jeremiah Johnson) personally support and endorse Donald Trump's personal moral decisions or anything he has publicly said regarding politics (including the past).
4. Donald Trump is a devout Christian and His life aligns with biblical principles.
What the article does say:
1. Donald Trump is going to be used by God as a trumpet in America to expose darkness and perversion.
2. Christians must look past/through his bantering and listen for the truth that God is going to make known through him.
3. God can use anyone He chooses to fulfill His purposes and plans in the earth. Nebuchadnezzar, Cyrus, the Jews who crucified Jesus, or Donald Trump among many.
After reading through about 1,000 pieces of mail in the last 24 hours, here is my conclusion:
Some Christians appear to be absolutely infuriated at the thought or prophetic word that God is going to use Donald Trump as a Trumpet to expose darkness and bring truth because of His moral background and political views. Perhaps God not being limited, subjected, and dependent to who human beings think He should use for His glory reveals their own issues with God, not a prophetic word.
I, like many of you, was shocked by the word I received regarding Donald Trump. Trust me when I say it was given with fear and trembling.

Again, I am not called to prophesy what I think or what my opinion is. I simply deliver the word of the Lord and encourage the saints to test and judge what has been spoken.

I will publicly repent to the body of Christ if what was prophesied does not come to pass.

Johnson's July 15 prophecy led to enormous response, including heavy criticism. Johnson has a chapter on his 2015 prophecy and the subsequent controversy in his book *Trump, 2019, and Beyond*, released in 2019. These statements from Johnson (copied from a third-party website) were originally on Facebook but were taken down.

July 29, 2015 Jeremiah Johnson
Donald Trump Is the New Word of God?
Benjamin Corey at Patheos site

Benjamin Corey mocks the Jeremiah Johnson prophecy from *Charisma:* "I'm not going to lie, what I just read is the dumbest thing I've read in my life. I'm not trying to be overly or unnecessarily critical, either. It just really, truly, is the dumbest thing I've ever read. I had to read it three times to make sure it wasn't the Onion."

After quoting Johnson, Corey writes, "God has given Trump a tender heart to help the poor and immigrants? People will be blessed by his compassion? Apparently God hasn't been watching the news. Or seen his twitter feed. Or met him."

Late July 2015 Steve Bremner
Judging Prophetic Words with Discernment
SteveBremner.com

Bremner critiques Johnson prophecy from July 15; Bremner later admits error. [See his November 2016 post "Wiping Prophetic Egg Off My Face."]

August 6, 2015 Donald Trump
First Republican debate (Cleveland, Ohio)

August 7, 2015 Donald Trump
Trump attacks Megyn Kelly.

August 7, 2015 Larry Tomczak
"Fresh from the Frontline: Why Donald Trump Is Dominating"
The Christian Post

Ten reasons for Trump's popularity are given.

August 7, 2015 Prophecy News Network
PROPHECY! Donald Trump Shall Become the TRUMPET?
PNN News and Ministry Network

A radio show mentions the meaning of Trump's first and last name and references Jeremiah Johnson's prophecy about Trump but does not argue that Trump will be president.

August 10, 2015 Jeremiah Johnson
Critique of Jeremiah Johnson: Trump Shall Be the Trumpet
Ave Maria Radio

The Catholic writer at Ave Maria Radio applauds Catholic "apostolic authority in the Catholic Church that can, in principle, say Nay to this 'prophet.'" The Ave Maria Radio Facebook page announces the radio piece the same day.

August 11, 2015 Jeremiah Johnson
"Firestorm Erupts Over Trump's 'Bible Connection'"
Joe Kovacs at WND [World Net Daily]

Coverage of Jeremiah Johnson's dream about Donald Trump.

August 21, 2015 Donald Trump
Huge rally (Mobile, Alabama)

A photo of Sydnie Shuford at the rally went viral and was used to trash Trump supporters.

Fall 2015 Fusion GPS
Washington Free Beacon hires Fusion GPS to do research on Trump and several other Republican candidates.

[See Michael Horowitz Inspector General report, December 2019, p. 129, note 212.]

August 26, 2015 Donald Trump
"Donald Trump Plans Meeting with Evangelicals"
Reid Epstein at *Wall Street Journal*

August 28, 2015 Michael Brown
"An Open Letter to Donald Trump"
The Christian Post

"There's often a fine line between confidence and arrogance, between self-assurance and pride (often, the line is anything but fine), and, to many of us following you with interest, you seem to have crossed that line. Pride really does kill! So, my heartfelt suggestion to you, sir, is that you humble yourself before your Creator, that you recognize your sins and shortcomings, asking Him for forgiveness through the cross, and that you ask Him to help you to be the kind of man that America (and the nations) need at this critical time in world history."

September 4, 2015 Joel Belz
"An Arrogant Blowhard"
World Magazine

"With more than 20 men and women from the two major political parties now vying to be nominated to a try for the presidency in the 2016 general election, it's admittedly a little tricky to sort out better from best. But in this unique lineup, it shouldn't be so hard to identify the fraudulent worst."

September 14, 2015 Robert Jeffress
Donald Trump has rally (Dallas, Texas)

Trump met Robert Jeffress, pastor of First Baptist Church (Dallas), for the first time. Trump thanks Jeffress for his support.

September 16, 2015 Donald Trump
Second Republican debate (Simi Valley, California)

September 17, 2015 Russell Moore
"Have Evangelicals Who Support Trump Lost Their Values?"
New York Times

Donald J. Trump stands astride the polls in the Republican presidential race, beating all comers in virtually every demographic of the primary electorate. Most illogical is his support from evangelicals and other social conservatives. To back Mr. Trump, these voters must repudiate everything they believe.

Jesus taught his disciples to "count the cost" of following him. We should know, he said, where we're going and what we're leaving behind. We should also count the cost of following Donald Trump. To do so would mean that we've decided to join the other side of the culture war, that image and celebrity and money and power and social Darwinist "winning" trump the conservation of moral principles and a just society. We ought to listen, to get past the boisterous confidence and the television lights and the waving arms and hear just whose speech we're applauding.

September 2015 Kim Clement
Kim Clement has stroke.

September 25, 2015 Donald Trump
Value Voters Summit, Family Research Council (Washington, DC)
CNN

A straw poll from the summit showed the following percentages for preference to go to the White House:
Ted Cruz 35
Ben Carson 18
Mike Huckabee 14
Marco Rubio 13
Donald Trump 5

September 26, 2015 Molly Worthen
"Donald Trump and the Rise of the Moral Minority"
The New York Times

"Mr. Trump's popularity among the evangelical rank and file suggests that even if his Christian critics can offer appealing models for a new 'moral minority,' they may have hit a political dead end. On the campaign trail, anger and xenophobia play better than repentance and grace."

September 28, 2015 Donald Trump
Major coverage of religious leaders praying for Donald Trump:
    Praying for Donald Trump (YouTube clip from Don Nori)
    Donald Trump Prays with Religious Leaders (YouTube clip)
    CNN coverage
    David Brody on CBN NEWS
    Jessilyn Lancaster Charisma News report

Paula White set up the meeting at Trump Tower. This is the meeting where Darrell Scott, a major Black leader, met Lance Wallnau.

October 3, 2015 Lance Wallnau
Meeting Donald Trump: An Insider's Report
Facebook

October 6, 2015 Kenneth Copeland
"Did Kenneth Copeland Really Endorse Donald Trump for President?"
Jennifer Le Claire at *Charisma News*

This is about controversy over a September 28 prayer meeting for Trump.

October 7, 2015 Mark Taylor
America, America [#3 in list]
Sord Rescue

America, America 10-a7–15 The spirit of God says, "America, America, oh how I love thee America, America, oh how I have chosen thee! For as England was to the D-Day invasion, so shall America be for my end time harvest. For England was the Headquarters, the hub from which the D-Day assault was launched, so shall it be for my America for the end time harvest. For as England had men, women, equipment, food, money, weapons, and supplies of all kinds which poured in from all over the world, so shall all these things pour into my chosen America.

America I have chosen you as the launching platform for the world-wide assault on the spiritually oppressed peoples of the earth. People will say how are we chosen? It's as if America is frozen. Am I not the God of the universe and all of creation? I have heard the cries of my people that have sought my face, and I WILL HEAL THEIR NATION! People will ask how will I do this. I shall do this in two parts."

First- The Spirit of God says, "Army of God, out of the darkness! I COMMAND YOU TO ARISE AND TAKE YOUR PLACE! For I have given you extra time, mercy and grace. Go, Go, Go, do not slow down. Begin to take and hold your ground, for there is no more time to waste. America will once again be the great light. The enemy will say, "Oh the Light, the Light it shines so bright, there is nothing else left to do but take flight." And indeed they will. The sign will be, a mass exodus in the natural as the spiritual flee."

Second- The Spirit of God says, "The gate keeper, the gate keeper, the President of the United States is the spiritual gate keeper. I have chosen this man Donald Trump and anointed him as President for such a time as this. Can you not see this? For even in his name, Donald- meaning world leader, (spiritual connotation faithful). Trump- meaning to get the better of, or to outrank or defeat someone or something often in a highly public way.

This man I have chosen, will be a faithful world leader, and together with my army, will defeat all of America's enemies in the spiritual and in the natural. You will see it manifest before your eyes. I will use this man to shut gates, doors, and portals that this past president has opened. He will open gates, doors, and portals this past president has shut. My army shall not be silenced; they will begin to see he is the one I have chosen. They will begin to rally around him and keep him covered in spiritual support, and as you gain ground they will say America is not frozen.

The seeds, the seeds, why is no one asking about the seeds? What about all the seeds America has sown since her birth? America has never received her harvest. For I will use President Trump and my army to bring back to America all that she has sown. This will be used for my harvest. America will prosper like never before in her history as a nation. All of the financial seeds you have sown around the world, food, clothing, 90 percent of my gospel that has gone through out the earth, has come from my chosen America. Her blood has been spilled on foreign soil to free the oppressed so that my gospel could go forward. America your harvest is here! It shall parallel with your spiritual harvest in the natural, so do not fear."

The Spirit of God says, "The border, the border, is a 2000 mile gate, that's flowing across with demonic hate. I will use my President to shut this gate and seal it shut. It must be shut. Then I will use him and my army to root out evil structures that are still there, to the point that the government will begin to call on my army. They will prophetically locate these structures so they may be dismantled before any evil can take place.

Opec, Opec take a hike, for I am tired of your evil energy spikes. When my President takes office you will shake and quake, you will say America no longer needs us and that is true, for she will be energy independent for my red, white and blue. For a sign will be given when prices go low, for a gallon of gas will be one dollar and below."

The Spirit of God says, "The Supreme Court shall lose three, and my President shall pick new ones directly from MY TREE!

Are you still not convinced that he's my anointed, and that he's the one I have appointed? Why can no one figure it out, the news media, the people, and the so called wise. Why, when he's attacked, do his poll numbers rise? Those who attack him, their numbers go low, even to the point of a big fat zero. It's simple to see, this man I have appointed, for in my word, is your answer. I said 'do not touch my anointed, especially my prophets.' If you are still not convinced about what my word says, another sign will be given. It will be a WARNING TO ALL, especially those who will NOT LISTEN."

The Spirit of God says, "The sign will be El-Chappo, El-Chappo, your evil reign has come to an end. Who do you think you are attacking my anointed? Turn yourself in and repent and I will spare you. If you do not, you and those that follow you will surely die a very public death for the entire world to see. For no one touches my anointed. I the Lord am an all seeing and all knowing God. I will be the one to disclose your location, the den, the den, that you and your vipers hide in. For time is short and the spirit of death is at your door, and the world will see your dead body and the red shirt you wore."

October 10, 2015 Lance Wallnau and Darrell Scott
Trump holds rally (Atlanta).

Pastor Darrell Scott (New Spirit Revival Center in Cleveland, founded by Darrell and his wife, Belinda) invited Lance Wallnau to join him at the Atlanta rally. Wallnau and Darrell Scott met at Trump Tower in September.

[See October 12, following, on Lance Wallnau for his support of Trump at Atlanta rally.]

October 11, 2015 Lana Vawser
Dream Regarding United States Election—Call to Prayer!
Lanavawser.com

Firstly, I want to preface this word by saying that I do not have a political agenda for the United States of America. I am simply one person in Australia who has a huge heart of love for this beautiful nation and to see the destiny of the United States established and the Kingdom of God extended, releasing a huge wave of revelation of His goodness and love. I also want to say that I do not base what I am about to share on any 'policies' that I have heard, but simply what I believe the Lord revealed to me in a dream concerning the candidates. This word is not in any way to 'sway' anyone in their political views, but simply to release a revelation from the Lord that I believe needs to be covered in prayer.

I had a dream recently where I was in a political arena and I saw Donald Trump and he was passionately putting forward his policies. In this dream I could not "hear" what he was saying, I just remember seeing him speaking with great passion.

Suddenly, I was lifted above the United States of America and I saw the nation as if I was looking at a map. Written across the United States of America was the word "TRUMP" in big letters.

As I looked at this word suddenly the letters began to rearrange and the word went from "TRUMP" to "TRIUMPH."

I then heard the Lord speak loudly in my dream "TRUMP SHALL LEAD THE UNITED STATES OF AMERICA INTO TRIUMPH!!!"

As I was waking up out of the dream I heard the words "TRUMP SHALL LEAD THE UNITED STATES OF AMERICA INTO VICTORY!!!"

As I came to the end of typing this dream I heard the words "Angels of triumph have been assigned to Trump."

I believe the Lord is inviting us to seek His heart and to partner with Him in prayer to see the United States of America brought back into a place of godly victory and triumph in whichever way that manifests.

I am simply releasing that which was released to me.

Standing with you in prayer my friends in the United States of America, Lana Vawser.

October 12, 2015 Lana Vawser
Note from Lana
Lanavawser.com

Over the past 24 hours I have received lots of messages and comments, sadly many sent with great verbal attack, concerning the dream I released about Donald Trump and I feel I need to clarify something. Many have interpreted this dream as the Lord telling me that Donald Trump would be the next President. I have not said that but I do believe the Lord IS using Donald Trump in this season.

I simply released that which was given to me so the people of God can pray and continue to seek His heart for their nation.

October 12, 2015 Lance Wallnau
My Unusual Saturday with Trump
Facebook and Scribd

Wallnau gets mistaken for Michael Cohen in TV interview. After clarifying his identity, Wallnau states, "Donald Trump is anointed in this season to break things open. Like Jeremiah of old he has an assignment to tear down and to uproot and to plant. He has broken up a demonic cartel of political correctness and now it is up to you and me, each of us to move forward in our own sphere and knock down the obstacles that are silencing us and holding us back from what we are called to say and do."

October 13, 2015 Rick Joyner
"The Trajectory of Donald Trump"
Morning Star TV

Joyner emphasizes Trump's popularity in relation to border security, economy, and Trump being the most honest of all the candidates. He compares Trump to King David. We are in the first stage of the End Times, Joyner argues.

October 13, 2015 Mark Taylor
Don't Be Deceived, Get in The Fight [#4 in list]
Sord Rescue

The Spirit of God says, "The Clintons, the Clintons, your time has come to an end for you both are being omitted for the crimes you have committed. Hillary's is no great secret and they will be her downfall, but Bill's will be exposed one after the other and it be a windfall. For this time, you will not escape prosecution and restitution for the rape and prostitution. You thought no one saw, but I the Lord see it all, and now this will be your downfall."

The Spirit of God says, "Beware, beware, the enemy roams about seeking whom he can devour and this sitting President is doing just that in this hour. He's full of lies and deceit and is very hateful; he spreads division and corruption with every mouthful. Beware when he says, 'Look over here what the right hand is doing,' to divert your attention from what the left hand is doing, is his intention. This is a setup from this President and his minions, from the hate, the division, and Hillary Clinton. Why can no one see this? A sign will be, he will try and take the guns so the people can't rise up and stop him when he tries to run. He will not succeed for this is the peoples right, but make no mistake it will be a fight."

The Spirit of God says, "My Army, My Army, rise up and take to the fight, and I will stop this that has already taken flight. For this is a war over America and not to be taken lightly. You will have to fight, but America will shine brightly. Take the fight to the enemy and you will be victorious for all to see and America will be loved once again, even by some that used to be her enemies. My Army, continue to war, pray and fight with a shout, and I will remove this President that has become a louse! Then you will see the man I have chosen, Donald Trump, when he takes back MY WHITE HOUSE!"

October 17, 2015 Marko Joensuu
The Trump Prophecies and the Urgent Need for Prophetic Reformation
Mentoringprophets.com

This is a critique of the prophetic movement.

October 20, 2015 Kenneth Storey
The Donald Trump Prophecies
YouTube

Storey speaks about Lance Wallnau's meeting with Trump and praises Trump as the best candidate in terms of facing the establishment.

October 28, 2015 Donald Trump
Third Republican debate (Boulder, Colorado)

November 7, 2015 Mark Taylor
Time Is Up [#5 in list]
Sord Rescue

The Spirit of God says, "I am neutering this sitting President, I am neutering this sitting President in this hour, so his evil and corrupt ideologies and theologies can no longer reproduce in this country I call MY UNITED STATES OF AMERICA! For this man who holds the title called the President of the United States, will begin to lose his grip from it and be stripped of it, for I the Lord God will rip it from him. This man who calls himself Commander in Chief, is nothing more than a lying deceitful Thief!"

The Spirit of God says, "Time is up for those who are corrupt! For I shall begin to remove those who stand for evil in leadership and stand in the way of my agenda. Judges, Senators, Congressman and women of all kinds, even in the local, state and federal lines. Even the Supreme Court is not immune from their corrupt and evil ways, for I will remove some and expose their backdoor deals which have been at play. For my America has been chosen as the laughing platform for my harvest, and she will be a light unto the world once again as I clean up that which is the darkest. Fear not America your greatest days are ahead of you, arise my Army and fight and watch what I will do for you!"

November 10, 2015 Donald Trump
Fourth Republican Debate (Milwaukee)

November 23, 2015 Donald Trump
"Donald Trump Comments on ISIS and Register of Muslim Immigrants from Syria"
Politifact.com

November 30, 2015 Lance Wallnau
Meeting with Black Pastors at Trump Tower

This is the meeting where Lance Wallnau stated that Trump was a Cyrus figure.

December 1, 2015 Michael Brown
"Why Evangelicals Shouldn't Support Donald Trump"
The Christian Post

"Yet there's something that concerns me even more when it comes to Evangelicals supporting Donald Trump and that is the issue of pride, the sin that is often at the root of a host of other sins (Isaiah 14: 11–15), the sin which God resists (James 4: 6), the sin which leads to destruction (Proverbs 16: 18). Trump seems to have little understanding of what it means to ask God for forgiveness, while his very open, unashamed boastfulness is part and parcel of his persona. Trump and pride seem to walk hand in hand, quite comfortably at that. So, while I do understand why many Americans are behind Donald Trump and while I do believe he could do some things well as president, I cannot understand how Evangelicals can back him, especially when we have a number of solid, God-fearing, capable alternatives."

[Brown did a video on November 27 to make the same argument.]

December 7, 2015 Donald Trump
Press Release Calling for "Complete Shutdown of Muslims Entering the United States Until our Country's Representatives can Figure out what is going on."
The New York Times

December 7, 2015 Tony Perkins
"Conservative Titans Meeting Today to Discuss 2016 Endorsement"
Tim Alberta at *National Review*

Perkins endorses Cruz, who was chosen as best candidate by dozens of evangelical leaders.

December 15, 2015 Ted Cruz
"Inside the Secret Meeting Where Conservative Leaders Pledged Allegiance to Ted Cruz"
Tim Alberta, *National Review*

Cruz emerged as the favorite, Rubio second.

December 15, 2015 Donald Trump
Fifth Republican debate (Las Vegas)

December 17, 2015 James Dobson, Ted Cruz
"James Dobson Endorses Ted Cruz"
Ryan Lovelace at *Washington Examiner*

Dobson said of Trump's faith, "If anything, this man is a baby Christian who doesn't have a clue about how believers think, talk and act."

III. Nomination and Victory
2016

January 13, 2016, Johnny Enlow
A True Year of Jubilee
Elijah List

Enlow talks about the significance of the year of Jubilee, he talks about perfection and completeness. He mentions that it is of significance that Trump turns 70 in the year of Jubilee.

I will clearly state that the Lord hasn't shown me who will be the next president of the United States. Let me also state that I personally have my doubts that it will be Donald Trump. I think many feel that God is saying something through the appearance of Mr. Trump on the political scene, but most also admit that they aren't necessarily saying he'll be elected president. If Trump is a trumpet or shofar sound that God is using, then we must follow the Biblical pattern.

The shofar was never the thing God was doing, rather it was only that which activated, facilitated, or proclaimed what God was doing. The trumpet was not the Year of Jubilee itself, but the declaration of it. The appearance of Trump in the political arena has clearly made this election a hybrid like no other. Normal rules are out the door. The candidates that seemed best positioned in terms of resources and organization haven't seen that translate directly into the typical advantages we'd expect to see.

As it relates to Trump's primary political stances, I believe that many of them represent what God is judging in the United States, as opposed to what He's endorsing. If you draw up a Kingdom blueprint for who God would place in the position of authority as president, you wouldn't pick a three-times married, divider, polarizer, and significantly challenged in the fruit of the Holy Spirit, brash individual. A recent survey has said that 50% of Americans would be embarrassed to have Trump as president. I believe he's presently operating as a bull in the china shop of the 2016 elections. Ultimately, will he run the shop or just initiate its rebuilding? I don't know, but I do believe the process will reveal that God has been much more sovereign than many of us imagined and that Donald Trump will prove out to have been used strategically for the purposes of God.

January 14, 2016 Donald Trump
Sixth Republican debate (North Charleston, South Carolina)

January 18, 2016 Donald Trump
Convocation address at Liberty University

Trump got mocked later for saying "Two Corinthians" instead of "Second Corinthians" in his address. Trump was applauded at the event for a strong defence of religious liberty.

January 22, 2016 Donald Trump
"Conservatives Against Trump"
National Review

Twenty-two major conservative leaders, including Cal Thomas, R. R. Reno, Katie Pavlich, and Glenn Beck, give their reasons for opposing Trump.

January 26, 2016 Jerry Falwell Jr.
"Here's the backstory of why I endorsed Donald Trump"
The Washington Post

January 26, 2016 John Paul Jackson
John Paul Jackson and President Donald Trump
Lou Comunale at News2morrow

In a 2012 TV show, John Paul Jackson interprets a woman's dream about a bulldozer crashing through the White House. Comunale suggests that Jackson is talking about Donald Trump as the bulldozer. However, Jackson does not mention Trump at all.

January 28, 2016 Donald Trump
Seventh Republican debate (Des Moines, Iowa)

January 28, 2016 Mark Taylor
Defeated Enemy [#6 in list]
Sord Rescue

The Spirit of God says, "There is an army arising from the dust and ashes from many battles and enemy clashes. This army that's arising is coming in my glory and light, and that battle that's about to unfold shall put the enemy to flight. For my army is about to hit the beaches and shores of every country and nation afar, and they shall drive back the army of darkness at the sound of my shofar! For my army will be young and old and will save over 1 billion souls."

The Spirit of God says, "There is nothing that the enemy can do to stop this that I the Lord God have started, for it is now time for the army of darkness to be departed. For the souls of this nation and all over the world are crying out to me. My Army! Bring them in, and I will save, deliver, and comfort thee. Arise! Army of God! Arise! Your work is not complete, for the kingdom of darkness is in for its biggest surprise, complete and utter defeat! Arise! My Army! Get in the fight, I say with great emphasis! Over take, terminate, and destroy the Army of darkness with Extreme Prejudice!"

Your Supreme Commander GOD!

February 1, 2016 Donald Trump

Trump comes in second in Iowa caucus after Ted Cruz.

February 5, 2016, Kenneth Copeland, Ted Cruz

Copeland endorses Ted Cruz.
Right Wing Watch

Copeland speaks about Ted Cruz in words addressed to Cruz's father: "I believe, with all my heart, that his son is called and anointed to be the next president of the United States."

[Note: *Huffington Post* reports on the same development in a June 21, 2016, reference following.]

February 6, 2016 Donald Trump

Eighth Republican debate (Manchester, New Hampshire)

February 9, 2016 Donald Trump

Wins New Hampshire primary

February 13, 2016 Donald Trump
Ninth Republican debate (Charleston, South Carolina)

February 13, 2016 Antonin Scalia
Antonin Scalia dies.

February 18, 2016 Pope Francis
"Pope Francis Harsh on Trump's Christianity"
CNN

Trump Responds to Pope
YouTube

Trump claims that political leaders told the pope that he isn't a good person, but he insists that he is a good Christian and proud to be so. He argues that no religious leader should have the right to question anyone's faith.

Pope: "A person who thinks only about building walls, wherever they may be, and not building bridges, is not Christian."

February 24, 2016 Mark Taylor
"Do Not Fear America" [#7 in list]
Sord Rescue

The Spirit of God says, "Why do I sense fear in my people about the future of America? Have I not said, 'I have heard your cries and will heal your land?' Stand firm! Do not falter, put on the full armour of God! Rake the enemy over the coals, for the end time battle is on for my 1 billion souls!"
The Spirit of God says, "Do not fear that my servant Justice Scalia has been taken, for some are crying out, why have I forsaken. For I will show myself strong to prove that the so called wise are wrong. For some will say that this is a miracle, for I am just getting started, this is not even close to the pinnacle, for what I am going to do with My America. For do not my people have eyes to see and ears to hear the two signs I gave, when they carried my servant's body up the steps of the courthouse where to rest he was laid? Read the signs! Read the signs that were for all to see, and understand the words in the prophecy."

The Spirit of God says, "5, that's right 5 Supreme Court Justices will be appointed by my new president, my anointed. I will choose 5 through my anointed to keep those alive. I will stack the court with those that I choose, to send a clear message to the enemy, that you lose! This is the miracle that I will perform, so that MY COURT will be reformed."

The Spirit of God says, "The cries, the cries that I have heard from the womb, have reached my eyes and ears like a sonic boom! The five I appoint and the reform that shall take place, the great I AM shall take on this case! For it is my will and my way for all those that have prayed, that MY COURT SHALL OVERTURN ROE VS WADE!

The Spirit of God says, "America, get ready for I AM choosing from the top of the cream, for I AM putting together America's dream team, from the president and his administration, to judges and congress to ease Americas frustrations!"

The Spirit of God says, "Rise up my Army and get in the fight, for this is the generation that's taking flight. This is the generation of warriors that those of old wanted to see, and the enemy will have no choice but to flee. Rise up! Stomp the enemies head with bliss; send the enemy back to Hell and into the abyss. This is the generation of warriors that all of Hell has feared to face and see, but I AM and all of Heaven is cheering you on with glee!"

Your Supreme Commander, GOD

February 25, 2016 Donald Trump
Tenth Republican debate (Houston)

February 26, 2016, Jeremiah Johnson
Prophetic Dream about Marco Rubio

Johnson talks about how Clinton and Obama have an unholy connection and wish for an Islamic regime. This view is based on dreams that Johnson had after Obama was elected in 2012.

Johnson also reports on a dream from February 25, 2016:

"Marco Rubio is carrying a Thomas Jefferson anointing for this generation. He will break the back of tyrants and restore the patriotic spirit in America. I love His courage and heart and you must know that he is very special to me."

As the Holy Spirit spoke these words to me as I watched Marco speak to the crowd, I immediately saw what looked like oil begin to be poured out upon His head from heaven. He was covered from head to toe in it and the Spirit of God spoke to me again in the dream and said, "I have anointed Marco as a forerunner of forerunners for the Hispanic community in America. He will lead the charge in the fight for freedom and restore the Malachi 4: 5–6 revolution among his people. He is a pioneer of pioneer's and will gain continuous favor in America in the years ahead. The father's in America will turn to this son (Marco) and this son (Marco) shall turn the hearts of his brothers to the father's."

Marco finished his speech to the people and walked off the stage with his family. I thought I was hidden in the dream, but he walked right up to me and said, "I need the prayers of the body of Christ now more than ever. See to it that this is accomplished."

Johnson says that his dreams about Rubio and Trump were not endorsements of either candidate or a prediction about who would win the November election.

[The above material is from Johnson's website, which is now defunct.]

February 26, 2016 Max Lucado
"Does Donald Trump Pass the Decency Test?"
The Christian Post

Famous Christian author warns about Trump in op-ed.

March 1, 2016 Max Lucado, Anita Fuentes
Max Lucado Warns Evangelical Christians about Donald Trump
YouTube

Evangelist Anita Fuentes reports about Lucado. "Could it be that Trump is a wolf in sheep's clothing?" asks Fuentes, in sympathy with Lucado's warning about Trump.

March 1, 2016 Donald Trump
Super Tuesday: Trump wins in Alabama, Arkansas, Georgia, Massachusetts, Tennessee, Vermont, and Virginia.

March 3, 2016 Donald Trump
11th Republican debate (Detroit)

March 6, 2016 Max Lucado
"Pastor Max Lucado Baffled Over Evangelical Trump Supporters"
National Public Radio

March 7, 2016 Rich Vera
On Trump
SidRoth.org

Vera mentions that when Trump was younger God marked his life and set him apart. Trump will be used by God to dig up a lot of dirt. There will be days of revival in America.

Transcript of Vera: "And the Spirit of the Lord came from my left side and said, "I'm going to corner him in a place that I'm going to cause him to call on my name and I'm believing him to take things out and put him in positions that he will call on my name."

March 10, 2016 Donald Trump
12th Republican debate (Miami)

March 14, 2016 Rodney and Adonica Howard-Browne
"Why I (we) decided to back Trump"
Facebook

Lance Wallnau shared this post on Facebook the same day.

Here is the text:

Update—the comments on this post confirm to us several things—people just read "Trump" and never read what we had to say at all—The (drive-by's) who don't know us or our hearts and wanted to slam us could now come on this page and spew venom—it is evident that many are under the control and influence of the mass media propaganda- they have been hypnotized and are living in a trance.

Personally we are not swayed by the opinions of others—we stand by our statements and do not retract one thing. Selah! People need to wake up!

To our Friends—we love you and thank you for your kind words and support—to our enemies we love you, forgive you and pray for you. Postscript:

There is a lot more we could say; however, we knew many wouldn't read our comments, just see the word "Trump" and manifest. Unfortunately, there is a lot that people don't know. For the kind words people have left, thank you. For the unkind words, thank you. It's called free speech. Thank you for responding. Unfortunately, because of the large number of comments and our busy schedule we have not been able to read all responses. So far it has been mostly good, with some bad and ugly—and whilst we lost about 100 followers, we gained over 600 more. Thank you.

Why I (we) decided to back TRUMP

Our comments and observations, as private citizens:

Coming from outside America (and having become citizens of the USA) we see things a little differently—we see it from a global perspective—from what is happening globally. We know that the Bible tells us that the devil's end-time plan is a one-world religion, one-world money system, and one-world government—a "new world order" (NWO). This is a plan that threatens every freedom we have and hold dear.

Christianity and the Bible is a threat to this global plan. So is anyone who thinks for themselves. The American Constitution—the document that made America the great nation it is—stands in the way of this global agenda. This is why it has been under attack—from our own president, and others, on down. We realize that it is the New World Order's Agenda to destroy the United States.

If you want to see things in this country stay as they are, please read no further. If you know we need a change, and you want a change, then this is what we have to say about it:

We cannot vote for Clinton. She has no scruples, has broken the law on multiple occasions, has extreme views on abortion, etc. , and works only for those who pay her.

Sanders is a Socialist/Communist. He, and those who follow in his footsteps, will take the country the way of Venezuela and the old Soviet Union. Communism is a failed ideology that has never worked anywhere it's been tried.

Unfortunately, it seems that whether we have Democrats or Republicans in charge, we keep going in the same direction. The people who actually run the country behind the scenes, continue to run America into the ground. The vast majority of politicians we elect fulfill their own agenda and do not stand up for the people who elected them.

Kasich is not going to win at this stage. He is a GOP insider and is for Common Core. He also received money from ungodly billionaire George Soros.

Rubio has the worst absentee voting record in the Senate. Either he is disengaged, or he doesn't want anyone to know his true stance on the issues. What kind of a president would he be? He tells his voters to vote Kasich in Ohio and he wants Kasich to tell his voters to vote Rubio in Florida—they can't win on their own merit.

The biggest vote against him is that he was the establishment's favorite. The one they could control to do their bidding. America has had it with The Establishment. They have not delivered what they promised. They are all in on the shell-game. The shell- game, with no pea.

Cruz. Our first hesitation concerning him started at Celebrate America DC 2014 at Constitution Hall. He was scheduled to speak, and cancelled at the last minute, because his office said he was being groomed for the presidency and he did not want to be associated with something that could reflect negatively on him. Why would a Christian be ashamed of a soul winning event?

The second thing—or red flag—is that he claims to be a Christian, but gave only one percent of his income to charity. Where your treasure is, your heart is. You have to put your money where your mouth is.

The third (huge) problem is the fact that his wife was part of the Council for Foreign Relations (CFR)—an arm of the NWO—and Goldman Sachs—the "money changers."

She (and he?) is for the TPP and open borders—both of which threaten America's sovereignty.

The fourth and final thing—that sunk it for us—was when he joined the Bush's. He brought in Neil Bush (Jeb's brother)—the man who was involved in the billion-dollar savings & loan fraud—to be his (Cruz's) financial director.

That's it for me—I am done—he has thrown his hat in with the Bush crime syndicate.

The only place I would put him is in the Supreme Court—if he can prove he loves the Constitution as much as he says he does.

The only one left—who is not bought and paid for is TRUMP. While I understand some people's reaction to this might be shock—I can only speak from personal experience. I met Mr Trump twice in a 20- year period— once in the '90's and the last time was two years ago. Both times were chance encounters—not planned. He did not know who I was—I found him to be a humble person and he treated me with kindness—that's all.

I believe him when he says that he is tired of the direction the country is going in and felt like that if no one else was going to step up, then he felt like he should. I believe that his popularity is due to the fact that he is NOT a politician, but he is one of "we the people" just as we are. We are all tired of being manipulated by politicians, liberals, and the media.

Trump does not censor his words—like politicians do—he says what he thinks—which appeals to people. I am not saying I agree with everything he has said, or that he knows everything he is signing up for, but I do believe that he will put knowledgeable people around him who share the same values as we patriotic Americans do.

People have lambasted him on his language. We have it on good authority that Hillary and George Bush—to mention only two—have very vulgar mouths behind the scenes. Trump isn't perfect, but at least we can see all his faults. They are not hidden behind a veil of smugness. Trump has not been bought out by private interests. He made his own billions and he is spending them on his campaign.

A mark of a person's standing is who backs them and who attacks them. The New World Order and the establishment are spending tens of millions to take him down. When the Pope attacks him, plus two former Mexican Presidents and other world leaders—then that tells me he is a threat to the New World Order and the One World Government. When the world's financial elite met in Davos, Switzerland, and said they are afraid of Trump—I said that's good enough for me.

Trump is bad news to the New World Order and the One World Government, spoken about by George Bush (Snr) in his "1000 points of light" speech.

Trump is good news to American Sovereignty.

Because of his stance on immigration, he is labeled by the left as a racist and Hitler—something they use in the UK against Nigel Farage and

UKIP for the same reasons. If you are a leftist liberal and you don't have a valid argument to support your opposing view—just call people names and label them: racist, misogynist, Hitler, fascist, etc. Most people don't even know what those terms mean. The problem is that too many Americans are illiterate when it comes to history—particularly their own. If you don't know history, you don't know when you are being lied to. We should hear what the candidates say—in their own words—and not believe the twisted versions. We need to think for ourselves and not be open to being manipulated.

Immigration should take place, but should take place legally—open borders are not the way to do things.

We are in the final hour now—the final grains of sand are slipping through the hour glass. We stand on the brink of a one-world government, one-world religion, one-world money system, and the rise of the antichrist.

I will say that a Trump presidency will give us a stay of execution, only.

All the nonsense stirred up in the main stream propaganda media: the lies—racism stirred up, etc. , is all a ploy to take Mr. Trump down. My concern is that, even if he becomes the nominee, he will be in danger—I fear for his life.

The GOP wants a brokered convention—to steal the nomination from the people's choice. Personally, I don't think they want Cruz either, but they have co-opted him.

I am shocked at how violently people are responding to each other over their choice of presidential candidate. Even Christians are ripping into each other. You are perfectly entitled to freely choose the candidate you feel represents your values. On the other hand, please be respectful of other people's opinions and choices.

This is a free country and we are thankful that we have the 1st amendment, which guarantees freedom of speech. Freedom of speech means being respectful of other people's freedoms to say what they want to say, as well.

I leave these points for your consideration—pray for America, vote, and let's see what happens.

All our love
Private Citizens Rodney & Adonica

March 15, 2016 Marco Rubio
Marco Rubio withdraws from presidential race.

March 17, 2016 Donald Trump
Donald Trump's statement on Christianity
YouTube

Christianity is being chipped away in this country, and he won't let it happen.

March 21, 2016 Rick Joyner
"Is Trump the One?"
MorningStar Ministries

Pro/con on Trump.

Joyner states that more than 50 percent of Evangelicals are open to Trump: "Even if you don't like many of the things Trump says, the sense that he will fight back, and fight hard, is more appealing to Republicans now than the empty rhetoric and promises of those who claim to be conservatives but did not act like it. The establishment made Trump inevitable. The more the establishment tries to stop him, the more inevitable he will be."

March 21, 2016 Rodney Howard-Browne
"Donald Trump is the New World Order's Worst Nightmare"
Singapore Christian duplicates Howard-Browne's Facebook post from March 14: "Trump is bad news to the New World Order and the One World Government, spoken about by George H.W. Bush in his '1,000 points of light' speech. Trump is good news to American Sovereignty."

March 24, 2016 George Papadopoulos
George Papadopoulos, Trump advisor, meets in London with Professor Joseph Mifsud, who introduces him to a Russian national.

This is a key event in the Trump-Russia collusion theory that comes to dominate U.S. politics and the Mueller investigation.

March 31, 2016 Donald Trump, George Papadopoulos
Trump meets with foreign policy advisors. George Papadopoulos talks about connections to arrange meeting with Trump and Putin.

April 2016 Fusion GPS
Fusion GPS hired by Perkins Coie on behalf of Clinton and DNC

[For data on Russian connections, Fusion GPS, the Mueller report, see list of websites in resources section.]

April 12, 2016 Mike Thompson
Mike's Heavenly Vision
YouTube

This vision discusses the spirit of Jezebel and its characteristics and the spirit of the Pharisees and its legalism. God's hand is on Trump, and the dogs of hell will be out to get him. Thompson says it is not an absolute that Trump will be the next president.

April 14, 2016 Donald Trump
"Donald Trump's Prosperity Preachers"
Elizabeth Dias at *Time*

April 18, 2016 Mark Taylor
"God's Man: Firefighter shares April 2011 Vision of President Trump"
TruNews with Rick Wiles [Show lasts 1.08.44.]

Trump is God's anointed man. The enemy will be scared of him. Ties with Israel will be stronger than ever, and Israel will flourish.

This is the first public interview with Taylor.

April 18, 2016 Steve Cioccolanti
Donald Trump End Time President
YouTube

Churches should talk about politics; Trump is self-funded; why Trump is popular; what if it's God's will for Trump to be president. The future president has the mandate to fulfill God's plan for the USA.

April 19, 2016 Donald Trump
Trump wins New York primary.

April 20, 2016 Mark Taylor and Rick Wiles
"Self-Proclaimed Prophet: God Will Make Donald Trump President and Kill His Enemies"
Brian Tashman at Right Wing Watch

An attack on Taylor and Wiles (Tru News).

April 21, 2016 Michael Brown
Donald Trump Is Not Your Protector: A Warning to Conservative Christians
www.askdrbrown.org

If you're a Trump supporter, you might say, "I know he's not a Christian and I don't even think he's a real conservative, but I'm voting for him because I believe he's the best man to fix our economy and protect our borders." I beg to differ, but I can respect that position. But please don't look to him to be a defender of conservative Christian values or a protector of religious freedoms. Barring dramatic divine intervention in his life, you will be sadly disappointed. Be forewarned.

April 22, 2016 Mark Taylor
"Trump for Next President"
Charisma News

In a report, Bob Eschliman claims that God showed Taylor in 2011 that Trump would be president and the dollar will once again be the strongest currency. The enemy will be afraid of him running as presidential candidate. Spiritual and financial success will run parallel.

April 26, 2016 Hillary Clinton
Papadopoulos was told that Russians had thousands of emails related to Clinton.

April 26, 2016 Mark Taylor
Purging the Temple [#8 in list]
Sord Rescue

The Spirit of God says, "The 501c3, the 501c3, those that are eating of it are not eating from my tree! From when I told Adam and Eve do not eat

65

from the Tree of the Knowledge of Good and Evil for you shall surely see, so it is with those that eat from the 501c3. For this demonic document that you have signed has now made you spiritually deaf, mute, and blind. Woe to those who continue to use this demonic system for you will be exposed and purged from this evil cistern."

The Spirit of God says, "Can you not see that you are taking a bribe? They will say it's all about the money, and for that you shall be kicked from my tribe! Taking a bite from that apple has taken you from a spiritual body to a brick and mortar, and has place you under the New World Order. For how can you be a part of my spiritual body when you have cut off my head? For those that don't turn will surely fall as dead. Tear up the contract, repent, divorce Baal, and re-marry me, and I will remove the spiritual blindness so you can once again see. Come out of this! Come out of this before it's too late, for my judgements are on those systems that I hate. Come out now for I will no longer tolerate!"

["501c3" refers to an allowance in the Internal Revenue Code for religious and charitable organizations to have tax exempt status.]

May 3, 2016 Ted Cruz
Ted Cruz withdraws from presidential race.

May 6, 2016 Lance Wallnau
Is Donald Trump America's Cyrus?
Strang Report

May 6, 2016 Mike Thompson, Mark Taylor
A Few Words about Mark Taylor
www.studygrowknowblog.com

This article is a summary of the charismatic movement and how prophets and apostles have been common among them. The charismatic movement is strongly based on experience rather than intellectual reasoning.

May 6, 2016 Russell Moore
"A White Church No More"
The New York Times

As of this week, the nation faces a crazier election season than many of us ever imagined, with Donald J. Trump as the all-but-certain nominee of the Republican Party. Regardless of the outcome in November, his campaign is forcing American Christians to grapple with some scary realities that will have implications for years to come.

This election has cast light on the darkness of pent-up nativism and bigotry all over the country. There are not-so-coded messages denouncing African-Americans and immigrants; concern about racial justice and national unity is ridiculed as "political correctness." Religious minorities are scapegoated for the sins of others, with basic religious freedoms for them called into question. Many of those who have criticized Mr. Trump's vision for America have faced threats and intimidation from the "alt-right" of white supremacists and nativists who hide behind avatars on social media.

May 7, 2016 Lana Vawser
"I Heard the Lord Singing Regarding Donald Trump"
www.lanavawser.com

Recently, the Lord surprised me as I heard Him singing and I heard him singing concerning Trump. I heard the Lord singing in the same melody to the old song by Billy Haley and The Comets, "Shake, Rattle and Roll."

Yet as I heard the melody, I heard the Lord singing:

"I am using TRUMP to shake, rattle and roll. I'm using TRUMP to shake, rattle and roll ... I'm using TRUMP to shake, rattle and roll"

I could hear it over and over and over again.

The heart of this word is not a prediction of the outcome of the US Election, but I did feel the Lord highlighting that He is USING Trump right now to bring a SHAKING, a RATTLING and there will be a ROLLING. He is using him to shake things up to MAKE ROOM for a much needed change.

May 9, 2016 Donald Trump
Twitter

"Russell Moore is truly a terrible representative of Evangelicals and all of the good they stand for. A nasty guy with no heart!"

May 9, 2016 Donald Trump
"Donald Trump's Feud with Evangelical Leader Reveals Fault Lines"
Elizabeth Dias at *Time*

Trump attacks Russell Moore, a Southern Baptist leader who opposes him. Robert Jeffress, pastor of First Baptist Church in Dallas, defends Trump.

May 20, 2016 Donald Trump
"Exclusive: Evangelical Leaders Plan Meeting to Test Donald Trump's Values"
Elizabeth Dias at *Time*

[Meeting was held June 21. See the following.]

May 22, 2016 Anita Fuentes, Mark Taylor
"Fireman Prophecy" of Trump is a False Prophecy. Here is why …
YouTube

Evangelist Fuentes speaks against Mark Taylor's prophecy.

May 24, 2016 Donald Trump
"Top Evangelicals Send Invites for Trump Meeting"
Tim Alberta at *National Review*

The report is about a June 21 meeting arranged by Tony Perkins, Bill Dallas, and others.

May 25, 2016 Donald Trump
United in Purpose and My Faith Votes Organize "A Conversation with Donald Trump and Ben Carson"
PR newswire

A press release announcing a June 21 meeting.

May 26, 2016 Donald Trump
Trump clinches enough delegates to assure party nomination.

May 27, 2016 Lana Vawser
Intercessors Arise and Trump the Enemy's Plans Against Trump
LanaVawser.com

Recently as I sat with the Lord, I felt an urgency in the Spirit concerning Donald Trump. I felt the Lord sounding an alarm to the intercessors across the world to increase intercession for him.

I am an Australian, who loves the United States of America, and I have released this word simply as I heard it and as with other words I have released concerning Donald Trump, I am releasing them without agenda.

As you read this word I want to encourage you to read it with an open heart despite your political views, or opinion concerning Donald Trump, I encourage you to go to the Lord and simply just pray for him. Whether he becomes the next President of the United States of America or not, I believe the Lord is sounding an alarm that he needs increased intercession right now.

So as I sat with the Lord I heard the words "INTERCESSORS ARISE AND TRUMP THE ENEMY'S PLANS AGAINST TRUMP." Instantly I saw thousands upon thousands of intercessors responding to the call from His heart to go deeper into intercession for Donald Trump.

I was taken into a vision and I saw Jesus leading His intercessors that had responded to His call into this deep, dark, dungeon. Jesus lead them into this dark dungeon in the spirit and I saw a large wooden table and upon the table was large pieces of paper that had lots of writing and blueprints upon them. Jesus then turned to the intercessors and He said "These are assignments and attacks of the enemy against Donald Trump, TAKE AUTHORITY OVER THEM IN MY NAME! ." I could not see any details but I knew in this encounter that the Lord was uncovering and foiling the plans of the enemy before they could even be put into action. There was a new level of discernment and insight the Lord was releasing in the spirit to His intercessors to release greater angelic protection to Trump. As the people of God prayed, I saw these attacks being foiled and the fire of God falling upon them, before they could even be put into action.

Whether Donald Trump becomes President or not, the Lord has been using him to shake things up, and I felt the heart of God today, that whether you agree with him, like him or not, that the Lord is highlighting the need for greater levels of intercession over him and into his life.

INTERCESSION WILL POSITION DONALD TRUMP FOR AN ENCOUNTER WITH ME

As I sat with the Lord on this word, I felt the atmosphere around me pregnant with encounter. I then heard the words "INTERCESSION will POSITION Donald Trump for an ENCOUNTER with ME!!."

Not only will the deeper level of intercession the Lord is calling His Church into regarding Trump, it will see plans and assignments of the enemy foiled in the spirit and greater angelic protection, but also position Donald Trump for an encounter with Jesus.

These are the days where discernment is really needed to hear and see what the Lord is saying and doing. Without agenda, we must seek the Lord's heart and what He is saying whether we agree or not.

Whatever the outcome of the election in November, I felt the Lord is raising an alarm in the Spirit to pray for Donald Trump to see VICTORY over the plans and assignments of the enemy before they are put into action.

WISDOM WILL COME UPON MY PEOPLE CONCERNING TRUMP

I then heard the words 'wisdom will come upon My people concerning Trump." In the place of intercession the Lord is going to release greater wisdom to His people on how to pray and how to battle in the spirit. This wisdom that will be released from on high will defy natural understanding and logic, but as the heavenly wisdom is put into practise there will be victory in the Spirit.

The words then surrounded me 'Wisdom will come upon Trump.' I felt the Lord wants to release wisdom upon Trump. As I sat with the Lord, I had this moment where I had this sense that Donald Trump has been asking the Lord for wisdom like Solomon and the Lord is answering his prayers. I felt the Lord pursuing Trump to reveal His heart to him and wisdom would flow.

As the body of Christ, can we stand TOGETHER and respond to the Lord's invitation?

I'm in, I hope and pray you will join me,
Lana Vawser

May 31, 2016 Mario Bramnick
Bramnick on Hispanic pastors meeting with Trump in Trump Tower
Strang Report

June 2016 Fusion GPS

Fusion GPS (under contract to law firm Perkins Coie, paid by DNC) hires Christopher Steele (former British spy). Steele writes pre-election reports from June through October 2016 and a final report in December. These reports become known as the Steele dossier.

June 2016 Dan McAdams
"The Mind of Donald Trump"
The Atlantic

My aim is to develop a dispassionate and analytical perspective on Trump, drawing upon some of the most important ideas and research findings in psychological science today.

Presidential candidates on the campaign trail are studies in perpetual motion. But nobody else seems to embrace the campaign with the gusto of Trump. And no other candidate seems to have so much fun.

The real psychological wild card, however, is Trump's agreeableness— or lack thereof. There has probably never been a U.S. president as consistently and overtly disagreeable on the public stage as Donald Trump is.

... I can find no evidence in the biographical record to suggest that Donald Trump experienced anything but a loving relationship with his mother and father. Narcissistic people like Trump may seek glorification over and over, but not necessarily because they suffered from negative family dynamics as children.

[Note: See the interview with McAdams at the December 8, 2019, entry.]

June 1, 2016 Frank Amedia

Frank Amedia reports that the Lord told him in summer 2015 of Trump win in Republican nomination
Strang Report

The interview took place on May 26, 2016, the day it was announced that Trump had won the nomination.

June 9, 2016 Mark Taylor
Mark Taylor reads his "Commander in Chief" prophecy by phone on the *Jim Bakker Show,* "Shocking Prophecies for the Election" (Day 1) [25-minute mark].

Bakker calls Taylor "the unknown prophet." Don and Mary and Taylor all regard the death of Supreme Court justice Scalia to be suspicious.

[Note: Don and Mary Colbert are guests on the show. Don Colbert is Jim Bakker's doctor and Mark Taylor's as well. Mary met Mark Taylor while he was visiting her husband's medical office.]

June 9, 2016 Donald Trump
Controversial meeting in Trump Tower (Jared Kushner, Donald Trump Jr., and Paul Manafort and Russian lawyer Natalia Veselnitskaya)

June 10, 2016 Donald Trump
Trump speaks at Faith and Freedom Coalition conference (Washington, DC)
Susan Milligan at *U.S. News and World Report*

June 12, 2016 Donald Trump
Pulse nightclub shooting [Omar Mateen] in Orlando

Trump references the Mateen case in talking about gun rights.

June 12, 2016 Mark Taylor
Shatter and Scatter [#9 in list]
Sord Rescue

The Spirit of God says, "The Illuminati and ISIS have merged and are attacking the pulse of this nation, for they are responsible for the list of assassinations. For the New World Order is shaking and quaking, for they will go down in flames a blazing. For they are trying to kill this nation before my chosen one takes office through depopulation, finances, and assassination.

My army, my intercessors arise and take the fight to the enemy, stop the assassinations, stop the attacks to the pulse of this nation."

The Spirit of God says, "The Illuminati, I the Lord God shall expose the Illuminati because of who they want to be. They shall say we will be the world leaders like a shot!

Not so fast, for I the Lord God will shatter you like a clay pot. Shattered and scattered my wind will send you back to the one who sent you. For you think you are wise craving power, money, and the prize.

You so called wise have been fooled by the lust and the lure of the prize to the point that the one who sent you now seeks his payment, and this too you will soon realize. For your days are numbered and short, Woa to you when you have to stand before him and report. For this will be for all to see for when you serve the god of this world it will bring you low, repent or you shall be cast into the fire below."

The Spirit of God says, "Why do the prophets of doom and gloom keep saying that this is the end? For they are misreading the season of time we are in. For those that keep speaking this with words that bend, are aiding the enemy making the people lay down their arms, give up, lose hope, stop fighting and saying we will just ride this out to the end. For you are never to stop fighting or lay down your arms for any reason.

Stop listening to those who commit spiritual treason. For life and death are in the power of the tongue, for this treasonous talk is even affecting the young. Stop aiding the enemy and start talking about what I the Lord God and my Army are going to do. Grab the enemy by the throat and make him fluster. Look him in the eyes and say, "Is that all you can muster?" Choose this day whom you will serve, for I have given you the victory and the choice is yours."

Your Supreme Commander, God

June 12, 2016 Mark Taylor
Babylonian Prison [#10 in list]
Sord Rescue

The Spirit of God says, "There's a beast in the east that's trying to arise that thinks he's the best, but I have one in the west that will give him a godly surprise and take him down to the least. For this beast that has risen is no surprise, for my church is in a Babylonian prison, come out of her or it will be your demise!"

The Spirit of God says, "The chaos and clatter that the earth is in, is directly related to the Babylonian box that the so called church is in. For my earth is moaning and groaning for my sons and daughters to arise with bliss. Where is my Army that will send this beast back to the abyss? For how can you take on a beast when you're deaf, mute, and blind? For all beasts are ancient and old, and lurk about seeking an enemy whom they can steam roll. For this beast has no teeth and lurks in the brush, trying to lure you into an ambush. Do not attack until you come out of her that Babylonian stem, or you will fall prey and be decimated beyond comprehension."

The Spirit of God says, "For when my people realize the curse they are under, and come out, break the curse, then they will plunder. For as they come out of her with a mass exodus, there I will be, to restore her back to my body and I as the head she will have power, authority, and unity again and the enemy shall fall as dead! For you wonder why the world is so perverse, it's because my church has forsaken her first love and is under a curse. Come out of her now don't walk but run and do not wait, before you cross the point of no return for then it's too late. Come back to me, come back to me and make me your first love I have dearly yearned, for some it's already too late, for they have not learned."

June 12, 2016 Mike Thompson
Mike's Heavenly Vision Part 2
YouTube

God wants the president elect to shake things up. The spirit of Jezebel is coming from Europe to go against the United States. Politics shouldn't be allowed in the church. Thompson said that God showed him that the new president is Trump.

June 14, 2016 Jill Steele
Trump Call
www.steelefaith.com

Let me first qualify this word by explaining a few things to you. The Lord spoke this to me on May 16th. It was extremely clear, and as I wrote and received, I kept wondering exactly who Cyrus was in the Bible. I thought I knew he was a King of Persia, but really could not place any specific information about him. Further, I had not been closely following the presidential race because the candidates have been hard for me to like. Trump was especially offensive to me for various reasons, and I had avoided listening to him. This word is not about a political party, nor is it intended to engage argument in any way. Maybe all of this is exactly why I received this word; because I have no desire to be involved in anything political, but only to serve God as He calls me to do. All I know is it came as a very strong word of the Lord and I wrote it EXACTLY word for word as I received it, as I do every word He gives me.

"TRUMP CALL! Trump is My Cyrus! Yes, you heard Me correctly! He is the man who will reveal Me in many ways. And as he does, all will see Me in a new way!

THIS man, (as Cyrus), who does not know Me, means well. And not for his own gain, but "for the people" he truly does purpose.

His stand is a GRANDSTAND, but his heart is in its place as he does have NO NEED for place, order, favor, or money. He has already been those things to many and so his breaches are sealed. There is no other reason, but to serve his country, (and true now, his God)- as I will use him for My purposes."

June 14, 2016 Democratic National Committee
Two Russian hacker groups are expelled from DNC systems by Crowdstrike, a security firm.

June 14, 2016 Mark Taylor
"Trump Chosen by God: Prophecy from 2011 Claims Trump Was Chosen by God to Save America"
Taylor Berglund at *Charisma News*

[*Charisma News* played the entire Tru News interview in their article.]

June 16, 2016 Mark Taylor
"How Donald Trump Could Easily Fulfill This 2011 Prophecy"
Charisma News

[*Charisma News* played a video segment from the Jim Bakker Show in their article.]

June 16, 2016 Jim Geraghty
"There Is No Other, More 'Presidential' Donald Trump"
National Review

"Trump won the backing of 45 percent of Republican primary voters. A delegate insurrection against his nomination in Cleveland would of course be politically painful. But is anyone certain that the pain of ditching Trump and replacing him with another Republican — any other Republican — would be worse than the pain of officially tying the party's fortunes to him through November?"

June 17, 2016 Eric Metaxas
Author Eric Metaxas Asks If American Democracy Will Survive
Stream.org

Trump "may well be our only hope."

June 19, 2016 Mark Taylor
"Charisma News Exposed for Promoting Prophetic Fraud"
Church Watch Central

This article states that the prophecy Mark Taylor read on the *Jim Bakker Show* on June 9 "was not in the original prophecy." This is not true.

[Note: Charismatic and Pentecostal prophets are regularly attacked. This and the next entry from David Pakman are two examples.]

June 20, 2016 David Pakman Show, Jim Bakker
David Pakman Show mocks Jim Bakker and prophecy.

June 20, 2016 David French
"Don't Bend Your Knee to Trump, Evangelicals"
National Review

Tomorrow, hundreds of Evangelical leaders will gather in New York City to meet with Donald Trump. I must confess that I don't understand their purpose.

I suspect that it will be exactly the kind of meeting that Trump wants: One where he can mouth a few platitudes and those Evangelicals who are desperate for power and influence will emerge gravely pronouncing themselves "satisfied" that he is in their corner. Of course, they'll maintain their "reservations" — including their professed distaste for his racist rhetoric, disrespect for women, and habitual lying — but they'll fall in line.

Evangelical leaders: If you back Trump, for the rest of your days, you will be forced to live with having had a hand in fracturing our nation on the basis of race, discarding the sanctity of marriage, and scorning honesty itself — all for the chance, the remote chance, that Trump will make one or two decent Supreme Court picks. You will be selling your integrity for the most meager of returns.

Christians have had to take tougher stands in darker times before. They do so in other nations today. This decision, by contrast, should be easy. Trump is not worth your consideration or even one moment of your time. Let others bend the knee.

June 21, 2016 Donald Trump
"Ahead of Meeting, Evangelicals Sense Leverage Over Trump"
Tim Alberta at *National Review*

June 21, 2016 Donald Trump
"Trump's Meeting with Evangelical Leaders Marks the End of the Christian Right"
Michael Farris at *The Christian Post*

Today, a candidate whose worldview is greed and whose god is his appetites (Philippians 3) is being tacitly endorsed by this throng.

They are saying we are Republicans no matter what the candidate believes and no matter how vile and unrepentant his character.

They are not a phalanx of God's prophets confronting a wicked leader, this is a parade of elephants.

In 1980 I believed that Christians could dramatically influence politics. Today, we see politics fully influencing a thousand Christian leaders. This is a day of mourning.

June 21, 2016 Donald Trump
"Trump's Meeting with Evangelicals"
Elizabeth Dias for *Time*
"Donald Trump Meets with 1,000 'Enthusiastic' Faith Leaders in New York City"
Alex Swoyer at Breitbart
"10 Points to Take Away from the Meeting with the Evangelicals"
Larry Tomczak at *Charisma News*
"Trump Is Surrounding Himself With Evangelical Pastors"
Emma Green at *The Atlantic*

The meeting was spearheaded by United in Purpose, Bill Dallas and My Faith Votes, and Johnnie Moore. Samuel Rodriguez, president of the National Hispanic Christian Leadership Conference, had positive interaction with Trump at the meeting.

June 21, 2016 Donald Trump
Inside Trump's Closed-Door Meeting, Held to Reassure 'The Evangelicals'
Sarah McCammon at *NPR*

June 21, 2016 Kenneth Copeland
"'Donald Trump's New Evangelical Adviser Was Sure God Had Chosen Ted Cruz to Be President' Oops."
Huffington Post

This report references a January meeting where Copeland was talking about a Ted Cruz presidency.

June 22, 2016 Donald Trump
"Who's Who of Trump's 'Tremendous' Faith Advisers"
Kate Shellnutt and Sarah Eekhoff Zylstra at *Christianity Today*

This article contains a list of all the faith advisors.

June 22, 2016 Donald Trump
"Trump Struggles to Close the Deal with Evangelicals"
Tim Alberta at *National Review*

"The Bible is full of men and women that repeatedly made grave errors," says Gary Bauer, the longtime activist leader and 2000 presidential candidate who also backed Cruz in 2016. "Who is it that they're holding up as this paragon, a man or woman without sin that they could have nominated for president? There's only one person who fits that description, and when he returns the election will be canceled."

June 22, 2016 Richard Land
"Why I Joined Donald Trump's Evangelical Executive Advisory Board"
The Christian Post

June 22, 2016 Eric Metaxas
Response to Trump Meeting with Evangelicals
The Mike Gallagher Show

June 22, 2016 Mike Gallagher
#NeverTrump Needs a Name Change
Townhall

And I ask fellow Americans who continue to be mystified at the destructive efforts of some of their former allies in the Republican Party to borrow a page from history and call them what they are: "Republicans for Hillary." Never again will I call them part of the Never Trump movement. This game of pretending that to be Never Trump doesn't lead to a President Hillary Clinton has to end.

June 23, 2016 Donald Trump
Pentecostal Leaders Pack Out Trump's New Christian Advisory Board
Aysha Khan at *Charisma News*

The article lists all members of Evangelical Executive Advisory Board:
    Michele Bachmann—former U.S. House member
    A.R. Bernard—senior pastor and CEO, Christian Cultural Center
    Mark Burns—pastor, Harvest Praise and Worship Center
    Tim Clinton—president, American Association of Christian Counselors
    Kenneth and Gloria Copeland—founders, Kenneth Copeland Ministries

James Dobson—author, psychologist and host, "Family Talk With Dr. James Dobson"

Jerry Falwell Jr. —president, Liberty University

Ronnie Floyd—senior pastor, Cross Church

Jentezen Franklin—senior pastor, Free Chapel

Jack Graham—senior pastor, Prestonwood Baptist Church

Harry Jackson—senior pastor, Hope Christian Church

Robert Jeffress—senior pastor, First Baptist Church of Dallas

David Jeremiah—senior pastor, Shadow Mountain Community Church

Richard Land—president, Southern Evangelical Seminary

James MacDonald—founder and senior pastor, Harvest Bible Chapel

Johnnie Moore—author, president of The KAIROS Company

Robert Morris—senior pastor, Gateway Church

Tom Mullins—senior pastor, Christ Fellowship

Ralph Reed—founder, Faith and Freedom Coalition

James Robison—founder, Life OUTREACH International

Tony Suarez—executive vice president, National Hispanic Christian Leadership Conference

Jay Strack—president, Student Leadership University

Paula White—senior pastor, New Destiny Christian Center

Tom Winters—attorney, Winters and King Inc.

Sealy Yates—attorney, Yates and Yates

June 24, 2016 Johnnie Moore

"Prominent Christian Johnnie Moore Reveals What 'Really Struck' Him About Trump During This Week's Evangelical Meeting"
Billy Hallowell at *Deseret News*

Moore mentions Trump's commitment to religious liberty. The article also mentions pro-Trump statements from Franklin Graham but also includes Evangelicals like Russell Moore who were opposed to Trump.

June 27, 2016 Bill Clinton

Bill Clinton and Loretta Lynch meet on her plane at Phoenix airport. This informal meeting became very controversial because of conspiracy theories.

June 27, 2016 Lana Vawser
"This is the Season of Solutions!!!"
LanaVawser.com

As I saw the news this week concerning Donald Trump inviting some evangelical leaders to be part of his advisory board, the Lord spoke to me and said to me that this was a prophetic picture for the body of Christ. A prophetic picture that there is about to be an increase in the people of God being "called for" to minister and give wisdom to people of great influence.

June 29, 2016 Tony Suarez
Suarez On Why He Joined Trump's Advisory Board
Strang Report

June 30, 2016 Michael Brown
"Why I'm Actually Rooting for Donald Trump"
Stream.org

June 30, 2016 Julie A. Smith
Can This Nation Be Turned Back to God?
Elijah List

July 5, 2016 James Comey, Hillary Clinton
"F.B.I. Director James Comey Recommends No Charges for Hillary Clinton on Email"
Mark Landler and Eric Lichtblau at *New York Times*

"Although we did not find clear evidence that Secretary Clinton or her colleagues intended to violate laws governing the handling of classified information, there is evidence that they were extremely careless in their handling of very sensitive, highly classified information."

Comey's full statement is at fbi.gov.

July 6, 2016 Donald Trump
"Conservative Pastors Are Distancing Themselves from the 2016 Election"
American Culture & Faith Institute

Provides numbers on pastors favouring a presidential candidate and participation in election event.

July 8, 2016 Johnny Enlow
A Word to the Older Generation: Refire, Don't Retire
Elijah List

Enlow uses Trump as an example of an older man who is refired.

July 8, 2016 Mark Taylor
Operation Let My People Go [#11 in list]
Sord Rescue

The Spirit of God says, "When Donald Trump is elected, a sign will be given. The earth shall quake because of who I have selected. It's a shift, a shift in the power structure that is taking place and another sign will be given when it falls without grace. A lightning strike and a great wind shall topple the sol called great monument, and they will not be able to mend. It will be a sign that the Luciferian reign and ungodly powers are coming to an end. I have had it with time and truth that bends. When it topples and shatters the capstone the builders accepted will be exposed for all to see and the one they rejected who is me. For these ungodly powers I the Lord God will expose! From the Illuminati to the Cabal, they are beginning to decompose. For those that speak of myths of wrath to come are creating fanaticism, and they will go down to the abyss with a cataclysm."

The Spirit of God says, "The timeline, the counterfeit timeline that they have used, you shall see it and how it's been abused. For the counterfeit timeline that they have used to lead my people astray, will be exposed and seen because my remnant people have prayed. You people who speak with time and truth that bends. Woa to you for you forgot about my remnant and that's my surprise, and now it's your end and it shall be your demise! For the counterfeit spiritual compass that is pulling and magnetizing my people off course as it be, will be turned back by my true army, and pointed true north, and back to me."

The Spirit of God says, "Woa to those that have tried to enslave my people, for now I will topple your so called steeple. It has stood for so long, that beast of old called Babylon! For this new world order that seeks to destroy, forgot about my true army that's being deployed. My army rise up and take on this beast, and I the Lord God will take him down to the least. For this beast is roaring trying to intimidate, through assassinations, division, and hate. Rise up! It's time to battle against this beast with extreme prejudice and you will terminate!"

Your Supreme Commander, God.

July 8, 2016 Paula White
"Paula White on Donald Trump's Christian Faith"
Napp Nazworth at *The Christian Post*

"My observation and experience is that faith has been instrumental in his life. Like many Christians, his understanding of the Bible has grown and is growing. So, while I can't give you a specific chapter and verse, I know of his love for the Word of God."

July 12, 2016 Johnny Enlow
A Word to the Older Generation: Refire, Don't Retire
Spirit Fuel [This prophecy was also given on The Elijah List on July 8.]

July 13, 2016 Glenn Kennedy
"God says Trump wins by landslide IF"
YouTube

"The only thing stopping Donald Trump from being president is Donald Trump."

July 14, 2016 Peter Wehner
Republican Presidential Politics
Peter Wehner at *Washington Journal* (C-SPAN)

Wehner, a major political analyst, argues that Trump is a terrible candidate for president.

July 15, 2016 Chris Lehmann
"How the Prosperity Gospel Explains Donald Trump's Popularity with Christian Voters"
The Washington Post

Compares Trump with prosperity preacher Joel Osteen.

July 15, 2016 Mike Pence
Mike Pence chosen as vice president

July 18, 2016 Mike Thompson
Heavenly Prayer Challenge Part 3
YouTube

This is about a vision about two opposing ideologies fighting within the United States. An angel gave Thompson a slightly different version of the Lord's Prayer, which says, "Let your will be done in the United States as it is in heaven."

July 19, 2016 Donald Trump, Paula White
Official nominee for president [Republican National Convention was held July 18–21 in Cleveland, Ohio]

Paula White gave the benediction at the end of the first night of the convention. On July 20 Ted Cruz created a fury for not endorsing Trump in his speech.

July 20, 2016 Various Prophets
Donald Trump Prophesied to Become Our Next President
The Investigator's Report (YouTube)

July 22, 2016 Donald Trump
"Why These Evangelical Leaders Are Firmly Against Trump"
Huffington Post

Religion reporter Carol Kuruvilla profiles eight Evangelical leaders opposed to Trump: Russell Moore, Eric Teetsel, Peter Wehner, Thabiti Anyabwile, Reid Ribble, President Carter, Max Lucado, and Jim Wallis.

July 22, 2016 Kenneth Storey
Donald Trump and the Restoration of America
YouTube

July 22, 2016 Democratic National Committee
WikiLeaks releases thousands of hacked emails from DNC.

July 27, 2016 Donald Trump
Trump at a press conference: "Russia, if you're listening, I hope you can find the 33,000 emails that are missing. I think you will probably be rewarded mightily by our press."

July 28, 2016 Wayne Grudem
Why Voting for Donald Trump Is a Morally Good Choice
Townhall.com

July 29, 2016 Dutch Sheets
"America Will Choose Her Destiny with These 7 Ideals"
Charisma News

This article elaborates on a few thoughts regarding the upcoming election and what voters should consider before they vote for the new president.

July 31, 2016 FBI Investigation
"Code Name Crossfire Hurricane: The Secret Origins of the Trump Investigation"
New York Times

This article is about the start of the FBI investigation of the Trump campaign. The FBI used Stefan Halper as a source in the investigation. Halper's identity was kept hidden until May 17, 2018, when it was reported by Chuck Ross at *The Daily Caller,* and May 18, reported by Ken Dilanian for *NBC News*. Ross used Halper's name in a March 25, 2018, article about his meetings with various Trump officials, but there was no mention of an FBI connection.

August 1, 2016 James Dobson
August letter

The article discusses how religious freedom became part of America's constitution and how it is being chipped away at. Trump would reverse that. Dobson was criticized for saying that Trump was led to Christ by Paula White.

August 2, 2016 Hank Kunneman
More Christian Prophets Are Confirming that Trump is Our New President
Sid Roth Show (YouTube)

The video has over 1 million views; it talks about Obamacare being reversed while persecution is coming everywhere. The year 2016 will be dark, with gloom, clouds, and thick darkness, and it will be powerful; it will be a year of reform. There will be inner turmoil within Russia. The spirit of Jezebel wants the White House and America. There will be a great revival among Muslims.

August 3, 2016 Dutch Sheets
What Should Christians Consider When Voting?
Elijah List

August 4, 2016 Jill Steele
A New Wave of the Flag
His Kingdom Prophecy

From a vision from July 4 weekend:

I submit to you the vision I was given asking you to pray for understanding and to pray for Donald Trump. Also, I was completely blown away because I was so sure the 'Trump Call' word God gave me back in the spring would be the end of my political words. (Smacking myself in the head here), I should have known better. And right now, things couldn't look worse for Trump... but God...

We were in the regular Saturday night service at our church. For holidays, we observe and incorporate many traditional celebrations. There was nothing remarkable about the service at this point. It was a basic observance of Independence Day. After we stood and sang "America the Beautiful," our pastor asked us to bow our heads as he prayed. As soon as I bowed my head and closed my eyes, I saw Donald

Trump standing at a podium, and beside him, a HUGE American Flag WAVING vigorously. Then the Holy Spirit said, "There is a NEW WAVE of the FLAG COMING!" At that moment, Donald Trump raised his hands and bowed his head. I actually thought, Wow! He is going to pray with us! But instantly, the Lord impressed on me that he was bowing his head to receive his anointing! Then, I saw more of the podium and I looked more closely at it because there was a big circle on the front of it and I couldn't tell what was on the circle. Suddenly, it became clear that it was the Presidential seal. Yes, it was Trump standing at the presidential podium. And that was the end of it.

August 8, 2016 Eric Holmberg
"Trump as Cyrus? Really?"
The Apologetic Group

August 10, 2016 Mike Thompson
Purpose of Mike's Heavenly Visions Part 4
YouTube

Thompson warns about an antichrist spirit in America.

August 11, 2016 Donald Trump
Pastors and Pews meeting (Orlando, FL [David Lane, organizer])

Trump focuses on repealing the Johnson amendment.

August 11, 2016 Jim Garlow
"If You're On the Fence About Your Vote, This Pastor Clarifies How the Very Future of America Is At Stake"
Charisma News

August 13, 2016 Henry Gruver
Prophetic Vision
Gruver on radio with Hagmann and Hagmann, "Watchmen Unleased" (YouTube)

In a dream, Trump visits Gruver's home and is dressed like a king. Gruver claims he received the vision of Trump in March 2016.

August 15, 2016 Peter Strzok
Controversial text from FBI Agent Peter Strzok: "I want to believe the path you threw out for consideration in Andy's office — that there's no way he gets elected, but I'm afraid we can't take that risk. It's like an insurance policy in the unlikely event you die before you're 40."

This text from Strzok to Lisa Page is the most famous of the thousands of emails related to the Trump-Russia collusion controversies. President Trump has argued that the text indicates treasonous intent.

August 15, 2016 Sadhu Sundar Selvaraj
Prediction of Trump Win
YouTube

"Trump will become President. He will be used to clean and purify the nation. As hard as he is, he has been prepared for this. As Cyrus was used to discipline Israel and then to restore Israel, likewise Trump will be used in the U.S. He will be used to curb violence. He will be God's mouth and hand for this nation."

August 15, 2016 Jim Garlow
Garlow on November Election
Strang Report

August 16, 2016 Lance Wallnau
"Prophecy: God Sent Donald Trump to Wage War Against Destructive Spirits"
Charisma News

When I first heard Donald Trump speak, he was returning from a trip to Iowa where he met "evangelicals." Asked what he thought about them he replied, "Well, they're interesting." He sounded like he had encountered a rare bird species never seen in Manhattan.

With 15 candidates running, and many of them strong Christians, it didn't seem likely that Mr. Trump, the business man outsider, would go very far. But I heard the Lord say something: "Donald Trump is a wrecking ball to the spirit of political correctness." That was the first word I heard about him.

August 17, 2016 Lance Wallnau
Part 1: Trump as Wrecking Ball to the Spirit of Political Correctness
Part 2: How is Donald Trump Like King Cyrus
Strang Report

August 17, 2016 Lance Wallnau
"Donald Trump Key to Isaiah 45 Prophecy?"
Charisma News

Wallnau reflects on his meeting at Trump Tower where he first met Trump:

Trump scanned the room and said: "I think we had such a long period of Christian consensus in our culture and we kind of got... spoiled. Is that the right word?" Then he turned the tables on us and said something shocking: "Every other ideological group in the country has a voice. If you don't mind me saying so, you guys have gotten soft." Ouch! That's the line I won't forget. Then in a moment of reflection he corrected himself, "I mean, we, myself included, we've had it easy as Christians for a long time in America. That's been changing."

The Spirit impressed upon my mind "read Isaiah 45."

To be honest, I didn't recall what the chapter was about. I opened a Bible and began to read "Thus sayeth the Lord to Cyrus whom I've anointed." Cyrus, I thought? Who is he in relation to all this? I recalled that he was a heathen king who was indispensable to the protection of the Jews but was frankly confused as to what God was saying.

With 15 candidates running, many who were clear conservative evangelicals, why would God be talking about Cyrus? I quickly looked up the number of the next president. I confirmed that Barack Obama is number 44. The next president will indeed be number 45. I kept reading Isaiah 45.

[Wallnau states in this piece that his first meeting with Trump was on December 30, 2015. Actually, Wallnau was first with Trump on September 28, 2015, at a meeting where various religious leaders prayed for Trump. Wallnau wrote about this in a Facebook post on October 3, 2015.]

August 18, 2016 Lance Wallnau
"Is Trump Himself a Prophet? This Businessman Says Yes!"
Charisma News

From my perspective, there is a Cyrus anointing on Trump. He is as my friend Kim Clement said three years ago: "Gods Trumpet." I predicted his nomination and I believe he is the chaos candidate set apart to navigate us through the chaos that is coming to America. I think America is due for a shaking regardless of who is in office. I believe the 45th President is meant to be an Isaiah 45 Cyrus.

Right now I'm recalling the last words I heard him speak at a rally in Atlanta before the nomination. "I have to tell you. Get ready folks," he warned. "The distortions of the news media and hundreds of millions of dollars in attack ads are coming. Who knows how much damage they will do? I really wonder about that. You have to get ready. They're coming."

How much damage will they do? We are about to find out. He is looking more and more like a man under siege. I for one will stand with him. With Cyrus Trump. I wonder how many will join me? Are you willing to become the missing grassroots needed in the final weeks? Everything is at stake.

August 18, 2016 Lance Wallnau
Donald Trump and Common Grace
Strang Report

August 18, 2016 Kat Kerr
Trump Will Win!
Lou Comunale post on News2morrow

August 19, 2016 Mark Taylor
The Luciferian Reign is Over
Komorusan714 (YouTube)

God isn't done with America; God will purge the land, expose corruption; the church has become apathetic; Trump knows a lot more than people think.

August 23, 2016 Steve Strang
Interview with Trump
Strang Report

August 26, 2016 Mark Taylor
Donald 2016 Trump Prophecy
YouTube

The 501c3 Tax Exempt Non-Profit Organization is said to be demonic. Blame for the state that America is in is put on the most prominent pastors because of their tax-exempt status. Christians are losing legal battles because they agreed to be under a bribe, which was the basis of 501 c3; it has had demonic influence and caused pastors to be timid. Trump will expose the Illuminati; ISIS is taking orders from Illuminati. Conspiracy theories are Satan's prophecies.

[Mark Taylor is criticized strongly by various Conservative Christians for his opposition to the use of 501c3 by churches.]

September 3, 2016 Wayne Jackson
Interview with Bishop Wayne Jackson
Fox2detroit.com

Don Lemon talks with Bishop Jackson about Trump's visit to his church.

September 4, 2016 Mike Thompson
Favour of God is Upon the Unlikely Part 5 [published on September 4, 2016]
YouTube

Trump is a wrecking ball, a bulldozer. Thompson says he will vote for him and that God is using Trump whether he becomes president or not.

September 6, 2016 Jim Garlow
"Will Obama's Betrayal of Israel Bring America Down?"
Charisma News

September 7, 2016 Jim Garlow
"Could Donald Trump Reverse the Curse Over America?"
Charisma News

September 9, 2016 Hillary Clinton
"Hillary Clinton Creates Controversy over her 'Basket of Deplorables' Comment"
Time

"You know, to just be grossly generalistic, you could put half of Trump's supporters into what I call the basket of deplorables. Right?" The racist, sexist, homophobic, xenophobic, Islamaphobic—you name it. And unfortunately there are people like that. And he has lifted them up."

"Clinton Offered a Partial Apology for her Comments"
Politico

September 9, 2016 Donald Trump
"Family Research Council Values Voter Summit"
Politico

Trump was introduced by actor Jon Voight.

September 14, 2016 Paula White
"Meet the Pastor who Prays with Donald Trump"
Elizabeth Dias at *Time*

September 18, 2016 Reyna
Donald Trump—Prophetic Vision

She saw a vision in which God was aligning Donald Trump to himself.

September 19, 2016 Lou Engle
Call to Pray
Elijah List

This is about a vision of Trump crying (Ezekiel 22:30, "I looked for a man to stand in the gap").

September 21, 2016 Darrell Scott
Pastor Darrell Scott leads prayer for Trump at Cleveland conference.
YouTube

September 23, 2016 James Dobson
"Why I Am Voting for Donald Trump"
Christianity Today

September 26, 2016 Donald Trump
First presidential debate (Hempstead, New York)

September 28, 2016 Norman Geisler
"Six reasons to vote for Trump"
Christianity Today

September 28, 2016 Patricia Green
Patricia Green Predicts Trump Presidency
YouTube

Green says that the Lord also told her on June 9th, 2016, that Trump would be president.

September 29, 2016 Donald Trump
Trump meets with Evangelicals at Trump Tower.

[For details on the meeting, see the December 2, 2019, article "False Idol — Why the Christian Right Worships Donald Trump" by Alex Morris at *Rolling Stone*.]

September 29, 2016 Lance Wallnau
God is Raising Up Trump
Strang Report

Wallnau sensed an anointing on Trump at first meeting.

September 29, 2016 Donald Trump
"Torn Over Donald Trump and Cut Off by Culture Wars, Evangelicals Despair"
Laurie Goodstein at *The New York Times*

This coverage is of Dick and Betty Odgaard's public ordeal over their unwillingness to rent out their chapel for a gay couple's wedding.

"… the Odgaards and other conservative evangelicals interviewed in central Iowa say they feel as if they have been abandoned. Many say that they have no genuine champion in the presidential race and that the country has turned its back on them. Americans are leaving church, same-sex marriage is the law of the land, and the country has moved on to debating transgender rights. While other Americans are anxious about the economy, jobs and terrorism, conservative Christians say they fear for the nation's very soul. Some worry that the nation has strayed so far that God's punishment is imminent."

September 30, 2016 Lou Engle
A Word About the Elections
Elijah List

September 30, 2016 Lance Wallnau
God's Chaos Candidate releases in paperback and Kindle. [See Wallnau's site on book and video introduction.]

October 2016 Donald Trump, Mike Pence
Trump and Pence are on the cover of *Charisma* magazine. Almost the entire October issue is devoted to Trump and the election.

October 2016 Donald Trump
A Declaration by American Evangelicals Concerning Donald Trump
Change.org

This petition received 24,000 signatures.

A significant mistake in American politics is the media's continued identification of "evangelical" with mostly white, politically conservative, older men. We are not those evangelicals. The media's narrow labels of our community perpetuate stereotypes, ignore our diversity, and fail to accurately represent views expressed by the full body of evangelical Christians.

Donald Trump's campaign is the most recent and extreme version of a history of racialized politics that has been pursued and about which white evangelicals, in particular, have been silent. The silence in previous times has set the environment for what we now see.

October 5, 2016 Donald Trump
Trump visits International Church of Las Vegas's Kairos School of Ministry.

October 5, 2016 Lance Wallnau
"Why I Believe Trump Is the Prophesied President"
Charisma News

I predicted his nomination, and I believe he is the chaos candidate set apart to navigate us through the chaos that is coming to America. I think America is due for a shaking regardless of who is in office. I believe the 45th president is meant to be an Isaiah 45 Cyrus.

Trump is much like Churchill, lifting a warning voice about the unravelling of America at a time when the ruling class, buttressed by the media, want to deny there is anything wrong! In all likelihood, Trump is intuiting that which is on the horizon if changes are not made. Like Churchill, the opposition wants to exile him for sounding an alarm in his disturbingly blunt manner. The media assault on Trump is unprecedented.

Let my account provide an alternative viewpoint. I am thankful to Steve Strang for the courage to publish this potentially controversial piece. Trump is not a perfect man or a flawless candidate. But I do believe I've heard God.

[In this article Wallnau says he first met Trump on December 30, 2015. It was on September 28, 2015.]

October 5, 2016, Lance Wallnau
God is Raising up Trump
Elijah List

Prophetic word to Trump, given to his son: "If you will humble yourself and pray and call upon the name of the Lord, you'll be the next president of the United States."

October 7, 2016 Stephen Strang
"Is Lance Wallnau's Prophecy True? Is Trump God's Anointed Man to Lead the Free World?"
Charisma News

"Lance Wallnau believes God is raising up Donald Trump like he did King Cyrus in Isaiah 45. When the charismatic speaker/business consultant first said this long before the billionaire businessman received the Republican nomination, nearly everyone thought he was nuts. Now, Wallnau's analysis is ringing true with many Christians who are looking to make sense spiritually of this very strange election season."

October 7, 2016 Donald Trump, Billy Bush
Video from 2005 released where Trump makes vulgar remarks to Billy Bush about women.
Washington Post

October 8, 2016 Donald Trump, Billy Bush
Trump apologizes for comments on 2005 video.

October 9, 2016 Wayne Grudem
Trump's Moral Character and the Election
Townhall.com

October 9, 2016 Albert Mohler Jr.
"Donald Trump Has Created an Excruciating Moment for Evangelicals"
Albert Mohler Jr. at *The Washington Post*

October 9, 2016 Lance Wallnau
Prophetic Word on Donald Trump
Facebook

Wallnau states that Satan was behind the release of a disgusting video by Billy Bush. Wallnau claims that "God can do more with Samson than he can with Jezebel." He warns that people should "be careful how you touch the anointed vessel of God" and says that Trump is carnal, but the other side is demonic.

October 9, 2016 Donald Trump
During the second presidential debate, Trump denies engaging in unwanted sexual advances towards women. [The debate was held in St. Louis.]

October 9, 2016 Lana Vawser
An Encounter with Jesus Concerning the US Election and Donald Trump
LanaVawser.com

Recently I had an encounter with the Lord where He showed me an assignment of the enemy that is about to be released into the body of Christ in the United States of America regarding the US election that is about to take place in a little over a month.

Before I share this encounter with you, I want to state this and make it clear that since I felt the Lord speak of Donald Trump in this encounter, firstly I am not releasing this word from any "political standpoint" of reviewing any policies or agendas. I am simply releasing this word from an encounter that I had with the Lord and felt a strong urgency to release it.

Secondly considering the video released yesterday from 2005, I want to say firstly that the Lord DOES NOT condone sin, and by releasing this encounter I am not condoning Donald's past actions, but felt an urgency to publish this encounter as a warning to the body of Christ. As I pondered this encounter in light of yesterday's video, I felt a stirring from the Lord to not focus on the past but what God is saying TODAY in THIS SEASON right now.

I was standing in what looked like a "commission room" in hell and so much darkness around. I saw the enemy and he was about to release a horde of demons upon the earth into the United States with a specific target against believers.

What I noticed about these demonic spirits was that they had blindfolds in their hands and they were ready to "move." I asked Jesus what these demonic spirits were and he said that they were "spirits of deception."

I then heard ... "My people that are not pressing in for discernment, to hear My heart concerning the US election and who I have anointed for the next Presidential Term, will be brought to a place right now in this season where they will be blinded by deception. This army that is about to be released into the body of Christ in the USA are coming to blind people to the truth that I have anointed Donald Trump and Mike Pence and the people of God need to hear this so that they keep pressing in for discernment despite what the media and the 'natural world' says. Things are going to continue to escalate and pressure intensify to push Donald Trump out, but My people need to take their place and stand with Me to see My purposes come to fruition."

The sense surrounded me that this is a very strategic moment, a time of urgency and a time to pray even more fervently. The sense of 'laying down agenda(s) and simply seeking the heart of God for this new season for the nation of America that is approaching.

I felt this reminder from the Lord to His people in the USA to be praying for discernment right now and to lift their eyes up higher. Place not your eyes on 'media' or the 'natural' but really continue seeking His heart. I felt such a strong sense of an 'increase in onslaught' in this US election in this "last leg," and God's people are going to need eyes to see and ears to hear what the Spirit is saying more than ever before.

As I have sat with the Lord on this word, I have felt the Lord's heart for His people to not get "caught up" in what is going on in the "natural."

The very heart of this word ultimately was I felt a call from the Lord for His people to "come up higher." To not be bound up by what is being reported or what is not being reported. The fate of a nation does not hang on MAN, it's in the hand of the Lord and the ONUS is on the Church right now.

I believe Jesus is calling His people in light of everything going on in this messy situation in the USA with Clinton and Trump, to seek His heart above ALL ELSE.

Put your hope in Jesus. To cry out for the Lord to bring a cleansing and a turning in this nation. To really individually continue to seek out the heart of God and ask the Spirit of God to give eye salve so there may be clear spiritual sight regarding this election and the destiny of the USA.

"Also buy white garments from me so you will not be shamed by your nakedness, and ointment for your eyes so you will be able to see" ~ Revelation 3:18

This is not just about Donald Trump/Mike Pence, this is about the destiny and the fate of the United States of America. The Lord sees BEYOND today, and it's time to really seek His heart and His ways.

This is really a time of repentance for America and calling forth the plans and purposes of God in the nation and a surrendering of agendas to align with His ways, even when we don't understand. It's time to stand in the gap more than ever before for a move of God in the nation. I felt that this is a very strategic moment right now, the fate and destiny of the nation hangs in the balance.

October 10, 2016 Andy Crouch
"Speak Truth to Trump"
Christianity Today

"Strategy becomes idolatry when we betray our deepest values in pursuit of earthly influence. And because such strategy requires capitulating to idols and princes and denying the true God, it ultimately always fails. Enthusiasm for a candidate like Trump gives our neighbors ample reason to doubt that we believe Jesus is Lord. They see that some of us are so self-interested, and so self-protective, that we will ally ourselves with someone who violates all that is sacred to us—in hope, almost certainly a vain hope given his mendacity and record of betrayal, that his rule will save us."

October 10, 2016 Donald Trump
"Evangelical Leaders React to Tape of Trump's Vulgar Remarks"
Sarah Eekhoff Zylstra at *Christianity Today*

Most prominent Trump supporters stuck with Trump while a few went public against Trump, including James MacDonald.

October 11, 2016 Kenneth Copeland
Christians Who Don't Vote for Trump Are 'Going to Be Guilty of Murder'
Right Wing Watch

"Nobody will take God's nation away from God."

October 11, 2016 Norman Geisler
Norman Geisler on Why He's Supporting Trump and Not Changing His Mind
Christianity Today

October 11, 2016 Donald Trump
"Evangelical Magazines Decry Trump: 'Someone who violates all that is sacred to us'"
Julie Zauzmer at *The Washington Post*

News about *World* and *Christianity Today* articles against Trump.

October 11, 2016 Lana Vawser
Pray for Discernment in Elections
Elijah List

"This army that is about to be released into the body of Christ in the USA are coming to blind people to the truth that I have anointed Donald Trump and Mike Pence, and the people of God need to hear that they need to keep pressing in for discernment—despite what the media and the 'natural world' says."

October 11, 2016 Marvin Olasky
"Unfit for Power: It's Time for Donald Trump to Step Aside and Make Room for Another Candidate"
Marvin Olasky and the Editors at *World*

October 13, 2016, Jack Graham
"What Donald Trump's Evangelical Advisors Tell Him"
The Christian Post

October 14, 2016 Franklin Graham
Facebook

"A lot of people are slamming evangelicals for supposedly giving Donald J. Trump a pass. That's simply not true. No one is giving him a pass. I'm certainly not, and I've not met an evangelical yet who condones his language or inexcusable behavior from over a decade ago. However, he has apologized to his wife, his family, and to the American people for this. He has taken full responsibility. This election isn't about Donald Trump's behavior from 11 years ago or Hillary Clinton's recent missing emails, lies, and false statements. This election is about the Supreme Court and the justices that the next president will nominate. Evangelicals are going to have to decide which candidate they trust to nominate men and women to the court who will defend the constitution and support religious freedoms. My prayer is that Christians will not be deceived by the liberal media about what is at stake for future generations."

October 14, 2016 Jorge Parrott
Jorge Parrott, a mission worker, speaks to Donald Trump
Facebook [Film done by John Boneck]

Parrott refers to him as "President Trump."

October 17, 2016 Donald Trump
"A Christian Conservative Backlash Against Trump Seems to Be Building"
Lisa Wangsness at *Boston Globe*

October 18, 2016 Derek W.H. Thomas
Viral sermon hints at God's hidden purpose for Trump: 'Would you vote for Cyrus the Great?'
WorldNet Daily

October 19, 2016 Mark Taylor
Full Circle [#12 in list]
Sord Rescue

The Spirit of God says: "Russia, that's right Russia, I will use Russia, the United States of America and her allies, to take on the 4th Reich called ISIS. For it has come full circle again, that's right again. The New World Order is trying to rise and take it's place, just like they did in WWII, America and her allies came in from the west and Russia from the east, so shall it be again to slay this so called beast, and it will be brought down to the least. Some will say, "Why would I use Russia? Am I not the God of the cosmos? I will use anyone and any nation I choose, whether some like it or not! I will not be put in a box!"

The Spirit of God says: "The ties that were severed between America and Russia, will begin to mend and they will take on this so called Goliath and with one stone shall slay it and all those that are behind it. For it is not just ISIS they will fight, but the Elite, the Globalists, and the Illuminati who will be exposed by my light. For they are an enemy to the world and my agenda. They shall fall with a mighty blow, so that my gospel will begin to flow. For they wear their flag as if it were a prayer shawl, so they will be taken down with my Shock and Awe! For freedom and liberty will begin to ring, and the people will begin to sing, as healing and light come from my wings. My people rejoice and shout, for my gospel is coming and will go through all the earth, and all the nations will know this is why My America was birthed!"

October 19, 2016 Wayne Grudem
If You Don't Like Either Candidate, Then Vote for Trump's Policies
Townhall.com

October 19, 2016 Lana Vawser
I had a vision where I saw a divine "reset" and the Lord release an invitation to "lift up your eyes" coming into the US election time!!
LanaVawser.com

I had a vision recently where I saw the hand of the Lord come down upon the nation of America and upon the body of Christ in the USA and He pressed a huge button that was gold and shining and it said "RESET" across it.

I saw that there was a simultaneous "RESET" that was about to happen in the nation and in the body of Christ in the nation. As this "button" was pressed, I saw what looked like "sound waves" being released from this button that was activated and the sound waves where moving through the nation and in the body of Christ.

As the "sound waves" pulsated through the nation and the church I could hear Matthew 11:15 and Revelation 2:29 being declared loudly, over and over.

"Whoever has ears, let them hear." ~ Matthew 11:15

"Whoever has ears, let them hear what the Spirit says to the churches."
~ Revelation 2:29

As I was listening to these Scriptures being declared over the nation and the body of Christ, I could feel the invitation flowing from the heart of God to His people to come deeper in surrender, to lay down agenda's and seek out His heart for He was bringing about a *"MINDSET RESET"* in the nation of America and in the body of Christ.

I then heard the Lord say *"The way the United States is viewed and the MINDSET that has been established in the nation is about to CHANGE and I want My people to agree with My heart and be on the same page. The same page that I have set the stage for a great REARRANGE."*

As I heard the word *"REARRANGE"* instantly a vision opened up in front of Me and I saw a HUGE CHESSBOARD. I watched as the hand of the Lord moved pieces from the front to the back and pieces from the back to the front. It was happening in the nation and the Church of America all at the same time.

I watched as He moved pieces in directions many people did not like, nor did they expect, and I could see many on the sidelines of this chessboard and they were looking at the pieces being shifted, shaped and moved and they were shouting and throwing stones at them. As these stones were being thrown I saw a word written on the stones and it said *"DECLARATIONS."* These declarations being shouted were attempting to stop the *"shifting and moving"* of the pieces because they were not moving in the way that was expected . The Lord then says to me *"Lana, where are their eyes, where is their focus?"* I looked and noticed the eyes of these ones were on the *"pieces"*, how they look and their movements. So I answered the Lord *"They are on the pieces."* He then says to me *"Yes, in this critical moment for the United States of America, My people need to make sure that they are pressing deeper into My heart than ever before. They need to make sure that their eyes are on Me and not on the "external." For My people will not understand My ways and the way I am shifting things around if their eyes are on the natural. They must come lower still, in a place of surrender, no agenda and seek My heart as I release greater insight, strategy, blueprints and keys for this nation. I am about to release the greatest "RESET" upon the nation of America that they have seen and I am inviting My people deeper still. I am about to RE-ESTABLISH what has been lost. I am about to RE-ESTABLISH life. I am about to RE-ESTABLISH hope, but it will be in a way that may look unexpected. Darkness may surround, shaking may be heard, but as My people press deeper into My heart, they will HEAR the sounds of life."*

A vision then opens in front of me and I see myself standing in a room and I see Donald Trump on one side of the room and Hilary Clinton on another. I can see them both speaking, but I cannot hear what they are saying. The sense surrounds me that they are debating or releasing their policies. As this is taking place I see above them a great spiritual battle taking place in the heavenlies. There is a MAJOR WAR going on in the spirit. I can see angelic hosts, I can see demonic figures and there is turbulence, shaking, the storm in the spirit is violent.

I then notice the people of God standing all around Trump and Clinton in a U shape. I see MANY crying out and in fervent prayer as they can see the violent storm taking place in the spirit in this critical moment, but I then see MANY of God's people with their eyes on each other and they are fighting and throwing stones at each other. They are tearing each other apart and not seeing what's actually going on in the spirit and taking their position to intercede.

I begin to wonder why the people of God are standing around these two Presidential Candidates in the shape of a "U" and instantly I hear the Lord saying ... "This is a critical moment. Get your eyes off U (YOU). Lift your eyes HIGHER! Ask Me for greater sight. Lift your eyes off U (YOU) and your agenda or expectation and keep your eyes on Me and partner with Me to pray for the DESTINY I have for the USA to be manifested in whatever form and way I choose. My people the enemy is using this election to bring division, hatred and poison amongst you. If you have your eyes on U (YOU) this division will continue. I have allowed this shaking to take place in the body of Christ to bring about an exposing of offenses and what is in the heart so I can HEAL YOU, set you free and take you deeper in Me. I have allowed this critical, violent shaking to show you My people, just how much you need to be continually cultivating your intimacy with Me, living in the renewing of the mind, and constantly crying out for discernment and spiritual insight and sight, even when your mind is offended. My people, My people in the United States, do not allow what is going on in the elections to DIVIDE YOU! This is your time to RISE UP!!!!! Come deeper! Come deeper! Come deeper! Trust Me! Trust Me and what I am doing!

Trust Me and what I am doing!" The Lord then continues "The U shape represents a divine U TURN! A TURNING OF DIRECTION!!!!! I am bringing a DIVINE RESET to the United States. I am setting things up again that have been broken and establishing things that are completely NEW, but in order to perceive the NEW that is about to BREAK THROUGH, the NEW that I am about to release into the USA, you must come deeper still without agenda."

"In the remaining weeks leading up to the election there will be an increase in angelic visitations, there will be an increase in encounters with Me, there will be an increase in prophetic dreams and signs and wonders releasing KEYS to you My people of My heart for the USA and My plans for what is to come. Leading up to this election, POSITION YOURSELF WITHOUT AGENDA or BIAS to SEEK ME as I am releasing CLARITY and INSIGHT on how to pray and declare for what I am about to do and going to do in the USA right now and the next DECADE. I am ENLARGING your sight My people, I am ENLARGING your vision. I am going to be releasing insight for the next DECADE in the United States, because what I am doing now, FAR SURPASSES an election or one or two Presidential Terms. There has been much warfare and turbulence concerning this election, because this is a TIPPING POINT ELECTION that as My people partner with My heart, will see DESTINY open up in more significant ways than EVER in the USA. The enemy knows this, so there has been great opposition and backlash. Seek Me, hear Me and call and decree My heart. Throw stones not at each other. Partner with Me in declaring and crying out for a DIVINE RESET and NEW BEGINNING! AGREE WITH ME! Pick up My Word and throw the stones at the enemy and the giants that stand before the DESTINY of the USA being opened up in a whole new way. It may be dark, and feel like the darkness is increasing, but My people, SEE, SEE, SEE with the eyes of My Spirit and SEE that I am setting the stage for LIFE! LIFE! LIFE!"

October 20, 2016 Steve Shultz
No Medical Situation Requires Abortion or Killing the Baby in the 3rd Trimester
Elijah List

October 21, 2016 Carter Page
FBI get warrant to monitor Carter Page as a Russian agent.

October 21, 2016 Kenneth Copeland
"You Ought to be Ashamed!"
Kcm.org

"The United States of America is the only nation in the history of this planet that was put together by a group of people for the express purpose of worshipping Me," saith the LORD. "I will never forget it! I created the nation of Israel," saith Jesus, "because I love them. The United States was created because they loved Me. You think I'm going to let some silly politicians put this thing under? You ought to be ashamed of yourselves."

October 23, 2016 Michael Brown
Why I Will Vote for Donald Trump
AskDrBrown.org

"One of my dear friends has spent hours with Trump and members of his family, and he has told me that in 55 years of ministry, no one has received him as openly and graciously as has Trump. Yet my friend continues to speak the truth to him in the clearest possible terms. While I am not one of those claiming that Trump is a born-again Christian (I see absolutely no evidence of this), the fact that he continues to listen to godly men and open the door to their counsel indicates that something positive could possibly be going on. It also indicates that these godly leaders might be a positive influence on him if he was elected president."

October 23, 2016 Jim Wallis
"Evangelicals aren't who you think"
Opinion Piece at *USA Today*

The truth is that most U.S. evangelicals do not support Trump. These Christians are victims of a sort of identity theft, as the national conversation conflates them with a narrow demographic of mostly older, politically conservative whites.

This embrace by many white evangelicals of a racial and pro-rich politics, which ignores 2,000 Bible verses that emphasize God's concern about injustice and the poor, represents worse than bad theology — it is idolatry bordering on heresy.

The concern for the vulnerable is at the heart of Jesus' life-changing and earth-shattering call. This historic moment, in which a diverse new evangelical generation confronts the immoral bigotry of the Trump campaign, is an opportunity to reclaim the true "evangelical" identity going forward. And that will indeed be "good news" for us all."

October 23, 2016 Wayne Grudem

"Wayne Grudem Backing Trump ... Again and For Good"
Michael F. Haverluck at *One News Now*

October 24, 2016 Dutch Sheets

"Dutch Sheets Shares Prophetic Insight for Church Dilemma Over Elections"
Jennifer LeClaire at *Charisma News*

October 24, 2016 Donald Trump

"The Guilt-Free Gospel of Donald Trump"
Daniel Burke at CNN

An informative piece on Trump's religious background, claims about faith, and friendship with Paula White.

October 26, 2016 Jim Garlow

If You Are on the Fence Voting for Trump
Strang Report

October 26, 2016 Kat Kerr

Watch and Pray
Elijah List

Kerr tells her listeners that "the Devil is terrified" because of God's plans for Trump. Kerr states that "God himself" has told her Trump will win and that "it will be a landslide." She urges "get on God's train, the Trump train."

October 27, 2016 Lance Wallnau
Lance Wallnau on Patricia King
YouTube

King promotes Wallnau's book *God's Chaos Candidate*. Wallnau recounts his trips to Trump Tower in 2015 and being told to look up Isaiah 45 and realize that Trump is God's Cyrus. Wallnau says Trump "is a test for the discerning of the Church."

Patricia King states that the church has been too silent and that Trump has given the church courage.

Wallnau states that "the gift of Trump is boldness" and that being in Trump's presence helped Wallnau be more courageous.

Wallnau says Trump is "Churchillian" and that "Trump is prophetically wired for chaos." Trump "is living with the most vicious distortion of stereotype I've ever seen."

October 27, 2016 Rabbi Curt Landry
Feast of the Tabernacle 5777
Elijah List

"We are in that final Trump. I have raised up Donald Trump to very blessed to have you called and he will come see you in your business you raise an awareness of the corruption and the doubt and the unbelief. I have raised him up as a mirror to expose that which is done in the undergirding. Yes, he was unclean. Yes, he has done some things, but I have got him born again. I have sanctified him. I have filled him with the Holy Ghost."

October 28, 2016 Dean Briggs and Lou Engle
Calling on the War Eagles and Intercessors
Elijah List

A call to pray for the upcoming presidential election.

October 28, 2016 Jim Garlow
The Wrecking Ball of Donald Trump
Strang Report

October 28, 2016 Hillary Clinton
FBI announces new investigation of Clinton emails.

October 29, 2016 Jim Garlow
Well Versed
Strang Report

October 30, 2016 Donald Trump, Denise Goulet
Trump attends International Church of Las Vegas. Pastor Denise Goulet
prays for Trump.

October 31, 2016 FBI Investigation
FBI sees no clear link between Trump and Russia.

October 31, 2016 FBI Investigation
Report on former spy who gave research memos to the FBI.

October 31, 2016 Frank Amedia
Prophecy for Donald Trump
Strang Report

Amedia tells the background to prophecy about Esther and Hamon on the
Jim Bakker Show.

Election Insight with Frank Amedia
Strang Report

November 2, 2016 Chuck Pierce, Dutch Sheets
Prophecy at International Church of Las Vegas
Elijah List

"History making moment … this is the beginning of saving a nation."

November 2, 2016 Frank Amedia
Discussion of Book of Esther and Haman hanging
Jim Bakker Show

Evangelist Frank Amedia uses the book of Esther to argue that Christians need to fight for Trump just as Esther fought for the Jewish people.

November 2, 2016 Lance Wallnau
On Las Vegas church meeting
Facebook

November 3, 2016 Denise Goulet, Pasqual Urrabazo
Prophecies from Las Vegas Church Trump Attended
Elijah List

"This is my son with whom I am well pleased…"
"God has given you the backbone and the courage to say yes to this challenge…"
"You have your hand on this man."

"Trump's Prophetic Destiny"
Charisma News

November 3, 2016 Hillary Clinton
"Has the F.B.I. Gone Full Breitbart?"
Abigail Tracy at *Vanity Fair*

Tracy argues that the FBI is biased against Clinton. [Later the FBI and James Comey in particular are targeted by Republicans as anti-Trump.]

November 4, 2016 Robert Hotchkin
Seven Words for the New Year
Patricia King Ministries

"The Lord spoke to me that Donald Trump has been a sign of this in the earth. His success in business opened a door for him to have an impact in the unrelated field of high-level politics."

November 4, 2016 Darrell Scott
What Trump Is Really Like
Strang Report

Trump Could Win by A Landslide and Become America's Greatest
President
Strang Report

November 4, 2016 Lance Wallnau
What God Is Saying During the 2016 Presidential Election
Strang Report

November 6, 2016 James Comey, Hillary Clinton
Congress told by Comey that there will be no criminal charges against
Clinton

November 7, 2016 Franklin Graham
It's All About the Supreme Court and Not to Vote is Wrong
Elijah List

November 7, 2016 Anita Fuentes
Anita Fuentes: Rabbi says Bible Codes Predict Trump Win
YouTube

November 7, 2016 Darrell Scott
Donald Trump Could Become a Great President
Strang Report

November 7, 2016 Franklin Graham
BillyGraham.org

Franklin leads in prayer about the upcoming election.

November 8, 2016 Frank Amedia
Haman is About to Hang
Elijah List report [includes video from Amedia's appearance on the *Jim
Bakker Show* on November 2, 2016]

Amedia states that there is an anointing to destroy the enemies of God in the next election just as the enemy of God (Haman) was destroyed in the time of Esther.

November 8, 2016 Donald Trump
Trump is elected 45th president of the United States.

November 8, 2016 Michelle Bachmann
America Stands 2016

Michelle Bachmann stated in the program, "It is the evangelical Christian that made the difference" (at 6.11.09 in tape).

November 9, 2016 Michael Brown
"Donald Trump: President by the Sovereign Intervention of God"
The Christian Post

November 9, 2016 Donald Trump
"How Evangelicals Helped Donald Trump Win"
Elizabeth Dias at *Time*

November 9, 2016 Mark Taylor
Post Election Interview
TruNews

Trump winning the election was a massive triumph for the body of Christ.

November 9, 2016 T.B. Joshua
"Prophecy of Clinton's Win Deleted After Trump Wins"
BBC

[His Facebook post was taken down.]

November 9, 2016 Garth Kant
"Signs of Divine Intervention in Trump's Victory: Bachmann prayed with millions that crucial moment tide turned"
WND

November 9, 2016 Robert Hotchkin
7 Prophetic Promises for 2017
Elijah List

The Lord spoke to me that Donald Trump has been a sign of this in the earth. His success in business opened a door for him to have an impact in the unrelated field of high-level politics.

November 9, 2016 Stephen Strang
Post Election: God Answered Our Prayers. Now the Work Begins.
Strang Report

November 10, 2016, Lana Vawser
Donald Trump and His Crown
Elijah List

"In the throne room of heaven ... Jesus says: it is time to come in ... during your presidential season I will make you like King David, a man after my own heart ... I will use you to unify ... commissioning room ... saw scrolls ... assassination attempts."

[Lana sent an email to Steve Shultz, founder of Elijah List, on October 19th.]

November 10, 2016 Various Prophets
"Meet the Evangelicals Who Prophesied a Trump Win"
Josh Hafner at *USA Today*

November 10, 2016 Israel
Sanhedrin Asks Putin and Trump to Build Third Temple in Jerusalem
Adam Eliyahu Berkowitz at Breaking Israel News

November 10, 2016 Donald Trump
"White Evangelicals Just Elected a Thrice-Married Blasphemer: What that means for the religious right"
Steve McQuiklin at Fort Myers News Press

November 10, 2016 Bill Johnson
"Why I Voted for Donald Trump"
Gospel Herald

"All elections are tough. This one more so than any other I can remember. And there very legitimate reasons for voting for or against any given candidate. Unfortunately neither Billy Graham or Mother Theresa were running for office. That leaves us with the responsibility to do our best with what we have. And I have done that, with a good conscience. I believe the outcome is from the Lord."

November 10, 2016 Jeremiah Johnson
Pastor Jeremiah Johnson's 14 Month Prophecy on Trump and the US Elections
Triple E forum

A recap of Johnson's controversial prophecy from July 2015.

November 11, 2016 Michael Brown
Trump: God's Sovereign Intervention
Elijah List

"We should pray for divine restraint on his life as well, lest this divine wrecking ball wreak havoc on the nation while tearing down what is wrong. May he be a divinely guided wrecking ball!"

November 11, 2016 Mark Taylor
The Prophecies Donald Trump Has Fulfilled
Jim Bakker Show

Zach Drew and his co-host mention some predictions for the future, mainly referencing Mark Taylor. Taylor claims the following:
>   Trump will build a third temple in Jerusalem.
>   The U.S. dollar will be the strongest in history.
>   Mainstream media will begin to agree with Trump.
>   Trump will appoint five Supreme Court judges.
>   One Supreme Court judge will die.

November 11, 2016 Bob Eschliman
Update on Prophecy on Trump
Charisma News

Firefighter prophet updates his vision for Donald Trump's presidency.

November 11, 2016 Steve Shultz
Kim Clement Totally Prophesied the Trump Presidency
Elijah List

November 11, 2016 Mike Thompson
"Trump wins!"
YouTube

God: 1, Devil: 0 "Jezebel has been trounced."

November 11, 2016 Kathi Pelton
An Open Letter of Love to my Non-Republican Friends
Spirit Fuel

President Obama has called for unity and support, Hillary Clinton has asked for unity and support, President Elect Donald Trump has asked for unity and support and now I am asking for that as well. Not agreement but an extension of love. Unity as Americans rather than riots of hate filling our streets and cities. Words of blessing rather than curses of hate. I have spent eight years pleaded with those around me who share my beliefs to not speak hate or curses over our more liberal friends and neighbors. I, and many others have asked them to pray for our president and to extend love in the midst of disagreement. We can rally for our causes without killing and hating one another. The Bible says that without love we are merely a "clanging gong or resounding cymbal." We are just noise! On either side, liberal or conservative, we are just noise when we are absent of love.

November 11, 2016 Steve Bremner
"Wiping Prophetic Egg Off My Face"
SteveBremner.com

Bremner admits error in his July critique of Jeremiah Johnson's prophecy.

November 12, 2016 Kim Clement
Codebreakers Prophetic Alert: Trump Prophecy
YouTube

A recap of Kim Clement's prophecies.

November 13, 2016 Prophet Sadhu
Prophet Sadhu Correctly Prophesied Trump Win—It's Now What Follows
Trump Election You Must Hear
YouTube

Revelation given on August 10, 8: 23 PM, according to Sadhu. He said he was caught up to heaven and received the message about Trump. He said he was also given a prophecy in 2008 that Obama would win.

[See entry about prophecy on August 15, 2016.]

November 14, 2016 Lana Vawser
An Encouragement to Keep Praying for President-Elect Trump
Elijah List

November 15, 2016 Aimee Herd
Direction on Praying for President-Elect Trump from 1 Chronicles 29
Elijah List

November 15, 2016 Donald Trump
"Why These Jewish Mystics Think God Helped Trump Win"
Sam Kestenbaum at *Forward*

This article is about Jewish leaders who want a third temple built in Jerusalem, including MK Yehuda Glick.

November 15, 2016 Michael Brown with Jeremiah Johnson
Brown interviews Johnson about his July 2015 prophecy that Trump is a Cyrus.
AskDrBrown.org

November 16, 2016 Jeffrey and Kathi Pelton
Understanding This Crucial Time: A Call to Prayer
Elijah List

November 16, 2016 Angie Stolba
The Restoration and Rebuilding of America
Elijah List

As it has been said, the Lord has chosen Donald Trump to be His wrecking ball. God is going to use this next president to bulldoze a system that will no longer be efficient in this season. The Lord is raising up Trump in this specific hour; He has placed within this man a warrior's spirit that will refuse to fear and be intimidated by politics or human agenda. I hear God saying, "I have given Donald Trump the ability to set his face like flint (Isaiah 50:7) and not be afraid of the mess or stirring up the tradition of man."

November 16, 2016 Doug Addison
Prophetic Word for the US and on the New President
DougAddison.com

Trump or Clinton?
Over the past year, I have been part of and overheard many counsel meetings in Heaven about the next President. For the first time in my prophetic experiences, I heard the name of the next President change on several occasions, as it was contingent on their character.

Last year I heard that Donald Trump was being called to be President, but pride was blinding his heart. In August, some other prophets and I heard that the presidency had fallen on Clinton because of Trump's pride. It is important to understand that God always has a plan to use anyone who takes this office. He showed me the plan for using the Clintons had Hillary been elected.

Election Day
On November 8, the morning of the elections, I was visited by a strong presence of the Lord at 5:00 AM and I received these prophetic words. I heard...

Prophetic word for U.S.
"O America, I still love you and see your zeal for Me. Satan has asked to sift you like wheat and the enemy has been waging war against you. But a remnant is going to arise to possess the land. Your sons and daughters are going to awaken from a sleep and rise up like a mighty army. They will be like David's mighty men (and women). Yes, women! I am moving on women in this hour. I Am going to do this and it will bring about great changes that are needed for this time.

"There is a shifting of power and the worldly political religious spirit is falling. From this will rise a fresh new move of My Holy Spirit that can not be contained. What I am going to do will confound the wise and not be understood through the current beliefs and thinking that many of My people have been holding to. I am going to bring the new wine of My power and presence and a new wineskin that will not look like or fit into the old."

November 17, 2016 Jeff Jansen
The Power of Throne Room Decrees
Elijah List

It was the result of the church praying that Trump won the election.

November 18, 2016 Steve Porter
Daniel, Joseph, and Mike Pence
Elijah List

Perhaps one of the secrets of Trump's success will be his faithful second-in-command, working behind the scenes to change the world. Second place tends to be far less visible than first place, but the man in charge needs his second to help him stay on track. In fact, that role has not changed since the days of Daniel and Joseph. Even now that impact is deeply felt, even from the shadows. On a daily basis there are right-hand men, influencing the decision makers, keepers of the deepest secrets, allies in battles of ethics while facing less than ethical men attempting underhanded things. It's the job of the second to seek peace, mediate, and offer wisdom and encouragement to maintain the course throughout the many challenges that lie ahead.

Mike Pence is God's second for President Trump. Already I've heard they are in sync, praying together for God's leading on a daily basis. How can we not get excited knowing that the two at the top are seeking God's wisdom to turn things around?

November 18, 2016 Aimee Herd
What's Your Mindset
Elijah List

God has chosen the most unlikely just like he chose David to be king.

November 20, 2016 Kanye West
"Kanye West Calls Out Beyoncé and Praises Trump in Onstage Tirade"
Joe Coscarelli at *New York Times*

West went on a rant at concert in Sacramento: "A lot of people here tonight felt like they lost. You know why? Because y'all been lied to. Google lied to you. Facebook lied to you. Radio lied to you."

November 20, 2016 Faith Marie Baczko
A Season of Reprieve
Elijah List

Recently I shared that the enemies of God were attempting to take us into a time of great chaos on Earth, and that God had chosen Donald Trump as His 'Reset' to take us into a time of a great awakening and victory, and that this would be a new season of strength, courage and increased authority in the Body of Christ.

I believe a Donald Trump presidency is God's warrant that will issue a far-reaching reprieve! I was overjoyed by the revelation of the coming relief and respite from the enemy's advances, and the possibilities that this would open to the Saints and to the world! However, I was also taken aback by the revelation and understanding that this is a time of reprieve, and that we have been given a window of opportunity to accomplish our mandate.

November 21, 2016 Stephen Powell
The Eagle Has Landed
Elijah List

Donald Trump is our Cyrus.

[The original link on the Elijah List is no longer available. There is a report from Bob Eschliman at *Charisma News* from the same date that provides information.]

Here is some of the piece, quoting Powell:

The day after Trump's election, he said he saw "two peacocks come together as one mighty bird," which then took off into the air with "an incredible sound of power," while a large eagle landed on the ground at the same time. He then heard the voice of the Lord, booming from the heavens, say, "The Eagle has landed, and now the prophet will soar."

He said the eagle landing represented God securing the presidency in the Cyrus anointing of President-elect Donald Trump. He said the double portion peacock is "the double portion seer prophetic anointing being released in the nation right now."

"This anointing is for the nation, and is being offered to the nation, to be received like never before," he wrote. "Prophetic authority is rising in our land and will influence our government in increasing ways moving forward."

November 23, 2016 Kim Clement
"Kim Clement dies"
The Christian Post

Lance Wallnau honored Kim Clement: "His word helped me know Trump was the guy…"

November 24, 2016 Rick Joyner (with Aliss Cresswell)
Prophetic Perspective of Trump Presidency
MorningStar TV

[Original taping on November 9]

November 24, 2016 Alveda King
Evangelist Alveda King with Post Election Prayers for the Holidays
Elijah List

November 26, 2016 Stephen Powell
Sound of the Trumpet Heard and Felt around the World
LionofLight.org

"I have chosen Donald Trump to forerun a new model of national leader, says the Lord; yea, even a new form of world leader, says the Lord. This man will batter through demonic barriers, even on the world stage, which no man or woman in world history, has been able to have the breakthrough in before, says the Lord. But I have anointed him for this time, and his strength is not his own. I have assigned my angels to assist him in the breakthrough, to remove every stumbling block, to extract every demonic levy, says the Lord. His sound will be heard and felt, and I will put my fear on entire nations who see, and fear, and do not understand my working in this man says the Lord. For he will demonstrate something that I have chosen him for, a unique office, a unique position, a unique role, says the Lord. And many will follow after him, not just in America, but in the nations, says the Lord."

November 27, 2016 Franklin Graham
Pray for Our New President
Elijah List

November 28, 2016 Jessilyn Justice
Ben Carson Has Big Ideas About Trump
Elijah List

November 29, 2016 Kim Clement
"Kim Clement Prophesied Trump's Presidency in 2007"
Charisma News

November 30, 2016 Lance Wallnau, Kim Clement
What I Learned from Kim Clement on Warfare and Worship
Elijah List

November 30, 2016 Chuck Pierce, Cindy Jacobs
Urgent Call to Prayer for the Electoral College Process in the USA
Elijah List

December 2, 2016 Jeremiah Johnson, Mark Taylor, Lance Wallnau, Kim Clement
Prophecy As Propaganda: the Trump prophecies as political persuasion
Mark Joensuu at Mentoring Prophets

Joensuu argues that prophecies about Trump from Jeremiah Johnson, Mark Taylor, Lance Wallnau, and Kim Clement are inaccurate.

The prophetic movement waits in one line for one "brave" prophet to stand up and declare a definitive prophecy about the Republican victory, whereas the more seasoned ones (once burnt) tend to make more vague statements, so that they don't get caught of a false prophecy if a Republican doesn't get elected, but they can participate in the victory if their candidate wins.

If the brave prophet gets it right, he or she gets the glory. If he or she gets it wrong, they are simply forgotten, or if they are famous enough, they will find a way to deluge the market with more prophesies so that the original prophecy is forgotten.

I might sound a bit harsh here. But that's the way things have been. I guess I have observed the prophetic movement for far too long.

December 2, 2016 Elaine Tavolacci
Prophetic Word for 2017
Facebook

"On Thanksgiving evening the Holy Spirit began to reveal some things to me concerning the New Year. This is what He showed me. Just as there is a changing of the guard in the White House and president elect Donald Trump has 4,000 cabinet positions to fill, the Lord is looking for many positions to replace in seats of great authority in spiritual gifts (1 Cor. 12:4–11) as well as the five-fold ministry of the body of Christ. (Eph 4:11–12). Many prophetic voices will be raised up from the pit to the palace. Get ready for an upgrade."

December 6, 2016 Johnny Enlow
Trump Quake: What's Next?
Elijah List

God has three major archangels assigned to Trump, including Gabriel. Trump's victory is tied to other prophetic signs, including Cubs winning the World Series.

December 6, 2016 Alveda King
The Greater Good: A Dream Unfolds
Elijah List

December 7, 2016 Elaine Tavolacci
Word for 2017: Get Ready for an Upgrade
Elijah List

December 8, 2016 Mike Thompson
Post Election Heavenly Vision Part 6
YouTube

Dogs of hell and a spirit of hatred and murder are still coming even though presidential election is over. There are lots of things behind the scenes that still have to be worked out.

December 12, 2016 Mark Taylor
"The Lost Art of War" [#13 in list]
Sord Rescue

The Spirit of God says: "Why are my people not repenting? You use generalized repentance, which has little to no effect, when you should be using target focused repentance and prayer. You don't use target focused repentance, because of your pride! Your haughty spirits and attitudes have caused you to fall into the enemy's pit. You're afraid of target focused repentance, because you will have to admit there is fault with you and your congregation. By not repenting, this is an abomination. My people have lost the art of war, for any true warrior of mine knows that waging an effective warfare, starts with target focused repentance and prayer."

The Spirit of God says: "Woe, Woe, Woe, to you leaders that have led my people astray. You, who are cowardly and afraid of offending, have sacrificed my truth and my people on the altar of Mammon. Repent now or you will not come out of that pit, for truly you have received your reward and that's all you will get. You honor me with your lips but your hearts are far from me. Because of your pride and your refusal to repent, there will be no hiding from this judgment. It's upon my church, especially the leadership. Your big fancy homes, clothes and cars, were made with money stained with innocent blood. This has allowed the enemy to come in on you like a flood. Even the Pharisees knew not to touch that money, but woa to you that continue to take it saying it's sweet as honey. The blood, the blood which cries out to me day and night, from the aborted babies to murdering of my prophets. The blood is on my churches' hands, and yet no repentance? I am looking for my true love, my pure spotless bride, and it grieves me her garments are stained because of pride. Where is she? Where is she my true love, I can no longer wait, my judgment is upon you, repent and come back to me before it's too late."

December 15, 2016 Nathan Shepard
Obama Will Be Last President
Survive the End Days

[This is an example of false prophecy. The web page concludes by stating, "World War III will hit by 2017." Nathan Shepard is a pen name.]

December 15, 2016 Anita Fuentes
God Has Allowed a Lying Spirit in the Mouths of These Prophets
YouTube

Fuentes speaks against prophets who are in favor of Trump.

December 16, 2016 Mark Taylor
"Energy, Energy" [#14 in list]
Sord Rescue

The Spirit of God says, "Energy, Energy, I am releasing new energy. For this new energy that I am releasing will make my America and my Israel, energy independent. For America and Israel will now be the top energy producers in the world. This new energy and the technology to capture it, will spring forth from the depths. This is the sign that will be given ... a massive volcano eruption will signal that this is the time for my America and Israel and the end of the energy corruption. OPEC, your evil regime will no longer be tolerated. You will no longer be needed, for you refuse to listen to my words and have not heeded. For when that ring of fire blows its top, it will be a sign to you that you will lose your stock and the covenant you have with that ring will be lost."

The Spirit of God says, "You countries that have dominated energy for decades, to move your evil agenda, are charged with this guilt. Your days are numbered and you will say, look how fast this was built. My America and my Israel will be one and because of this, you will be undone. Because of your rage, and the money you made from those countries you manipulated and attacked from within, you will now have to turn to those countries for help on a whim. For your wells will go dry and your finances too, for you will now be fed, from the Red, White, and Blue."

December 19, 2016 Kathie Walters, Bill Yount, Wanda Alger
Prayer Alert from Now Until the Inauguration
Elijah List

December 19, 2016 Jamie Rohrbaugh
7 Prayer Directives Regarding President-Elect Donald Trump and the Spirit of Elijah
From His Presence

That we would be faithful, Spirit-led intercessors who pray fervently for this brother.

That God would fill Mr. Trump with the spirit of Elijah (and amplify the Holy Spirit's work to the extent he has already received it), so that Mr. Trump would be a vessel in God's hands to turn the hearts of the fathers to the children, the hearts of the children to the fathers, the disobedient to the wisdom of the just, and help make ready a people prepared for the Lord.

That Trump would fully fulfill his prophetic destiny.

That Christians would see Mr. Trump with Holy Spirit-led vision.

That God's Word would be clear to him and that he would have a consistent flow of holy encouragement.

That we as Christians would 'touch not God's anointed,' but would instead treat him with the same mercy and grace that God gives us.

That Mr. Trump would receive the strategies and plans from Heaven that God wants to implement to touch every aspect of culture and society for His glory.

December 26, 2016 Chuck Pierce
Prophecy on Trump Presidency
Elijah List

Announcement of prophecy conference.

December 26, 2016 John Mark Pool
A New Level of Extreme Victory
Elijah List

December 29, 2016 Curt Landry
Is Donald Trump a Cyrus or a Nebuchadnezzar?
Elijah List

December 29, 2016 Barack Obama, Michael Flynn
Obama announces sanctions against Russia.
Michael Flynn discusses sanctions with the Russian ambassador to the USA.

December 30, 2016 Mark Galli
"The Church's Integrity in the Trump Years"
Christianity Today

"Our main political task in this new administration is more urgent than ever. Along with doing our civic duty as we see it (and we will see it differently!), we can speak charitably to one another about our disagreements, taking the time to find out what each of us really believes and why. We can stop saying implicitly or explicitly, "I have no need of you." And we can continue to literally break bread with one another, in our churches and in our homes, praying earnestly for one another, warmly calling each other brothers and sisters in Christ. Among the divinely inspired reasons for this familial metaphor of the church, there is this: you cannot divorce your siblings."

December 30, 2016 Jeremiah Johnson
2017 Prophetic Word: The Trump Presidency and the Increasing Polarization in the Church
JeremiahJohnson.tv

Predictions are made about Russia, China, Israel, and the church in relation to Trump.

Two days before Donald Trump was elected President of the United States, I received and published a prophetic dream in which a baby with the face of Donald Trump was brought to a church and given to an older woman who was a nursery worker at a church. The woman began to rock baby Donald and sing over him. This is what she sang, "Donald, you have a crooked way in you, but through the intercession of the Church, God is going to change you." She sang this tune over Donald several times and then I woke up.

IV. First Year
2017

January/February 2017 James Beverley
"Trump and Prophecy"
Religion Watch column in *Faith Today*

[This is a publication of the Evangelical Fellowship of Canada. The chronological and thematic work for this column led to the ongoing development of this current guide.]

January 4, 2017 Franklin Graham
God Let Trump Win
Emily McFarlan Miller at *Charisma News*

January 4, 2017 Lance Wallnau
The Year of the Clashing of Swords and Taking New Ground
Elijah List

January 5, 2017 Barack Obama
Obama had a meeting in the Oval Office about Russian collusion. Obama, James Comey, Sally Yates, Susan Rice, and Joe Biden were present. This meeting dealt with how to process the issue of Russian interference in the election with the incoming administration. The meeting remained secret until February 12, 2018, when news broke about Senators Chuck Grassley's and Lindsey Graham's February 8th request that Susan Rice explain her January 20, 2017, email to herself about the meeting.

    January 5, 2017 Meeting in Oval Office
    January 20, 2017 Sally Yates email about meeting
    February 8, 2018 Grassley and Graham letter to Yates
    February 12, 2018 Press release from Senator Grassley about request to Yates

January 5, 2017 Paula White
Trump's Spiritual Advisor Fires Back at Critics
CNN

January 5, 2017 Paula White
"Donald Trump Inauguration Prayer Speaker Paula White Says She's No 'Trinity-Denying Heretic'"
Samuel Smith at *The Christian Post*

White stated, "I also reject any theology that doesn't affirm or acknowledge the entirety of scriptural teaching about God's presence and blessing in suffering as much as in times of prosperity … In fact, I have preached and written as much on the lessons we must learn in times of trial in our lives as I have in times of abundance."

January 6, 2017 James Comey
James Comey briefs Trump about Steele dossier.

January 6, 2017 Johnny Enlow
The Ride of the Reformation Glory Train
Elijah List

"Rosh Hashanah 2015 to Rosh Hashanah 2016 brought us the 70th year of Jubilee and this unprecedented year of Jubilee brought us God's choice of Donald Trump as President of the United States and Leader of the Free World. Trump at age 70 became elected President of this nation during the Hebraic year 5777. On inauguration day he will be 70 years, 7 months and 7 days old. Because the Electoral College changed some votes it allowed Trump to end up with exactly 77 more electoral votes. 7 is the prime number of God and is why there are 7 spirits of God."

"Only if you are still out of tune spiritually (or motivated by an unnecessary fear) should this presidency still be a struggle for any of you. Outgoing president Barack Obama's legacy-tainting final acts against Israel are an immediate, major proof that the insertion of Trump as President was an urgent need for us and our nation. We will avoid many national catastrophes because of the proper honoring and care of Israel that our new president will see to."

"It is still almost surreal the level of betrayal that the Obama administration exhibited in its instigation of the UN vote against Israel. The pressuring of nations such as Ukraine to vote against Israel, and the intentional adding of language that includes Jerusalem itself— essentially

making it illegal for Israel to go to the Western Wall—and then the attempt to pretend to look passive in the process."

"It is so great of an injustice that if this is the last political act of President Obama and of Secretary of State John Kerry it will mark them forever. In fact, the authority has been given to President Trump to allow President Obama to have a positive legacy or to remove any legacy. If President Obama does not retreat from his pride, and he only has days to do so, he will have his entire legacy wiped out. God can fix even our past mistakes as we humble ourselves before Him, but when we up the ante into treacherous pride, there is no happy ending. Pride goes before the fall."

"Donald Trump as President will be the best friend to Israel that they have ever had. He will attempt to be fair to the Palestinians and try to negotiate a reasonable peace treaty, and the plight of the Palestinians is very important. However, Trump is a quick discerner of core intent and he will discover that those who represent the Palestinian people are driven by the unreasonable hatred of a demonic principality and have no real desire for peace or compromise."

"President Trump will then expose their hypocrisy and severely turn on them. Because Trump has Jewish family and friends who do see things clearly in Israel, he will not be subject to the deception most world leaders fall under. No country on the earth has been more unfairly and unjustly treated by the nations over the last couple of decades than Israel, and there is a now a larger spiritual bill to pay. The nations that have unjustly judged Israel are presently under limited grace for terrorism and the ones that just voted against Israel have just caused another decrease in grace over their nations."

With the election of Donald Trump as President, it marks the release of something new over our nation. A powerful train is coming in and the "smoke" that the train releases is a holy smoke of reformation glory.
Trump and the Angel Called "Union"

As I have stated before, I believe that Trump will be the most important President since Abraham Lincoln and that our nation will in the future have a "before Trump" and "after Trump" historical perspective. I believe that the United States' great angel named "Union" has been ordered to step in, as he has not been asked to step in since Lincoln's day. I also believe a great angel of Reformation that was from that day has also been released at this time, and it is for the 2.0 version of reformation.

Kim Clement, Bob Jones, John Paul Jackson, Jill Austin, Ruth Heflin, and John Wimber, they are all ecstatically happy and involved in what we are doing now. They are all still prophesying over us and pressing the Father on our behalf. For Believers in Christ, death is always swallowed up in victory.

January 10, 2017 Donald Trump
Intel chiefs presented Trump with claims of Russian efforts to compromise him.
Evan Perez, Jim Sciutto, Jake Tapper, and Carl Bernstein at CNN

The report at CNN states that a two-page synopsis of the Steele dossier was presented to Obama and Trump last week by four of the senior-most US intelligence chiefs—Director of National Intelligence James Clapper, FBI Director James Comey, CIA Director John Brennan, and NSA Director Admiral Mike Rogers.

[The CNN news report was updated on January 12.]

January 10, 2017 Donald Trump
These Reports Allege Trump Has Deep Ties to Russia (6.20 p.m.)
BuzzFeed reports on and publishes text of Steele dossier.

CNN Media Heads and Political DC Operatives Construct More Russian Madness (8.24 p.m.)
Theconservativetreehouse.com

Critique of CNN and Buzz Feed over Steele dossier.

January 14, 2017 Charles Shamp
Chasing the Wild Goose
Elijah List

I believe that we are about to see one of the greatest transformations of nations that any generation has ever seen. I believe the Lord is getting a hold of President-Elect Donald Trump in such a manner that he will chase the Holy Spirit with great passion and cause other nations to follow the United States. He will lead other leaders to fly above the turmoil and chaos to a place of unity and victory in the earth—a massive shift is coming. A global transformation!

The Holy Spirit continued to speak saying, "Prophet, you must prophesy to him. He is weary in well doing, but the joy of the Lord is his strength. We need him in the fight. Without the intercessor locking arms with the angels, God can't release Heaven on earth. It is the intercessor who helps bridge the gap and create the arc from Heaven to earth with the angelic realm. You must prophesy!"

January 16, 2017 Lana Vawser

Washington, DC! A MAJOR Release is Prophesied and Declared for America Starting Inauguration Day!
Elijah List

"It's going to all be roses now that Trump is almost in office."

I heard Jennifer LeClaire (Editor of Charisma Magazine) share this week at the POTUS SHIELD Conference. The Lord spoke to her that the curse and stronghold of the Jezebel spirit over the nation had been broken—but it was MORE IMPORTANT than EVER to continue to pray.

As God's people prayed for Mr. Trump, I saw the Lord place ACCELERATION BOOTS upon him. The prayers of God's people and the Spirit of God will come around President Elect-Trump in greater force as he progresses in his Presidential term.

The first day I arrived in Washington DC this week, I heard the Lord saying over and over, "WASHINGTON IS WAKING UP. WASHINGTON IS WAKING UP." The sense surrounded me of the importance right now of AGREEING with HIS DECREE!

A few days later, I could hear the sound of angels MARCHING into Washington DC on ASSIGNMENT to bring a great AWAKENING of His power and glory.

I saw a MIGHTY move of the Spirit of God in WASHINGTON DC bringing the GREATEST AWAKENING that has EVER been seen. An AWAKENING to the destiny that the Lord has ordained for this city. I could hear His heart, "WASHINGTON DC IS A KEY TO UNLOCKING THE RIPPLE EFFECT OF MOMENTUM IN THE NATION."

January 17, 2017 Donald Trump
"Did God Choose Trump?"
Lauren Markoe at ReligionNews.com

This is an analysis of various views of Trump and divine providence.

January 17, 2017 Donald Trump
"Trump's Apostles and Prophets Create POTUS Shield to Renew America's Covenant with God"
Peter Montgomery at Right Wing Watch

January 18, 2017 Jane Hamon
God Says: I Will Turn Things Around! This is a Comeback Year!
Elijah List

It is vital for the Church to pray as never before for the President, his cabinet, governors and local government and spiritually steward the reformation taking place in the land. Our mistake will be to put our trust in a man to save us. We must pray for God's wisdom on the man, but put our trust in the Lord.

January 19, 2017 MK Yehuda Glick
"MK Yehuda Glick Praises 'Miracle' of Inauguration in D.C. Church"
Sarah Posner at *Forward*

This has news of the inauguration prayer event and celebration. Glick makes a comparison between Trump and Cyrus.

January 19, 2017 Hank Kunneman
America, It's a Time to Celebrate! Out of the Oval Office a President and Vice-President Shall Join Their Hands and Pray Together! This is My Promise to You!
Elijah List

I have placed those in your House called White; this is My doing, this has been My saying, yet there are those who stand to despise, ignorant of that which I'm bringing to the room, to the House, by the way of My Holy Spirit.

January 19, 2017 Donald Trump
"The Story Behind Trump's Controversial Prayer Partner"
Katee Shellnutt at *Christianity Today*

January 19, 2017 Paula White
"Prosperity, Heresy and Trump: Inauguration Pastor Paula White Answers her Critics"
Emily McFarlan Miller at *Religion News Service*

January 19, 2017 Paula White
"Paula White, Trump's Spiritual Adviser, Says He Has 'a Hunger for God'"
Noah Weiland at *New York Times*

"I know that President-elect Trump has a personal relationship with the Lord Jesus Christ. We've had in-depth conversations about God."

January 20, 2017 Kat Kerr
Kat Kerr prays at inaugural prayer breakfast.
Facebook

January 20, 2017 James Robison
Robison blesses Trump at inaugural prayer service at St. John's Episcopal Church.

January 20, 2017 Robert Jeffress
Jeffress speaks at same service.

January 20, 2017 Donald Trump
Inauguration

Prayers at the inaugural were given by Reverend Franklin Graham; Cardinal Timothy M. Dolan, Archbishop of New York; Reverend Dr. Samuel Rodriguez; Pastor Paula White; Rabbi Marvin Hier; and Bishop Wayne T. Jackson.

January 20, 2017 Lana Vawser
"Donald Trump the Pioneer, Melania Trump an Esther"
LanaVawser.com

While I watched I felt the Lord speak to me, and He said "DONALD TRUMP, THE PIONEER!!!!!" Instantly I saw the winds of awakening blowing all around Donald Trump, and not only was the sense so strong that the Lord is working deeply in his heart and life bringing an awakening to him PERSONALLY, but as he has stood and PIONEERED a new way with COURAGE, he has been and is a FORERUNNER to what God is doing in the USA.

Many have asked me whether I believe the Lord is USING and has ANOINTED President-Elect Donald Trump, and I absolutely believe that He has and is. Many have asked me how the Lord can anoint and use someone they see to be having 'rants' on twitter etc, and I want to encourage you, that we are all on a journey. The Lord doesn't wait till we are perfect to use us. The Lord is looking at the heart, and I believe that Donald Trump has a genuine love and heart for the United States and the people of the United States to see change, healing and freedom come back to the nation again.

I also saw the AWAKENING of the ESTHER ANOINTING over MELANIA TRUMP. I saw a message inside her, a loud voice with such humility that the Lord is going to begin to release through her. The Lord is going to release a ROAR through her that is going to AWAKEN WOMEN to their destiny.

January 20, 2017 Kim Clement
Prophetic Alert about Inauguration
Elijah List

Against all the odds, the least likely candidate in presidential history, a political outsider, Donald Trump, has just been inaugurated as the 45th President of the United States. This event is not just a headline that is here today, gone tomorrow. This is a moment in history prophesied about by Kim Clement years ago starting in 2007, and many Biblical prophecy scholars believe this moment has been centuries in the making.

January 20, 2017 Kim Clement
Kim Clement Center: Trump, Missing Malaysian Jet and Your Bank Account
Elijah List

January 21, 2017 Mike Thompson
Trump Inauguration: Powerful Prophetic Era Begins!
YouTube

January 24, 2017 Lance Wallnau
Why are Liberals Mizrabels and So Discontented?
Elijah List

We need to get into the spirit of Elijah and speak the truth because Donald Trump is going to need surround sound in America with new voices rising up and intelligently mobilizing activists for the Book of Acts to deal with the false prophets.

January 24, 2017 Cindy Jacobs
ACPE Prophetic Roundtable: 2017—The Breakthrough Year Part 1
Elijah List

Fuller Theological Seminary is going to come into a time of renewal as in the days when C. Peter Wagner invited John Wimber to teach his signs and wonders class. The Holy Spirit will be poured out once again upon the professors. Other divinity schools such as Princeton will also be visited by God as young professors are touched by God's power and come into spiritual renewal. New wine curriculum will be introduced into seminaries and Bible Schools around the world. The renewal legacy of Peter Wagner combined with that of John Wimber is about to come upon a new generation.

[Note: This prophecy is important because of its emphasis on revival and a link to past leaders in the charismatic and Pentecostal worlds.]

ACPE Prophetic Roundtable: 2017—The Breakthrough Year Part 2

The greatest harvest of souls the earth has known is upon us. Hundreds of thousands will be saved. Many, many people will talk about the need for societal reformation and desire to be reformers. Young people will band together to form movements that display a passion to go into each area of their culture and see reformation. This will set the stage for the greatest outpouring of the Spirit and awakening the world has even known!

January 26, 2017 Lana Vawser
"I am Raising Up a Company of Women with Fire in their Beliefs!!!"
LanaVawser.com

As I have sought the Lord on this encounter as I slept, I believe He spoke to me that the GREATEST AWAKENING we have ever seen amongst women, is upon us right now.

A new day is upon women right now!

This week when I saw the women's march that took place in Washington D.C this week, something stirred in me. I was deeply grieved to hear and see what took place, but in the midst of it all, I felt the Lord quickening me to "pay attention" to it. It wasn't until pondering my dream this morning that I understood what the Lord was saying.

This was a very clear example of the "fire in the bellies" of women to stand in conviction and passion for what they believed in. While this protest was one of division and lack of honour for President Donald Trump, the Lord quickened to me that He is raising up women now who KNOW HIM, modern day Esther's, Deborah's, and Mary's to stand with PASSION and CONVICTION on their platform of influence.

The Lord kept highlighting PAULA WHITE to me. That the position of influence that the Lord has placed her in, in this season to advise President Trump, is a prophetic picture for the Lord raising women up to the frontline and into places of greater influence to bring change to nations. Their mouths FULL of the wisdom of heaven and discernment of His heart, and being CALLED UPON to release the strategy of heaven. This is only going to continue to increase more and more in this season.

January 27, 2017 Steve Shultz
Why I'm so Filled with HOPE—After the Inauguration of Donald J. Trump!
Elijah List

January 27, 2017 Donald Trump
Brody File Exclusive Interview: President Trump Relying on God Now More Than Ever
David Brody and CBN

January 27, 2017 Donald Trump
Travel ban from seven Muslim countries.

January 27, 2017 Nathan Shaw
ANZUS The East Gate, and the Alignment of the Nations
NZ Prophetic Network

I believe it is God's purpose for Australia, New Zealand and the United States to form a three corded strand of support for Israel.

[Note: ANZUS stands for Australia, New Zealand and the United States. This prophecy was on the Elijah List on January 27 but is deleted. It is on the NZ Prophetic Network for February.]

January 28, 2017 Patricia King
17 Prophetic Words for 2017
Elijah List

The Lord says, "Watch what I will do in Syria." Many individuals trapped in the deception of ISIS will wake up and see the truth. Many of them will be visited by the power of the Lord and as a result will risk their lives for His justice, righteousness, and glory.

January 28, 2017 Stephen Powell
Trump is Unstoppable
LionofFlight.org

"You Mr. Trump I have made unstoppable, not just for your nation but for Israel too, for you shall minister to her, you shall protect her, and you shall set an agenda with her, partnering together for the next stage in my plans, and in this also you shall not be gridlocked like prior administrations have, for I am with you, and with the progress you make on the state's side, so you will carry this unstoppable anointing across the sea."

January 29, 2017 Faith Marie Baczko
Let God Arise—Let His Enemies Be Scattered
Elijah List

An unprecedented, momentous and extraordinary year has now shifted into full throttle with the inauguration of Donald Trump as the 45th President of the United States. As the anointing of the Presidency has now fallen upon him, a REPRIEVE has begun, and God is moving to restrain and push back the powers of darkness.

God is about to ARISE over the Land of America in extraordinary ways! This year on August 21st, the Great American Solar Eclipse will occur! This will be the first total eclipse in four decades and will be visible only over continental United States—it will be the first time in ninety-nine years an American Eclipse is visible from coast to coast. The Eclipse will cross 10 States beginning in Oregon and ending in North Carolina, crossing a stretch of 70 miles; the next one will be in 7 years.

In a year characterized by a multitude of sevens, God is marking this incredible year of the Trump Presidency with the Great American Eclipse, a time where HE WILL ARISE within and through this nation to do great and marvelous things for all!

January 31, 2017 Lana Vawser
Call to Pray for the United States
Elijah List

The vision opened up before my eyes and I saw snakes (metaphorical picture of the enemy) slithering in the darkness and they were heading towards the BACKDOOR of the WHITE HOUSE.

It reminded me of the word I released recently about snakes looking for the "back door" in the lives of Believers. In this vision, the snakes were slithering in the darkness "under the radar" attempting to go unseen, coming from "unexpected places," and they were coming with a specific assignment to do whatever it took to hinder what God is birthing in the United States of America and through President Donald Trump. Their assignment was to stop the birthing and stop President Trump in whatever way they could.

In this explosion of such VICTORY, I watched as the GLORY OF GOD fell so heavily upon the White House. I watched as encounters with Jesus happened in the White House, the glory of God resting upon the

White House and flowing out into the nation. Such a strong sense of the Lord refining, purifying, cleansing and increasing surrounded me. Such a significant birthing and a "taking of the ground" was taking place. In watching the glory of God falling upon the White House, my spirit was filled with excitement that the glory of God is about to be seen across the United States like it has never been seen before.

In this vision I heard a sound that I heard also during the inauguration of Donald Trump when he was being sworn into the office of President of the United States. It was the sound of DEFEAT. It was the sound of the enemy shrieking. I heard such loud shrieks of pain in the "losing of ground" and the pain of hearing the name of Jesus being glorified and lifted high. I heard the shrieks of pain of the enemy in the breakthrough that is taking place in the new day dawning upon the United States and the shrieks of his pain in the NEW LIFE bursting forth.

January 31, 2017 Jonathan Cahn
"Last Words to Obama and Charge to President Trump"
Charisma News
[Also posted at Cahn Facebook page, January 31, 2017]

Cahn chastises the Obama administration for pushing abortion and same-sex marriage and for not supporting Israel.

America stood at the threshold in the face of an election that threatened to establish for ages the edicts of apostasy and the ways godlessness, and an open war against the people and gospel of God.

And then there was Donald Trump. There had never been a candidate like him.

And so in this last election, the pollsters couldn't believe what happened and the experts couldn't explain it. But there was a reason for what happened. Against all odds, the people of God gathered to pray for the election—in small groups and large gatherings, around the nation and across the world.

What was it that all the experts and pollsters missed? The answer was 3000 years old: If My people who are called by My name will humble themselves and pray and seek My face and turn from their evil ways, then I will hear from heaven, I will forgive their sin, and I will heal their land."

For the power of prayer is stronger than kingdoms. And God is faithful. And His promises are true.

And now to you, Donald Trump, who will shortly take your oath of office. As you are lifted up to become the most powerful man on earth, remember always that it is the Almighty who lifts up kings to the throne, and the Almighty who removes them.

Your authority comes not from man but from God, the King above all kings. Therefore, submit your life to His authority and by His authority you shall lead.

February 1, 2017 John Kilpatrick
Prophetic Words for 2017 and beyond
YouTube [PDF of the message]

Kilpatrick says the revelation was received in January.

"Trump ... Truman ... True"

"I have raised up Trump and have given him generals to lean on to help him defend the Jews and keep them in their land. General Eisenhower brought them in, and these contemporary generals will keep them there."

He then asked me, "How do you spell Truth?" I spelled it, "T-R-U-T-H."

The Lord said that He is changing the appetites of people. Instead of rejoicing in rumors and lies, the people will now become excited to hear truth again. They will love the truth and reject the lies, as well as the liars.

February 1, 2017 Kathie Walters
Gabriel and the Many Angels Standing in DC: Keep Praying
Elijah List

February 1, 2017 Lana Vawser
WITH THE NOMINATION OF NEIL GORSUCH, THE UNITED STATES IS ABOUT TO BECOME UN-TIED!!!! AS MY PEOPLE PRAY!!
LanaVawser.com

Today as I sat watching President Donald Trump's nomination of Neil Gorsuch for Supreme Court Justice, instantly, I felt the Lord's presence strongly all over me. I heard the words "THERE IS ABOUT TO BE ANOTHER DOMINO EFFECT OF MY POWER IN THE UNITED STATES AS MY PEOPLE INTERCEDE AND AGREE WITH ME!"

I had a vision of the this "DOMINO EFFECT" being set up in the spirit as God's people intercede and agree with what He is saying right now. There was such a heavy emphasis on AGREEMENT. I know very little about Neil Gorsuch, but when he stepped up to the podium I had the sense of the strategic positioning hand of the Lord.

I felt the Lord encouraging His people to pray and agree, that no matter what may attempt to come against the plans and purposes of God, that as God's people stand in the gap, any wolves prowling in the darkness, any opposition against what the Lord is doing, the battle that would intensify around this, would fall to the ground and there would be a clear passage and positioning of Gorsuch.

I had a sense of the positioning of Gorsuch in the nation of the United States is a prophetic picture of the release of an increase of the breaker anointing of justice into the United States. As the domino effect was happening, I was watching the hand of the Lord BALANCING THE SCALES OF JUSTICE in the United States and written across the scales was the word PURITY.

February 2, 2017 Rick Joyner
Bob Jones' Media Prophecy Coming True Before Our Eyes
Elijah List

Joyner says, "One thing Bob told me often was that the most dangerous terrorist organization was the media. He's proven right on that one, too."

February 2, 2017 Lisa Jessie
On Display: A Word to the Beloved Daughters of the Lord
Morning Time Light

Many have said that Donald Trump has been raised up as a "Cyrus" for our times. I fully believe in this and totally agree. One of the meanings of the name "Cyrus" is "one who humiliates his enemy in a verbal contest" or "one who humiliates with his voice." I believe this anointing is related to Donald Trump being raised up as a "wrecking ball to the spirit of political correctness" (Lance Wallnau). The biblical Cyrus "humiliated" Israel's enemies by using his voice (his royal decree) to release them to return and rebuild. Don't miss the prophetic significance of this! Not only is Donald Trump a wrecking ball to the spirit of political correctness, but he also carries a "builder's anointing" in the natural which is a signpost to a spiritual reality. I believe that for those with eyes to see, Donald Trump is an incredible "sign" and "wonder" of what God is doing in the spiritual realm in his kingdom and indeed, the natural and spiritual are intertwined.

I personally believe that just as Donald Trump has put his beloved daughter Ivanka on display in her role which seemingly does not "fit" the assigned role traditionally given or expected by the world, our Abba is actually putting his Church, his beloved Son's bride on display, and thumbing his nose at the principalities and powers which, until this moment in time, have run the show!

February 3, 2017 Kim Clement
Sunil Isaac reiterates Prophecy about Trump and Missing Malaysian Airplane
Elijah List

Two years and two months before Trump declared his candidacy in June of 2015, Kim prophesied in April 2013 about a Donald who would hold the American flag, an influential person that would win the election.

10 years ago, in April 2007, Kim prophesied I will raise up the Trump to become a trumpet and I will not forget 9/11. I will not forget what took place that day and I will not forget the gatekeeper that watched over New York who will once again stand and watch over this Nation.

10 years ago, in February 2007, Kim prophesied There will be a praying President, not a religious one, for I will fool the people, says the Lord. The one that is chosen shall go in and they shall say, he has hot blood. Yes, he may have hot blood, but he will bring the walls of protection on this country in a greater way and the economy of this country shall change rapidly.

This incident, this tragedy with Malaysian Airlines, has brought this nation to a place of fear. "We don't know!" You're not supposed to know!

What you have done, says the Lord, is you have ignored your reliance upon the King of life itself, the Lord Your God. Now you're at My mercy, says the Lord. Search as much as you wish. For all the nations stand before Me now without intelligence, without understanding. They know nothing.

The activity of demonic power and principalities is at high alert. They plot, they plan, and God says, I have kept the nations wondering. They said, "We know we have intelligence, we have equipment, we have the best!" What do you have to find the jet? What you need to look for is how they plot and plan against Israel, India, yes, against America, Canada, Great Britain, the Norwegian territories, Scandinavian territories; but Estonia, what are you doing? There are those praying, and demonic powers are terrorized.

I have no fear and I told you when the Malaysian jet went down, that I would stop them in their tracks. Ha! And where are they now? And I have comforted those who have mourned. But now the stench of debt has come to My nostrils in a nation where there is no excuse. America, I made you the wealthiest, blessed you beyond measure to the provocation of the East and the Middle East and the African nations to where they would all run here so they could get more of that prosperity.

The Lord says, "I stand with you to proclaim—you want death? I'll give it to you. Death to debt is My promise but I need somebody else on the top, for there is no fragrance, but a stench." I believe with all my heart— it's time for us to smile and rejoice for a season of wealth is coming upon us!

February 3, 2017 Ben Peters
Unexpected Benefits of the Trump Presidency
Elijah List

As the economy picks up people will have a more positive attitude towards the government and its leaders. They will recognize the spirit of wisdom on them. This will make them more inclined to believe what they have to say, creating a great platform for them to talk about their beliefs and convictions.

In addition, and this will be huge, God will release divinely inspired technologies to bless His Kingdom, Israel, America and the world we live in. This will give a powerful evangelistic opportunity to Christians who have been given scientific secrets. This will send shock waves into the scientific and academic world.

I believe there will be a mega-shift taking place in science and education, as the testimony of the inventors of new technologies get major airtime on TV, the internet and all other media available. They will declare that these technologies came from God the Creator speaking to them, rather than from their own intellect or scientific training. It will cause a major shaking and quaking, causing scientists with intellectual integrity to take a closer look at Creation Science and abandon their faith in the theory of evolution. Our public schools and universities will actually begin to present alternate views to evolution and students will be encouraged to think for themselves on the issue.

State laws, restricting or eliminating abortions will be upheld by a new Supreme Court.

The Jews, who have been taught to hate Christians and their religious beliefs, will begin to listen more and more until there is a great wave of acceptance of Jesus as their Messiah.

There is another Great Awakening coming, greater than anything America has ever seen. This will catch many Muslim leaders by surprise. Some will convert, as will huge numbers of their people.

There will be a reaction and somewhat of a civil war going on, with some being martyred by radical Muslims. This will actually expose those who are extreme radicals and allow law enforcement to arrest and incarcerate them. The Islamification of America will grind to a halt and more and more former Muslims will integrate into American life and become a huge blessing to our society.

But God will place godly and honest men and women in positions of authority and in science and education, that will find constitutional ways to reverse the belief systems that now permeate our society, including the belief that people are "born that way" and can't help it. Coupled with a major spiritual awakening, the shift back to the foundational principles of family life will take place, probably with lots of opposition, but it must happen.

Pornographic media will begin to lose its popularity. More clean and even Biblical movies and TV shows will be introduced and become very successful. Very quickly media will shift from being very anti-Christian to becoming pro-Christian.

News media will also begin to shift as the Awakening begins to impact those in control. Left-wing media will decrease and truth-seeking media will increase. Those perverting the news will be shunned by consumers and lose their collective voice. People will be so excited about miracles taking place in huge religious rallies that they will have to talk about it to keep viewers tuned in.

To accomplish all these blessings, there will be a major challenge from a very angry enemy. As fierce and angry opposition is raised to hinder Trump's policies and appointments from being empowered, so also the battles will rage in Christian lives to discourage and hinder us from achieving our divine victory.

February 4, 2017 Joni Ames
Godly Women Arise! It's Your Time to be Seen and Heard!
Elijah List

There truly has been a shifting of gears now that we, as a nation, have chosen a righteous president. Although the end results will be awesome, we are in the midst of a battle right now.

A few years ago, there were many prophecies saying that a civil war in the Church was coming. Even then, the Lord spoke to me that it would be a literal civil war in our nation. Basically, that is what we are now experiencing. We are at war with one another in our own nation.

While walking my dogs recently, I heard a loud "BOOM!" I looked up and all around and there was nothing there. In fact, even on the Charlotte, NC news that night, it was reported that many calls had come in where people heard the same thing. I mulled over it a few days, and finally the Lord reminded me of something He'd told me several years ago.

He said that as other women have "come out of the closet," there was coming a time when HIS women would explode forth from their PRAYER CLOSETS in such power and anointing that it will set the rest free. I believe THIS is that time. The explosion we heard was that.

There is warning in this as well. We don't have to scream and holler, pound on pulpits, act aggressively, etc. That kind of stuff will not produce the type of fruit the Lord is after.

We must, like Esther, seek the Holy Spirit regarding how to obtain favor for the purposes for which we are called.

We can't accomplish what God has called us to do by being like those who are out in the streets acting like a bunch of banshees. I use that term because a banshee is a demonic female spirit that calls forth death.

February 5, 2017 Charles Shamp
"The United States Embassy Will Move to Jerusalem"
Destiny Encounters

I heard the Lord say that two blessings will come to America when the US moves its embassy from Tel Aviv to Jerusalem. First the Lord will pour out a blessing over the United States Dollar, it will soar to new heights and secondly I saw the name David come out for the door and the Lord said there will come a man like David from the United States, a military man who will have a great mind. The Lord will give him wisdom and he will crush ISIS and remove its head, he will lead the US to victory over this darkness.

February 7, 2017 Johnny Enlow
Amazing Superbowl 51 Message
Elijah List

MVP Tom Brady: He is Mirroring What Trump Will Do for America
Tom Brady was the MVP (most valuable player) of the game and came back from being hit and sacked multiple times… . Meaningful numbers are all over the place with Brady. He is 39 years old … . that it tied in with the 39 stripes Jesus took. and that a great healing is coming to our nation, as counterintuitive as that can seem for some. By His stripes we were and are healed.)

Brady is also a #12 and that is the number of government. Tom took a lot of heat for being a supporter of Trump believing he could help our country be better and stronger.

It is also part of the prophetic message of this Super Bowl that the Patriots owner Bob Kraft is a Jew and also a friend of Donald Trump. The recurring theme of patriotism and care for Israel will be with us for the foreseeable future as something God desires us to pick up on.
Final Score 34–28: Psalm 34:2–8
And finally all the above recovery takes place as we operate out of the truth of Psalm 34:2–8.

So in a nutshell, here is your Super Bowl message: 2017 is a year orchestrated by God for you to have amazing recoveries from amazing contradictions. It is a year where He will also greatly use the man He put in as President. You don't have to love him or everything he does, but there is wisdom in respecting and honoring who God puts in. God wants His people thinking patriotically towards America because there is a specific "lead nation" call that is on us. The other nations are held back in some capacity until we step into ours.

February 7, 2017 Lou Engle, Matt Lockett
After 50 Weeks of Prayer: Is the Supreme Court Nominee God's Champion?
Elijah List

During Inauguration week, my team and I hosted a Native American friend from California who came to DC to pray. When he heard about our year-long prayers for the "champion," he felt led to look at the list of Supreme Court nominees which had been narrowed to three front-runners.

As a Native American, the meaning of names carried much weight; it was only natural for him to notice the significance of the meaning behind someone's name.

He was shocked when he saw that the name Neil means "champion." This fact really intrigued us. We began to wonder, "Is Neil Gorsuch the champion that God had in mind?" I laughed a little when I asked my team: "Were we praying for him by name all along and didn't even know it?!"

February 12, 2017 Lana Vawser
"I had a Vision and I saw Ephesians 3:20 On Fire across the United States of America"
LanaVawser.com

Today as I sat in worship, enjoying the Lord and pondering the word that I felt to release for the day, I was completely surprised by what the Lord said and did.

I heard the words "I am now giving Donald Trump a double portion of victory and triumph for all that has come against him. Double for the trouble!"

A fire then burned in my spirit that the Lord wanted this word released and decreed. I began to seek the Lord about this double portion and what He was wanting to say.

Instantly, I heard the words "For the sake of the breakthrough, healing and increase of the nations. For the sake of the Kingdom and My name and Glory being extended across the earth."

The sense surrounded me so strongly that the Lord is using President Trump right now to break ground, to break ground that has not been broken before, and where it seems impossible, rivers are going to spring forth in the dry lands.

I AM DOING SOMETHING TOTALLY NEW

"Behold, I will do something new, Now it will spring forth; Will you not be aware of it? I will even make a roadway in the wilderness, Rivers in the desert." ~ Isaiah 43:19

I felt the Lord's heart for the pioneering that is taking place in the nation of the United States and President Trump being used to bring about an unprecedented level of breakthrough.

DOMINO EFFECT BREAKTHROUGH

I then heard the words "All of hell is frantic over what I am doing in the United States because the breakthrough taking place in the nation is releasing the DOMINO EFFECT BREAKTHROUGH into other nations all across the world. My plan and picture is so much bigger than every one can see. The redemption, healing, freedom, increase and breakthrough that I am orchestrating and bringing into the United States is going to flow like a river and into all over nations in the earth."

THERE IS AN ELIJAH AND THE PROPHETS OF BAAL SHOWDOWN OCCURRING IN THE SPIRIT OVER THE UNITED STATES RIGHT NOW

"There is an Elijah and the prophets of Baal showdown occurring in the spirit over the United States right now. It is war, and where things look completely impossible, I am looking for those places, and in a moment, I will send My fire from heaven that will crush the impossibilities in the United States and testify My name and power to the ends of the nation. I am the One and Only true God!!!! My victory and triumph will be

displayed LOUDLY against the enemy and what stands against My plans. My people, you MUST STAND and you MUST pray, you MUST worship over the nation. You must NOT leave your post. Cry out, cry out in this war, cry out in this war and watch and see My fire fall in POWER to testify of My greatness and My power to bring LIFE all around."

THE SEASON OF "UNDONE"

"Donald Trump and the United States of America are carrying a BREAKER ANOINTING in this season, that I am about to release in POWER throughout the earth in increased ways. I am looking for My people to lay down their offences, to lay down their agendas, to lay down their expectations and continue to seek My heart and cry out for eyes to see and ears to hear what I am doing. What I am doing is COMPLETELY NEW, it has not been seen before and all the demonic forces are TERRIFIED and they are attempting to create roadblocks, chaos, fear, turbulence and terror. But I am calling My people to rise up in their place of intimacy with Me, to seek out My heart and hear what I am saying and ALIGN with My decree, even if it doesn't fit with your 'preconceived earthly ideas or expectations. My ways are higher, and I am bringing about a manifestation of My power, Glory and love in the United States and the earth that is going to mark this season, "THE SEASON OF BEING UNDONE." Undone by My love, My wisdom, My power, My Sovereignty and My power."

EXPOSING AND UNDOING

"In using Donald Trump in this season I am exposing and undoing MUCH in the body of Christ and the earth. The poison and what is carried in the heart is being exposed BECAUSE I want to bring healing. I want to bring restoration, I want to bring My people to a place where they can see Me and My hand even when I show up and move in a way that they don't understand. There is a great UNDOING taking place to invite My people into the NEW. The mandate is upon My people more than ever to seek Me, to truly cultivate their intimacy with Me, their secret place, to know Me, to know My heart and to be able to PERCEIVE the new thing that I am doing even when it offends or looks completely different to what they expect. I am moving powerfully in this season, and I am getting things done and I am inviting My people to join with Me in all I am doing."

"Many may kick and scream and throw accusations at one another, a strife rising to the surface in the body of Christ because of what I am doing, how I am using President Trump and what I am doing in the nation of the United States. How this grieves My heart and I long for My people to come together as one in unity. I know there are many who are disheartened, angry and disillusioned, but I say unto you, come to Me and let Me comfort you. Let Me love on you, let Me minister to you, let Me reassure you that I have got this. I am working, and ALL THINGS are going to turn out for your good and the good of the nation of the United States as My people continue to stand and intercede and agree."

I SAW EPHESIANS 3:20 BURNING ON FIRE ACROSS THE NATION OF THE UNITED STATES

As I sat feeling the Lord's heart so deeply for President Trump, for the people of God in the United States and the nation, I had a vision and I was taken up above the United States. It reminded me of the dream I had almost a year before President Trump was elected, where I saw the nation of the United States. Then came a great shaking and the word TRUMP changed to TRIUMPH and the Lord spoke to me that He was going to use Donald Trump to lead the United States of America into triumph.

This time, when I was taken above the United States again, I saw the Scripture reference EPHESIANS 3:20 BURNING ON FIRE across the nation. In the spirit, I saw the WALLS of the United States of America and I saw in this season the people of God and the watchman have been WOKEN UP in the shaking and they have been and continue to be positioned on the walls again. They are crying out for a move of Holy Ghost fire in the nation. Day and night, they are crying out. The more they pray, the more they cry out, the BRIGHTER and BRIGHTER Ephesians 3:20 BURNS.

God will achieve infinitely more than your greatest request, your most unbelievable dream, and exceed your wildest imagination! He will outdo them all, for His miraculous power constantly energizes you! —Ephesians 3:20 (The Passion Translation)

In this great awakening and shaking in the United States God is wanting to encourage and reaffirm to His people that what He is doing in their lives is FAR BIGGER than their greatest request, unbelievable dream, and wildest imagination. God is going to EXCEED THEM in their lives.

Then on a bigger scale, as the people of God continue to battle and intercede for the United States, where they continue to move in the awakening of their authority and sonship, standing together in Unity, the POWER OF GOD that is going to be demonstrated in the nation of the United States is going to be GREATER than could have EVER been hoped, imagined, or dreamed. God is doing something MORE GLORIOUS than could ever have been imagined. It's bigger than President Trump. He is just one significant piece to the divine puzzle. He is pioneering and breaking new ground, and the Spirit of God is coming in and bringing and going to continue to bring a great cleansing in the United States, a great uprooting and a positioning for greater breakthrough.

DON'T STOP PRAYING!!
The heart of this word was an encouragement for God's people to continue to pray for the United States and President Donald Trump. I never imagined releasing so many words about President Trump ever, but I know that there is a great war against him, and it is VERY strong, BUT the Spirit of God is stronger and AS GOD'S PEOPLE CONTINUE TO PRAY there is a DOUBLE PORTION of VICTORY and TRIUMPH that will be given to him to bring breakthrough and for the Lord to accomplish what He is wanting to.

There are going to be many, many more situations where things come up, trouble comes up and it looks bleak, it looks dark, and then SUDDENLY the DOUBLE PORTION MANIFESTATION of the POWER OF GOD releasing VICTORY and TRIUMPH will be seen and many will be left with jaws wide open declaring "How in the world did that happen?"

The Lord is revealing Himself as KING! King of Kings and Lord of Lords in the nations like never before in this season. It's just the beginning, the tip of the iceberg where we will begin to see heavenly breakthrough. The perfect justice, mercy, kindness and love of the Lord is going to be seen in the nations more and more than we have ever seen before.

God is using the United States and the breaking of new ground taking place there as a beacon of hope for other nations.

The greatest domino effect that we have ever seen in the nations is UPON US! This is a crucial time! We must repent and stop the offence, the bickering, the slandering taking place in the Church and pray like never before. We must continue to stand in the gap and repent on behalf of the nations.

Pray that GOD HEALS OUR LANDS in whatever and whichever way He chooses, with confident trust and expectation that He is doing something greater than we could ever hope, imagine or dream. It's all about Jesus, and His Glory invading the earth and the stage is being set for the greatest move of the Holy Spirit in the nations than we have ever seen."

"Then if my people who are called by my name will humble themselves and pray and seek my face and turn from their wicked ways, I will hear from heaven and will forgive their sins and restore their land."—2 Chronicles 7:14

February 13, 2017 Michael Flynn
Flynn resigned.

February 14, 2017 James Comey, Michael Flynn
President asked James Comey to shut down investigation of Flynn.

February 19, 2017 Cindy Jacobs, Perry Stone
Prophecies About President Trump and Future of America!
YouTube

Cindy Jacobs and Perry Stone are guests on Sid Roth's show *It's Supernatural*.

"Year of breakthrough…"
Cindy Jacobs: "Satan has a plan for America."

February 21, 2017 Alveda King
Roe Dies; First Lady Prays; Evangelist Dreams
Elijah List

February 23, 2017 Kim Clement
Trump, Dow 20,000 and the Dinar
Elijah List

Kim Clement's first prophetic utterance regarding the Dow reaching 20,000 was spoken in code years ago. Back in March 13, 2013, while I was giving a Codebreakers report on our House of Destiny broadcast,

Kim suddenly "interrupted" me mid-sentence as an unexpected prophetic word erupted from his spirit.

Kim proclaimed the following: "20,000! I'm hearing 20,000. 20,000— it will reach sooner than most people think. I don't know what 20,000 is—all I heard was 20,000. People say it will take years and years. The Spirit says, No it won't. It'll be sooner than most people think; it will be a shock—20,000!"

On a historic prophetic broadcast on February 22, 2014, Kim laid out prophetically our today, and what the future holds. During that prophetic flow, the following codes came forth. Kim prophesied about a future leader of America, and he stated, "I heard gold. I wasn't sure if this was attached to his name. He will restore the fortunes in this nation because of his brilliance." Kim went on to say, "This man will throttle the enemies of Israel."

This prophecy was declared one year and 4 months before a political outsider, Donald Trump declared, his candidacy in June of 2015. Trump subsequently, in a shocking turn of events, came out of nowhere to win the presidential election in November 2016. Fascinatingly, President Trump's branding for all his properties and assets utilizes gold, a prophetic clue given in code three years ago.

In the same prophecy from February 2014, Kim prophesied, "The giant of debt, the giants that have come, the brothers of Goliath, stand in glee watching America. Watch, I said 20,000. Look not to Wall Street; however, observe." Here is the key—according to prophetic instruction, we must "observe" the prophetic sign of 20,000. It is simply a sign.

In the same prophecy from February 2014, Kim prophesied about California and the following sign: "California, you are dying because of a drought. Watch My sign, watch the sign of rain for I told you there would be severe wind from above and all the states that are affected by this severe weather have been set up for a shaking of My Spirit and an outpouring of My Spirit. California, I am looking at you."

Connecting All the Prophetic Dots
Now for the fun part of Codebreakers, where we get to observe the signs, connect the prophetic dots to see and understand the prophetic message. Within a one week time period between January 20, 2017 and January 27, 2017, the following historic signs took place, all connecting to the prophetic word given in advance.

Sign #1: President Trump's inauguration, the man with the word "gold" associated with him, was inaugurated as President on January 20, 2017.

Sign #2: A few days later, on January 25th, 2017, the Dow Jones closed at 20,000 for the first time in history. CNN reported, "The historic milestone leaves the Dow up more than 1,700 points since President Donald Trump's victory in November. The achievement is evidence of how optimistic investors have become about the prospects for the U.S. economy."

Sign #3: The very next day, CNN reported the drought in California is almost over. "A series of potent winter storms that lashed Northern, and more recently Southern California, has erased the worst of the long-term drought that plagued the Golden State for three years." For the first time in 36 months, the US Drought Monitor report does not show any part of California with the designation of "Exceptional Drought." At its height, the Exceptional Drought area covered nearly 2/3 of the state and as recently as Christmas of 2016, approximately 20% of the state was still in the worst of the drought.

Are all these signs prophesied about three years ago, and all manifesting during a one week time period, coincidence?

FYI, there is no Hebrew word for coincidence. What I am trying to tell you is that God is up to something and now is the time for us to be alert, seeking for direction and guidance from our Lord, who takes pleasure in our prosperity. Psalm 35:27 states, "Let the Lord be magnified, Who has pleasure in the prosperity of His servant."

As stated in prophetic code, these signs indicate that prosperity is coming, not just financially, but spiritually and politically. Are you ready?

February 23, 2017 Mark Taylor
"God is Now in Control"
Before It's News

Taylor says that "Roe v Wade will die." He also states that the death of Scalia is a prophetic sign, as is the death of the woman who was central in Roe v. Wade. Taylor argues that the "spirit of deception" in America is the largest ever.

February 24, 2017 Mark Taylor with Sheila Zilinsky
(A CALL TO ACTION) Waging War With Prayer Against Witches and
Demons
YouTube

February 24, 2017 Mark Taylor
Roe v. Wade will die
YouTube, Mark Taylor Facebook

Obama is trying to set up a shadow government (3:00).
Talks about prophecy after Scalia died: "2 signs at his funeral … siren and
train."

[Woman in famous Roe v. Wade court case died.]

February 24, 2017 David Turner
Turner on Revelation From God That Trump Would Win
Strang Report

Turner released prophecy on video before election.

February 28, 2017 Donald Trump
Nomination of Neil Gorsuch.

March 2, 2017 Jeff Sessions
AG Jeff Sessions recuses himself from Justice Department campaign
investigations.

March 3, 2017 Mark Taylor
Spiritual Treason Prophecy [#15 in list]
Sord Rescue

*"I am looking for men and women of God to put their differences aside,
come together in unity, for this common cause in forwarding My Kingdom.
My Army is making great strides against the Kingdom of Darkness! Taking
ground! Holding ground! They will be an unstoppable force in the days
ahead. Unify, unify, unify! I am calling on My troops to unify now!"*

March 3, 2017 Lance Wallnau
Witches Cast 'Mass Spell' Against President Trump
Elijah List

March 3, 2017 Theresa Phillips
Prophecy Regarding First Lady Melania Trump
Sound Cloud

Melania is "about to become an Esther … will become a scholar on American history … she will become an icon to the millennials … she's about to change the fashion industry."

[This prophecy was given to Phillips in May 2016.]

March 4, 2017 Stephen Powell
The Trump Card for Israel
LionofFlight.org

"The Lord would say to you Israel I've raised up a storm for you, and in this storm will stand a man for you from across the sea, and he shall receive blow after blow after blow for you Israel, but he is anointed to shed the arrows with justice, to resist the pressures from the wicked one to bend and to bow to nothing that comes against you, I will bless you Oh Israel, for there is a man that I have given to you, to stand in My storm for you. For in this storm I shall cause a shiver, a shake, a fear, and a dread to fall upon your enemies in this next season, Oh Israel, oh apple of my eye. I will shake your enemies, they shall be in disarray, they shall be in confusion, for I shall be a tempest against them."

March 6, 2017 Jonathan Cahn
Messianic Rabbi Jonathan Cahn on Jim Bakker Show
Jim Bakker Show

Obama attacked Israel, so God ended Obama's reign.

March 7, 2017 Bill Yount
"Be Patient—I am Performing Major Surgery on Your Nation"
Charismamail.com

"Stop grumbling and complaining. It can delay and even cancel this kairos moment as your nation is on My operating table. Speak life and become love to every person. Embrace your opposition and enemies so they will experience My arms of love surrounding them. Protest the devil, not people."

March 7, 2017 Jon and Jolene Hamill

Jon and Jolene Hamill: A Dream over the USA: The Bulls versus The Sharks

Elijah List

This bull in my dream does not represent Baal but actually God's Throne Room antidote and conqueror of the Baal principality. In other words, His agent of breakthrough.

Biblically, one of the living creatures before God's Throne is fashioned in the image of a young bull (see Revelation 4:7). I have heard that the bull in the four living creatures is also called an ox, which represents the apostolic anointing. The ox goes ahead to break up the hard ground with the plow, breaking open the way for the seed. Psalm 92:10: "But you have exalted my horn like that of the wild ox; you have poured over me fresh oil."

By revelation from the Lord, the bull in the dream secondarily represents Donald Trump—a man with the strength and the bull-headed persistence needed to restore our land and security, even in the face of unprecedented resistance. Please pray continually supernatural strength for our new President.

March 9, 2017 Faith Marie Baczko

King Cyrus: Receiving our Marching Orders and the Beginning of Wealth Transfer

Elijah List

God has promised that we would have the best—He is now about to release the great transfer of wealth, long-awaited and prophesied over many years. All because the TIME has come to build, and the Kingdom of God is at hand—fast approaching!

Through the Trump Presidency, great favor is now being given to the Church in the US to accomplish God's mandate, as a season of prosperity has opened—I believe this will extend to the Church globally.

The Lord showed me that those in President Trump's Cabinet such as Rex Tillerson, Nicky Haley and Betsy DeVos have been in preparation throughout their lives for this notable moment of history, and will become a Cabinet that will transform America and change world History.

March 14, 2017 Donald Trump
"Trump's Dominionist Prayer Warriors Organizing to Build Christian Nation"
Peter Montgomery at Right Wing Watch

[Note: This article is referenced in Sunnivie Brydum's August 4 piece for Religion Dispatches: "A President 'Anointed By God:' POTUS Shield and Religious Right's Affair with Trump" and Stephen Strang's August 8 blog.]

March 16, 2017 Sunil Isaac
Codebreakers: Trump and the Media
Elijah List

March 17, 2017 Kathie Walters
Challenging the Status Quo: St. Patrick's Call to Ireland
Elijah List

I wanted to send this out again to the Elijah List readers not just for the history of St. Patrick's Day but because of a correlation I found between the mission of St. Patrick and our current President, Donald Trump. St Patrick was an amazing minister—such boldness to confront spiritual and governmental powers. When Patrick confronted the Druids who were connected to kings and rulers and political powers it made me think of our own president, President Trump, who is confronting the exact same thing. But ... the difference between St. Patrick and President Trump is that he has us—praying Believers—standing strongly behind him.

March 19, 2017 David Hughes
Interview with Mike Pence at Church By the Glades Pastor David Hughes [Coral Springs, FL]
YouTube

March 20, 2017 Tania A. Hall
The Prophetic Decrees that Call Forth Joel's Army
Elijah List

We can all agree that history is in the making as President Donald Trump and First Lady Melania reaffirm America's roots in the Christian faith by exalting the Lord back into His proper place in congress.

These mighty warriors that move in Kingdom power and glory will be endlessly dying to self and forever honoring each other. They will not seek a platform or be motivated by self-gain, but will take up their Cross, having known the Father's heart through intimacy and having committed themselves to whatever the Lord wants to do.

This new breed of miracle workers will be the dread champions of God. They will be brave and fearless, honoring their King and each other with selfless valor born of the Spirit. Forever yielding to the Holy Spirit, they will display outstanding qualities and true conviction, regardless of the persecution or attack. These selfless warriors are being called forth to bring revival and reformation to this generation.

March 21, 2017 Donald Trump
"Here's Why Trump's Evangelical 'Army of God' Should Matter to the DNC"
Donna Kassin at *Huffington Post*

[Note: This essay is very important since it is one of the few extended notices in mainstream media about the charismatic/prophetic element in Trump's support.]

March 21, 2017 Lance Wallnau
"Why Trump Is 'God's Chaos Candidate' and 'Wrecking Ball'"
CBN provides two video clips with Wallnau, one with CNB News and the other with Pat Robertson.

March 22, 2017 Donald Trump
"Did Trump Just Compare Himself To King Cyrus?"
Sam Kestenbaum at *Forward*

Trump quoted Cyrus on the Persian New Year (Nowruz): "Cyrus the Great, a leader of the ancient Persian Empire, famously said that 'freedom, dignity, and wealth together constitute the greatest happiness of humanity. If you bequeath all three to your people, their love for you will never die … On behalf of the American people, I wish you freedom, dignity, and wealth."

March 23, 2017 Donald Trump
"Does the 'Cyrus Prophecy' Help Explain Evangelical Support for Donald Trump?"
The Guardian

March 30, 2017 Todd Starnes
Interview on *The Deplorables' Guide to Making America Great Again*
Strang Report

Spring 2017 Donald Trump
"When Character No Longer Counts"
Alan Jacobs at *National Affairs*

This is a critique of Christian leaders who support Trump.

These leaders have replaced a rhetoric of persuasion with a rhetoric of pure authority — very like the authority that Trump claims for himself. ("Nobody knows the system better than me, which is why I alone can fix it.") Consequently, their whole house of cards may well collapse if the Trump presidency is anything other than a glorious success, and will leave those who have accepted that rhetoric bereft of explanations as well as arguments.

What is required of serious religious believers in a pluralistic society is the ability to code-switch: never to forget or neglect their own native religious tongue, but also never to forget that they live in a society of people for whom that language is gibberish. To speak only in the language of pragmatism is to bring nothing distinctive to the table; to speak only a private language of revelation and self-proclaimed authority is to leave the table altogether. For their own good, but also for the common good, religious believers need to be always bilingually present.

April 4, 2017 Mark Taylor
"Enemy's Timeline Denied by the Most High"
Jim Bakker Show

Bakker says he was told by God two hours ahead of official notice that Trump had won.
Trump's victory wrecked Satan's timeline.
Bakker states that Roe v. Wade will die.

April 8, 2017 Mark Taylor
"False Prophet Predicted Trump Would Win In 2012—But Religious Right Is Still Rallying Behind Him"
Christian Dem at Daily Kos

April 19, 2017 Diane Lake
Now is the Time for Miracles
Starfire Ministries

Several days before occultists first began calling for targeted global witchcraft against Donald Trump, I heard the Lord say that He's "stepping it up" with displays of "raw power" and was repeatedly directed to 1 Kings 18. This chapter contains the account of Elijah's showdown with the prophets of Baal. Elijah challenged them to "... call on your gods, and I will call on the name of the Lord; and the God who answers by fire; He is God" (v. 24).

A similar type of atmosphere now exists in our nation. There's a spirit of deception that keeps people deceived, but it feels like people are desperate for truth. As we believe that heaven rules, there's a "truth forecast"—God's building an army of reformers across the earth ready to stand for truth!

April 21, 2017 Mark Galli
"What to Make of Donald Trump's Soul"
Christianity Today

Some believe that Trump is a baby Christian who is making his way in the faith. While we would never presume to judge another's heart, we are deeply troubled by what is observable about Trump's spiritual health. Aside from his ethical breaches and questionable character, his attitude toward the sacred has been confused and cavalier.

Again, it is for God alone to judge the state of the heart. But the gospel of Jesus Christ casts the behavior of Trump in a transcendent light, and that light looks to us like darkness (Luke 11:35).

Not all evangelicals will agree with our assessment. But can we agree on this? To continue to attack or defend his policies depending on our assessment of the common good. And to do so as men and women who know themselves and Trump as sinners in the hands of a righteous God, who will brook no evil—and who will never fail to welcome the penitent.

April 22, 2017 James Comey
"Comey Tried to Shield the F.B.I. From Politics. Then He Shaped an Election."
Matt Apuzzo, Michael S. Schmidt, Adam Goldman, and Eric Lichtblau at *The New York Times*

April 24, 2017 Lance Wallnau
Passover Prophecy: Cyrus, Trump and North Korea
Elijah List

Donald Trump, the 45th President is walking through the Cyrus prophecy of Isaiah 45 even as we speak! It starts in verse 1: "To Cyrus, whose right hand I have held- to subdue nations before him and to loose the loins of kings..." Trump had no interest in Syria till his heart was moved by the sight of suffering children.

April 28, 2017 Lana Vawser
Triumph Over the USA
Elijah List

This week I was sitting with the Lord and the Lord spoke to me: "I am decreeing triumph over the United States of America." I watched as angels of triumph that had been positioned all across the United States began to stomp upon the nation with their feet.

I heard the Lord say, "There is a revival of courage being released in the United States." I saw an impartation of courage that is in the United States—and also resting upon President Donald Trump—that the Lord is beginning to increase and release into the nation. This revival of courage by the hand of the Lord was calling out the warriors in God's people.

April 30, 2017 Steve Strang
Why Culture Won't Change Without Radical Revival
Elijah List

May 1, 2017 Lance Wallnau
Donald Trump Prophecy For May, He Needs Prayer, Snakes Are Cornered
Bible Codes, Some Will Fall!
YouTube

May 3, 2017 Lana Vawser
"I SAW THE LORD SPEAK TO PRESIDENT TRUMP. YOU WON'T BELIEVE WHAT HE SAID!"
LanaVawser.com

Sometimes when God shows me a specific dream or prophetic experience, it does not necessarily mean the person in the experience had the encounter or if they did, remembers what I saw. It means this is what God IS DOING in this person's life

I had a vision where I saw Jesus leading President Donald Trump to a door. This door was labelled "INCREASE." When Jesus opened the door in the middle of the table was a drawing board. Instantly I knew where I was. It was the strategy room of heaven. The Lord grabbed a scroll off the shelf and He turned to President Trump and said "It is now time for this new scroll to be applied."

Jesus unravelled the scroll across the drawing board table and instantly I knew in my spirit that this scroll was a new strategy for the 'next steps.' Jesus turned to Mr Trump and said "Things are about to radically change, the United States of America is about to move onto a completely new page, I am now beginning to set the stage."

The sense surrounded me that the manifestation of restoration, freedom and increase was upon the United States of America in great increase.

It wasn't to say that the uprooting, the cleansing and the shaking was over, but there is coming a time where there will be an "adding onto," the increase of greater visible signs of restoration, healing and freedom in the nation. The sense surrounded me that the list of things that the Lord wanted to see accomplished in this season in the United States of America, a few of those things had been checked off and completed.

Instantly I remembered a vision I had of President Trump before he was elected where he stood before Jesus and Jesus placed a purple robe over him and a crown on his head. The heart of that encounter was the Lord saying that in Donald Trump's Presidential Term, that the Lord would make him like King David, a man after His own heart.

I saw a softness in President Trump's heart to Jesus, a willingness and longing to hear from Him and to hear His strategy and to walk the journey before him uprightly, and I had a strong sense of the Lord's delight and favour.

I felt the Lord highlighting the encounter from months before President Trump got elected, because the Lord wanted to show me something else in this encounter. As I looked back into that encounter, what stood out to me was the crown on President Trump's head. The crown at the time of the encounter, I believe the Lord was highlighting President Trump's kingship/authority upon the earth, but this time when I looked back into that encounter, I felt another highlight of the Lord.

As I pressed in to ask the Lord what He wanted to say, I heard the words "There will now be an increase of the crown of wisdom upon President Trump." I saw Jesus breathe upon the crown and as He did, it was like the whole room was filled with the tangible presence of the wisdom and strategy of God. The sense surrounded me that there is about to be a major increase of discernment and strategy upon the life of Donald Trump, that he is going to begin to see things he has never seen before, he is going to begin to see in ways he has never seen before, and he is about to move in ways he has never moved before and as he does, partnered with Jesus, there is going to be a great ushering of increase, abundance, favour, healing and restoration into the nation of the United States of America BUT the people of God MUST join and agree with the Lord and PRAY IT IN!

In this increase of wisdom and insight and leading of God that he will receive, if he continues to partner with God, there will be an even greater exposure of hidden things and a revealing of twisted truths, suddenly being seen for what they are. This wisdom and discernment, this heavenly insight that the Lord will reveal to Donald Trump, is going to carve pathways of breakthrough in the United States that have not been carved before and in areas that have not been carved.

I also saw that the Lord has showers and showers of blessings to be poured out on the United States of America, the rains of blessing, if President Trump takes heed of the wisdom, insight and discernment of God that will be released into his life in this season for the greater breakthrough and move of the Spirit of God in the United States of America.

PROPHETIC DREAMS GIVEN TO DONALD TRUMP RELEASING "TIPPING POINT KEYS"

As Jesus spoke with Donald Trump in this strategy room of heaven, I saw prophetic dreams opening up over President Trump and the Lord releasing keys to him as he sleeps. These keys are keys to unlock in a moment through the divine strategy of heaven, what has been locked away for generations. Each of these keys had the same inscription on them "Tipping Point." They were the very keys to activate the tipping points where the ground has been ploughed and prepared by the intercession of the saints, things held back for generations, that is FOR the United States of America, released and breaking through and out SUDDENLY.

I saw as Donald Trump put these "tipping point keys of strategy" into action, I saw people firing at him with accusation and offense, but he stood firm, full of resolve and burning conviction of what he had seen and heard and was unmovable. Even though these 'tipping point keys of strategy' had seemingly put him in the firing line more than ever, the protection of God over him through the prayers of the saints was greater than ever. I saw many with tongues like vipers and they were spitting poison at him because the 'way of strategy' was not what 'has been done, what is to be done or what should be done.' The atmosphere surrounded me so powerfully ringing 1 Corinthians 1:27 "But God chose the things the world considers foolish in order to shame those who think they are wise. And he chose things that are powerless to shame those who are powerful."

These very "tipping point keys of strategy" that the Lord was going to give to President Trump, many in the world would consider "foolish" but it was going to bring a great demonstration to the power of God and the wisdom of heaven. The power and breakthrough of God was going to be demonstrated loudly, and the most unexpected of strategies and plans would bear the greatest fruit of breakthrough and jaws would be left on the floor and the hand of God again clearly demonstrated upon President Trump.

I saw all of this taking place, and I am suddenly back into the strategy room of heaven, watching what is taking place. Jesus looks at President Trump and says "We are now moving into the next phase, where I am bringing restoration, increase and making greater space for the greatest move of My Spirit upon this earth and that is why the battle continues to rage and increase to seven times hotter than it was. The enemy is scared, but as he has come at you and the United States of America in seven directions, I will now send him scattered in seven directions."

The vision then changed and I saw the White House. I see huge warrior angels standing at the door of the White House. One of the warrior angels reminded me of Michael the Arch Angel and they had swords of fire in their hands. I looked over the White House and I saw a HUGE NET made of fire.

I then heard the Lord say "Many traps have been set to trip up, hinder, catch and trap President Trump and what I am doing in the United States of America. I have sounded the alarm, I have released the clarion call for My people to increase their intercession. I am opening eyes to see the results of intercession. There is a net of fire upon the White House, a net of My protection that is established through the prayers of the saints that is protecting all that I am doing."

I wondered why the Lord used the imagery of a "net" and then the understanding came to me. Where the enemy has set up "nets" and "traps" to try and stop and catch what God is doing in and through the White House and in the United States of America, the NET of the Lord's protection is swallowing up the nets of the enemy.

The Lord spoke again:

"My people continue to pray for President Trump's heart, that he will remain open to Me and My leading, that the enemy would not trap and hinder his heart and lead him in different directions. Pray for his heart, to continue to seek after Me, to be sensitive to me as I move him into this new realm of transition of strategy."

IT'S A NET OF HARVEST
The Lord then said to me:

"Where the enemy is attempting to create nets to TRAP, where the enemy is creating nets to STEAL, I am decreeing to the body of Christ, get ready to CAST OUT YOUR NETS in a whole new way, for the HARVEST is about to explode in a whole new way. What I am about to do in the United States of America, the fish are about to jump into the boat in a whole new way. As I am transitioning President Trump into a new realm of divine strategy, so I am transitioning my church into a whole new realm of divine strategy for the harvest and move of My Spirit upon this earth. In this season, just like I will begin to teach President Trump new strategies of "casting his net on the other side of the boat," so it will also be with you My people."

There was so much excitement in the atmosphere. These new strategies were going to bring a level of increase, breakthrough, freedom and restoration into the United States of America that was going to see the Glory of God displayed in powerful ways. It is not that the current and previous strategies were wrong, or to replace these strategies, but the sense was that a completion had taken place in the spirit of some things, increase added to some strategies and completely new strategies were being birthed.

The darkness and turbulence that surrounds is just an indicator of the transition, change and increase of breakthrough upon the United States of America.

There are winds of change about to blow across the United States and they will be blowing in from different directions and in different ways than have been seen before, but they are going to blow in by the Spirit of God a level of increase, restoration, revelation of truth, and rebuilding that is part of the "divine set up" and "setting of the stage" for the greatest move of the Spirit of God that is about to shift gears in the United States to release the sound of reformation and awakening and perfect positioning for further movement into the destiny of God for the nation.

I saw the Lord using a branding iron and the branding iron was on fire. As the Lord came down with His hand upon the nation of the United States with the branding iron at the same time I saw a mantle of fire falling upon President Trump, burning with the same fire on the branding iron. It was the Lord's fire.

As the branding iron stamped into the middle of the United States it burnt into the nation a word that was burning on fire and the word said "PURITY."

The Lord is moving, shaking, burning away, cleansing, refining and purging in many ways and through President Trump to bring the United States to its destined place—a place MARKED by the PURITY of God, and that is why there has been such an attack on the nation to bring anything but purity. But the Lord is calling His people to continue to cry out and contend for PURITY and RIGHTEOUSNESS in the nation. It will not come by the effort of mans hands, but by the cleansing fire of God.

The Lord wants the United States to move into the words He is decreeing over the nation. "A nation marked by PURITY!!!! His PURITY!!!!" A city on a hill that shines with the righteousness and Glory of the Lord and His ways, as an example to other nations of purity and holiness.

Keep decreeing and interceding people of God for President Trump, his heart and ears to hear the strategy of heaven, and that the nation of the United States would align with the Lord's decree over it.

May 3, 2017, Donald Trump
President Trump Hosts Faith Leaders at the White House
WhiteHouse.gov

The dinner was held on May 3rd, and the White House report was published on May 4th. Here is wording from the White House:

"Vice President Mike Pence opened the dinner by welcoming the group to the White House and thanking them for their unwavering support.

"My wife and I are here tonight to thank you—and to pray with you for our nation's future under President Donald Trump," he said. "Our nation's leaders have understood the high importance of prayer as far as the founding of America. In 1775, the Second Continental Congress established a day of fasting and prayer, so that 'with united hearts and the voices,' the people of America could offer up their petitions from their hearts into the heavens. And 65 years ago, in 1952, President Harry Truman signed into law a joint resolution of Congress to establish the National Day of Prayer—a day set aside each year for the American people 'to turn to God in prayer and meditation.' Every President has

issued a proclamation in honor of this day ever since—a tradition that President Trump is proud to continue."

"President Trump is a man of faith and a man of his word, and since day one he has taken decisive action to renew the hallowed promise of America," the Vice President continued. "He is a man of unshakeable faith in God and in the American people, and he is going to lead this nation to greatness. With your help, and with God's help, I have faith we will finish the task that we have started together."

At the conclusion of his remarks, Vice President Pence introduced the President, calling him a man of "courage, conviction and compassion."

"America is a proud nation of believers," the President said. "This evening, we are here to celebrate the renewal of religious liberty in America. Freedom is not a gift from government—freedom is a gift from God."

As the group listened, the President recalled the profound impact of his travels around the country. "There are five especially moving words that I hear from faithful Americans that always touch my heart," the President said. "'I am praying for you.'"

"Each of us in public life has a duty to protect our God-Given freedoms," he continued. "But for too long, the federal government has used the power of the state as a weapon against the faith community, bullying and even punishing Americans of faith."

The President then explained to the group that he is signing an executive order to check abuses of the Johnson Amendment, a provision in the U.S. tax code that prevents non-profit organizations, including churches, from being involved in political activity. The effect of the law is that many faith leaders have been intimidated into silence. In fact, 99 churches have come under IRS scrutiny for practicing their First Amendment right to speak on political issues.

The faith leaders, many of whom have had their voices silenced for decades under the Johnson Amendment, rose in applause.

"Those days are over," the President said. "You all should have the right of free speech, too. And you can rest assured; my administration will defend religious liberty for all our citizens."

May 3, 2017 Donald Trump
"Inside Evangelical Leaders' Private White House Dinner"
Elizabeth Dias at *Time*

May 4, 2017 Donald Trump
"Trump Signs Executive Order To Vigorously Promote Religious Liberty"
Kevin Liptak at CNN [The text of the order is available at whitehouse.
gov.]

In relation to policy, Trump ordered, "It shall be the policy of the executive branch to vigorously enforce Federal law's robust protections for religious freedom. The Founders envisioned a Nation in which religious voices and views were integral to a vibrant public square, and in which religious people and institutions were free to practice their faith without fear of discrimination or retaliation by the Federal Government. For that reason, the United States Constitution enshrines and protects the fundamental right to religious liberty as Americans' first freedom. Federal law protects the freedom of Americans and their organizations to exercise religion and participate fully in civic life without undue interference by the Federal Government. The executive branch will honor and enforce those protections."

May 4, 2017 Rick Joyner, Lance Wallnau
Rick Joyner and Lance Wallnau: "IT'S GAME TIME, Church Activation;
Seize the Moment!"
YouTube

May 8, 2017 Henry Gruver
The Trump Mantle: Conversation with Henry Gruver
YouTube

Gruver on Christian perspectives with John Parsons

May 9, 2017 Donald Trump, James Comey
President fires Comey.

May 10, 2017 Donald Trump, James Comey
Trump told Russian officials, "I just fired the head of the F.B.I. He was crazy, a real nut job. I faced great pressure because of Russia. That's taken off."

May 11, 2017 Lance Wallnau
The Month of Issachar
Elijah List

May 11, 2017 Martin and Norma Sarvis
Pray for Israel and for President Trump's Upcoming Visit
Elijah List

We believe that May 2nd was a day of historic significance and spiritual importance in Washington D.C. as some 100 leaders were invited to the White House to take part in a special event commemorating Israel Independence Day. A first of its kind, the ceremony was hosted by Vice President Mike Pence. Attending were many key governmental leaders, including Ambassador to the US Ron Dermer, US Treasury Secretary Steven Mnuchin, and senators and representatives from both parties. Also invited were a number of highly respected religious voices "who trumpet the cause of Israel." One of these was our friend Chuck Pierce, who called the meeting an "amazing breakthrough at the White House for Israel," and said, "In this time of nations realigning, let's give thanks for this official recognition of Israel's independence."

Pray ... That President Trump will allow himself to be humbled where necessary and that he will not presume himself capable of alone "solving" the difficult, complex difficulties in Israel, Judea and Samaria. Pray that he will allow God to use him and the country he represents in His way in bringing peace to the Middle East.

May 13, 2017 Donald Trump
President Trump speaks at Liberty University.

May 16, 2017 Stephen Powell
Trump Will Have a Highway Experience
LionofFlight.org

I hear the Lord saying, "Trump will have a highway experience." He will find his way in this in this presidency, for hidden in this season and in this hour is my way, the highest way, says the Lord, and Donald Trump will find it. He will find a way to govern which has not preceeded him for generations. He will find the way of the government of God in this season, for I the Lord have hidden it in his midst, and I will cause him to learn it, as I have taught him many other things along the path to the White House. He will not be outmaneuvered by the enemy, he will not be outsmarted. He will be given revelation from the heart of God, a wisdom to rule, an access point to the ways of God, as Solomon was given in his time and in his day.

May 17, 2017 FBI Investigation
Rod Rosenstein appointed Mueller as special counsel.

May 17, 2017 Bob Eschliman
The Lord Told me, the President's Life is in Danger
Elijah List

Jim Bakker said during a recent podcast interview with Charisma Media founder Steve Strang that God told him there will soon be an attempt on President Donald Trump's life, and that Christians need to be crying out in prayer for their president's protection. "There is going to be an attempt on our president's life very soon," he said. "We need to pray for the protection of our president."

May 17, 2017 Mark Taylor
They Will Try To Impeach Him But It Will Not Work
YouTube

May 19, 2017 Aimee Herd
In the Face of Political Confusion and Opposition in America
Elijah List

"Fellow Believers, who appreciate the important advances for the lives of unborn children and mothers, and religious freedom, made possible by this administration, must NOT lose heart! The intensifying darkness of the liberal and media hostility toward President Trump should cause us to pray MORE—not less—for his safety and success, and that of his family and entire team. God—through President Trump—is draining the DC swamp, and it doesn't *want* to be drained!"

May 19, 2017 Lance Wallnau
Divine Appointments and Revelations
Elijah List

May 19, 2017 Donald Trump, Israel
"Trump Plans First Presidential Overseas Trip to Israel, Vatican and Saudi Arabia"
The Washington Post

May 20, 2017 Johnny Enlow
God says, "I Played my Trump Card, I Will Win the Hand"
Elijah List

Last night I was awakened with an intense and fiery word from the Lord that I will attempt to convey. This is what I heard:

"Be not moved and shaken by the present shakings, rumblings and reactions coming out of DC. I did not go out of My way to affect this last election to then suddenly have it aborted. I played My Trump card and I will win the hand. This move does not require My Trump card to be perfect, as I have already taken all of that into consideration—as I always do—when I choose anyone for any assignment that I have.

"Jesus was the last man that had the character in place to actually sustain the call upon His life. Since then no one has had the character-base necessary for the great assignments that I have given out. Do not wrongly assume that I only call those who are qualified. I instead continually work to qualify the called, but I have amazing patience for that process. Yes, I am actively at work in upgrading My Trump card's character even through the fire he is going through.

"Do not find yourself having less patience than I do in your zeal for character and holiness. Human religious idealism has time and time again worked against Me as you choose to prioritize that which YOU see fit instead of what I am working on next. You must learn to stay out of judgment seats you don't belong in.

"You do not yet know how to cooperate with what I do on planet earth because you are often out of sync both with who I am and with what My agenda is. However, even as I call you higher to a place of wisdom and trust—yet I still have patience for you as you struggle to recognize

My present-day narrative. I am neither Republican nor Democrat. I am neither Conservative nor Liberal.

"Conservative-mindedness carries elements of anxiousness and fear that I do not carry. I am not on the defensive. I am not just trying to conserve principles and values. I am not wringing My hands at the sins of those who do not know Me. I do not have as My highest priority that society stop misbehaving. I am not angst-ridden in any way at all.

"I am more about liberating than about conserving. I am liberal in what I give out and My atmosphere is one that liberates. Where My Spirit is there is freedom. Even since the Garden of Eden, I have always trusted you with more freedoms than what you were then ready for. I am still the same God. I have always liberally given to society freedoms, provision, protection and opportunities that they do not deserve.

"I made the United States to be a melting pot for the nations. I made the nation to be a Promised Land of sorts for many nations. Yes, some basic safety procedures and processes need to be implemented, but I did not choose Trump because this was a priority of Mine. Yes, some protection of American values of freedom and tolerance need to be watched over but even this has not been My priority with My choosing of Donald Trump. He is in fact called to bring greater security to America, but much of that will happen through different means than presently being pursued.

"I Chose Trump For Purposes You Must Yet Be Patient to Watch For"
"I have chosen to play My Trump card as an interrupter of darkness and as a lead domino for national reformation—that will lead to reformation among the nations. The status quo of government had become entrenched on dark strongholds and I have played My Trump card as a disrupter of those strongholds. I have released Myriads of the hosts of Heaven to assist with that assignment.

"I chose Trump for purposes you must yet be patient to watch for. The hordes of Hell in media have rallied in mass under Leviathan but I will crush them under the forces that I have released under My trusted archangel Gabriel. He will be instrumental in devastating media outlets that do not position themselves as lovers of truth and goodness. There will be in-house fires that will not be able to be put out in some major media outlets. There will be the hanging by the very noose they have created for others.

"Do not be deceived by the look of power that the enemy in media presently seems to carry. Much of it will presently look very different. I have already beheaded the enemy in many places and much of the backlash you hear or see is the backlash, as it were, of a chicken with its head cut off. Its strongest kick is post-mortem—but it has already been dealt with. My Trump card is something I will continue to play, but it is a card I have already played as well. Much of the enemy's powerful-seeming backlash is the backlash of that which is beheaded.

"I Have Chosen Trump to Repair Your National Economy"
"I have chosen Trump and his unique skill-set to repair your national economy and to by extension, repair the economy of the nations. It is not a smooth uncomplicated process but it is a process I will help him with. It is the enemy who has been trying to destroy your economy and the nations' economies. He has been attempting that and even surreptitiously setting up for that in order to stop the massive harvest already coming in; and in aborting the age of reformation and era of renaissance that you are presently engaged in.

"I am saving you from much deeper conspiracies and from much darker futures than most of you can even begin to comprehend. Even you conspiracy followers only see the human elements involved and they are ever there from generation to generation with changing faces. Almost none of you have seen the dark hands behind the scene. It is why you must trust Me at this time though you are not used to trusting Me. You have created belief systems that limit My scope and scale of intervention on this planet and you are wrong in your assumptions of My Sovereignty being limited."

[This prophecy is repeated in a post on The Elijah List on September 27, 2019, along with three other prophecies.]

May 22, 2017 Donald Trump, Israel
Trump lands in Israel.

May 23, 2017 Donald Trump, Israel
Trump prays at the Western Wall.

May 23, 2017 Kim Clement
God Has Set Aside Trump as His David for This Nation
YouTube rebroadcast of February 22, 2014

May 24, 2017 Donald Trump
Trump visits Vatican.

May 25, 2017 Komorusan714
Trump Prepares The Way For Christ's Second Coming
YouTube

Trump's election stops the New World Order and represents an opportunity
for Christians to regain their heritage.

May 25, 2017 Frank Amedia
The POTUS Shield with Frank Amedia
Strang Report

May 26, 2017 Stephen Powell
Prophesies about Trump, the Media, and the Future of America
YouTube

Mainstream media is under divine judgment. The prophets of God will be
on major media.
Trump is not going to be impeached. Trump can be compared to Winston
Churchill.
The idea that Trump colluded with Russia is "complete garbage."

May 30, 2017 Charles Shamp
A New Prophetic Bird is Being Birthed in the Earth
Elijah List

May 30, 2017 Mary Colbert, Donna Howell, and Mark Taylor
Mary Colbert, Donna Howell and Mark Taylor: On Skywatch TV
YouTube

The three charismatic leaders talk about the opportunity Christians have in
light of Trump's victory.

May 21–28, 2017 Lance Wallnau
President Donald Trump — The UNBELIEVABLE story you've NEVER heard!
Elijah List [Given on Elijah List cruise]

Lance Wallnau recounts the prophetic messages in 2015 that caused him to consider Donald Trump as chosen by God. Wallnau states that God told him Trump would be a "wrecking ball" and that he was the Cyrus figure of Isaiah 45.
He states that Trump's election calls the Church to move from "escapism to engagement."
He also predicts that national media will be taking the Elijah List seriously.

May 31, 2017 Jennifer LeClaire, Mary Colbert, and Mark Taylor
Supernatural War for America on Skywatch TV
YouTube

June 2017 Donald Trump
"God and the Don"
MJ Lee at CNN

Article on Trump's association with Christian religion and churches

June 1, 2017 Christy Johnston
America, the Bells of Restoration Are Ringing!
Elijah List

Trump is a sign that it is time to set the nation on the same frequency it was founded on in 1776. George Washington, the first president, received a vision for the republic as a gift from God in 1777 in Valley Forge. Trump, the 45th president, has received a word from God about the restoration of this nation: To Make America Great Again. He has released a sound and a frequency which marks the beginning of turning back to the Lord.

I believe that in the seasons gone by, America has once again undergone a time of slavery, but it has been a more cunning, manipulative slavery—a perversion and captivity of truth. The lines of truth and justice have been so confused and muddied that those who stand for the Father's

truth and justice have been bullied and cast out, told to stay quiet ... but the Father's plans of restoration are unfolding. I see that His hidden plans are being unraveled to His leaders, His voices who will cry out in the streets, and commission an army of worshippers to ring the bells and release His mighty sound!

June 1, 2017 Tania Hall
The Greatest Awakening and a Billion Soul Harvest is at Hand!
Elijah List

I prophesy that this is a pivotal year for the Pentecostal movement globally, where great faith will ignite a double measure of the miraculous that was poured out at Azusa Street, for healing the nations of the earth.

This 111th year since the Azusa Street Revival is a pivotal year for the Pentecostal movement worldwide. 600 million people came into the Kingdom as a result of the Azusa Street Revival and a harvest double the size is coming—over a billion souls! The greatest awakening in history is at hand.

June 2, 2017 Chuck Pierce, Jim Bakker, Ramiro Pena
Chuck Pierce Releases Shocking Prophetic Word
Elijah List

We were praying together with a few others—Dutch Sheets, Cindy Jacobs, we were praying together in Washington, we were at the White House and Chuck prophesied that, and this was about a month ago, that we were going to have 10 months of struggle and difficulty and even war, struggle, in the White House, or at the White House, followed by three years of great success and progress.

Jim Bakker: "Who else could drain a swamp? There's alligators in the swamp—so you have to have a fighter."

Pastor Ramiro Pena: "He may be rough and tumble, but that's what we need right now. We don't need to elect a national pastor, we need a chief executive to right the ship and that's what I believe he's doing right now. "

[Note: In the preceding posting from the Elijah List prophecy, Steve Shultz states, "I'm not sure if you've noticed it yet, but today's prophets are getting much more specific, much more accurate, and much more profound in what they are seeing."]

June 2, 2017 Lance Wallnau
What's New with Trump
Elijah List

June 4, 2017 Joni Ames
Revival: Get Ready for the Adventure of a Lifetime!
Elijah List

Much has been said about Donald Trump's campaign slogan, "Make America great again." Well, the way to make America great again is to make the Church in America great again. Revive it. Restore it. Breathe life into it. Bring it back to being a living, breathing, full functioning organ again.

June 6, 2017 Mark Taylor, Mary Colbert, Jennifer LeClaire
Angels and Prophecies Day 2
Jim Bakker Show

Mark Taylor: "Comey was the clog in the pipe that's keeping the swamp from being drained … The new FBI director is going to drain the swamp."

June 8, 2017 Darren Canning
America, Get Ready for Blessing, Wealth and Gold!
Elijah List

In a dream a few nights ago, I saw President Trump. He was next to a person who I would describe as a working-class man. This man with the president, had not seen wealth in a long time. Suddenly, I saw his hand fill up with pieces of "gold." Wealth started coming into this man's life again!

The United States is about to see a new boom in its economy, and it will be greater than what we have seen during previous years. If you remember the dishonor from the previous administration toward Israel, it is no surprise the people of the USA were struggling the way that they were. The polar opposite was displayed recently, when President Trump was seen saying a prayer at the Wailing Wall, and meeting and honoring the President of Israel. Something has changed in America. God is going to bless it again!

June 9, 2017 Russell Moore
"Russell Moore, Baptist Leader Who Shunned Trump, Splits the Faithful"
Ian Lovett at *The Wall Street Journal*

June 12, 2017 Lance Wallnau
A Prophetic Word and Prayer
YouTube

June 16, 2017 Alveda King
"Father's Day Looms as Domestic Terror Massacre Rocks America"—a Call to Prayer and Nonviolence
Elijah List

June 19, 2017 Hank Kunneman, Kathie Walters
"President Trump Will Not Be Impeached!" Plus "God is Exposing Corruption and Will Save the Constitution"
Elijah List

"Do not think those who are speaking loudly, and loudly they are speaking, but they are not speaking by Me; and they have gathered in a place away from the White House, and they gather and they meet in secret.

"But oh I stand in the midst of them, and I hear what they say and I am watching the trouble that they are trying to create for this nation and for this administration, and I say, 'It shall not have its way!'

"For you will raise up from this place away from the White House and you will say, 'Impeach, impeach, impeach!' and you will seek to stir this up as a proverb in the land. No, this is foolishness!

"And so as I open the ground and I swallowed up those and that which was troubling a nation called Israel in the days of Moses and Korah, this will be swallowed up too. For there is a way, My way. And there is a day where the healing balm shall flow upon this land, and I shall unite it."
Hank

Kathie Walters mentions a dream she first had over a decade ago about the restoration of a ship that represented the U.S. Constitution. She then writes:

I had a second dream about 6 years ago, and again I was high up, like in a plane, looking down and the "US Constitution" was still lying on its side in the water. It was still rusted, but I saw the figure of a man in "overalls" and he was standing on the rusted side with this can of that anti-rust paint (like I saw in my first dream) and he was painting over the rust. So again I thought, "Good, the Constitution will be OK."

Then I wondered "who" that man was because he was in a dangerous place standing on the rusted side. The rust (corruption) could cave in on him, so I prayed that he would be able to apply that anti-corruption paint safely. Then it was as if the camera zoomed in and I saw who the man in the overalls was Donald Trump! I was a bit amazed as I only knew of him from seeing a couple of apprentice shows (this dream was six years ago).

When I first heard that Trump was considering running for President I was a bit surprised because he was not a politician, but then I remembered the man in the overalls who was helping with "repairing the corruption."

I didn't think about it anymore until I was in New Zealand ministering and was very busy. One night at a hotel, I suddenly awoke at 3am and was wide awake. I made some tea and turned on the TV. It was a whole program about the Trump family; I didn't know any of his family. So I started watching; they showed his whole family, even his grandkids.

As I started watching this show about the Trump family, this beautiful aroma came into my hotel room and filled the whole room. It was like sweet Almond oil. I smelled it and breathed it in the entire time the program was on for an hour. When the show finished the Almond oil aroma just drifted away. It was so awesome that from that day, I knew that although Trump didn't "look the part," he was called to make upright the "US Constitution." God told me He will protect the Constitution because He wrote it.

[This prophecy is repeated on a post from The Elijah List on September 27, 2019. It also features prophecies from other prophets.]

June 19, 2017 Jo Ellen Stevens
The Breaker Anointing Over Our Nation and Our President
Elijah List

Donald Trump has childlike faith.

"I have placed Donald Trump into your White House to show you how someone with curiosity beyond the normal can cause you to prosper. Many have tried to stop this from happening. Many, like the Pharisees of old, want it to stop!

"Watch what I will do with him and with America! I gave him a childlike faith and discontented spirit so that he would press past the naysayers and bring a bit of Heaven to earth in his thinking. Oh yes, he likes to build things from gold AND SO DO I. This is why all of the discontented follow him. This is what the discontented saw in My servant David and this is what I saw in Donald Trump. LET HIM DO MY WILL, AMERICA! He is a man after my heart like David because He has a childlike faith that if he can see it, then he can build it! LET HIM BUILD IT!"

June 20, 2017 Jon and Jolene Hamill
Key Dream: Baseball Practice with Trump—We Are Being Positioned for Victory!
Elijah List

"On May 21, 2016, I had a dream that has proven hauntingly prophetic. Donald Trump was leading his team IN A BASEBALL PRACTICE. This was the second of two dreams the Lord gave me to convey that Trump was His choice for President. In the dream he served as the owner, coach, and star player. But during practice, he hit the ball in a way that continually advanced his team. The other players became the true stars."

June 29, 2017 John Mark Pool
We're in a Season of Exposure, Closure and Victory
Elijah List

Our nation of America is being shaken! When the enemy's hand is revealed, the righteous right hand of God will demonstrate His lifting up a standard against evil for His Bride. As this is dealt with in very visible ways such as: recent special elections won for the conservative platform, chaos in Europe, and "fake news" finding nothing in their continual "witch hunts" in plans to destroy God's choice for our current President Donald Trump, what will remain is a shaking that multiplies our country with God's fruitfulness. Remember, the enemy is now in exposure for God's closure!

June 30, 2017 Mark Taylor
The Sharpening Report
YouTube

Taylor claims that Trump "is ten steps ahead of everybody else" and that "God is done with the news media," that 3,000 elite pedophiles have been arrested since the inauguration and that Hillary Clinton will go to jail. According to Taylor, former Justice Scalia was murdered. Taylor also prophesies that Roe v. Wade will be overturned, that Israel and the USA will be #1 in energy, and that the Washington Monument will be toppled.

July 6, 2017 Donald Trump
"Trump Defends Western Values in Warsaw, Poland Speech"
New York Times

July 7, 2017 Mark Taylor
"Satan's Frequency" [#16 in list]
Sord Rescue

The Spirit of God says, "Why are you tuned into the enemy's frequency? Why aren't you tuned into mine? Why do you listen to the doom and gloom? Do you not realize that they are tuned into the enemy's airwaves? I said go through out all the earth and preach my gospel, the good news! Then why is there so much doom and gloom?

Why are you siding and agreeing with the enemies plans? Repent!

You give more airtime to the enemies plans than mine, thus empowering his plans. Did I not say that life and death are in the power of the tongue? Then speak life! Why are my leaders searing the consciousness of my people with doom and gloom teaching? You who preach doom and gloom are robbing my people of hope and the will to fight. You are no longer saving lives but taking them. How you might ask? Your doom and gloom messages have robbed them of hope to the point of suicide! You prophets and pastors of doom and gloom now have blood on your hands! You are prophesying your own doom! Repent!"

The Spirit of God says, "The news media, the news media, you have become a stench unto my nostrils, there is no spirit of truth in you. I the Lord God will clean out the news media and bring back truth. The sign will be given when news outlets will go down, bankrupt, and I the Lord God will rebuild them using my righteous people to restore them. I am calling on my Army, those who are chosen to be journalists, investors, to get ready to take your place as I tear down and rebuild my news media."

The Spirit of God says, "Where are my billionaires and millionaires? Why are you not buying out these news outlets and taking control? That money I gave you was for my kingdom, to advance my kingdom in all areas of influence. Now is the time to move into my news media! I will now take back what belongs to me using my Army and the finances I have given them. Rise up my Army and take back my news media so the spirit of truth will begin to flow. This is a fight the enemy does not want to see, he has held this stronghold for too long and his time is up. Take this fight to the enemy and my Army will be victorious and my media will be brought back to me."

July 9, 2017 Lance Wallnau
Fresh Boldness Is Coming and a New Movement of Joy!
Elijah List

Wallnau argues that Donald Trump is a "reset" for America and the world. Lance prays for Trump's enemies to be scattered, including CNN, MSNBC, and Rachel Maddow.

July 9, 2017 Mark Taylor
Prayer of Repentance
"Satan's Frequency" [#16 in list]
Sord Rescue

Taylor offers a long prayer, including requests about his controversial contempt for 5013c. He also offers prayer for President Trump and his family:

"Father we repent for houses of prayer being in covenant with that entity called Baal, thru that demonic contract called the 501c3... . Father we repent for taking that blood money from the 501c3 that even the Pharisees knew not to take."

"Father we ask for your protection around president Trump and his family, we cover them with the blood of Jesus, we decree and declare Zachariah 2:5 around him and his family, a wall of fire with your glory in the center of it that no witchcraft, no voodoo, no hex, no vex, no word curse, no power, no principality, and no demon in hell can penetrate. Father your hand is upon this president and we decree and declare that he will not be impeached, assassinated, or harmed in any way and that no weapon formed against him or his family will prosper."

July 10, 2017 Lance Wallnau
How Trump Is Playing in China
YouTube

July 10, 2017 Rodney Howard-Browne
Pastor-Evangelist Rodney Howard-Browne was asked by Paula White to lead prayer for Trump in the Oval Office. White, Howard-Browne, and other Faith leaders were at a meeting in the East Wing with the White House Office of Public Liaison. Trump invited the group to the Oval Office.

July 11, 2017 Rodney Howard-Browne
Howard-Browne and his wife Adonica released photos and posts on Facebook about their Oval Office prayer and visit.
First Facebook post at 6:55 p.m.
Second Facebook post at 7:58 p.m.

[Note: The picture that accompanied Rodney and Adonica's post was of them laying hands on Trump as Rodney prayed for the president. The post reached over 2 million people. The picture is on the cover of this book.]

July 12, 2017 Donald Trump
Donald Trump and media reports on his meeting with faith leaders.

"Praying for the President: Evangelical pastor shares image of prayer circle laying their hands on Donald Trump's back in the Oval Office"
Chris Pleasance at *Daily Mail Online*

"Prayers for Trump"
The Drudge Report, Facebook

"Faith Leaders Pray for Trump in Oval Office, Enjoy 'Open Door' at White House"
Heather Sells, CBN News

"Photo Surfaces of Evangelical Pastors Laying Hands on Trump in The Oval Office"
Sarah Pulliam Bailey at *The Washington Post*

"Faith Leaders' Visit to Oval Office Is Blowing up the Internet"
Bob Eschliman at Charisma News [July 12, 2 p.m.]

Erin Burnett of CNN calls prayer image "pretty stunning … very strange"
Faithwire

"Something we don't see everyday here and the image of Donald Trump praying in the Oval Office and all of those hands on him. The president bowing his head in prayer in the Oval Office and all these people sort of, touching him, it's very strange."

July 12, 2017 Donald Trump, Pat Robertson
President Trump to CBN's Pat Robertson: Putin Would Have Been Happier with Clinton
CBN

July 13, 2017 Steve Strang
Did a Catholic Holy Man Name Donald Trump's Role in the 1980s?
Elijah List, *Charisma News*

July 14, 2017 Donald Trump
"Media Ridicule Photo of Evangelicals Praying Over Trump"
Fox News

July 15, 2017 Rodney Howard-Browne
"The Truth Behind the Oval Office Prayer Circle"
Fox & Friends, YouTube

July 17, 2017 Kevin Basconi
It's A Time of Prayer over America
Elijah List

I want to encourage you to pray for our president, Donald Trump. He will continue to be instrumental in making this spiritual shift possible in our nation. Prayer was instrumental in placing Donald Trump in office and the prayers of the American people were answered.

July 17, 2017 John Fea
"Trump Threatens to Change the Course of American Christianity"
The Washington Post

"Trump is different. His campaign and presidency has shed light on a troubling wing of American evangelicalism willing to embrace nationalism, populism, fear of outsiders and anger. The leaders of this wing trade their evangelical witness for a mess of political pottage and a Supreme Court nomination ... . Trump's presidency — with its tweets and promises of power — requires evangelical leaders to speak truth to power, not to be seduced by it."

July 18, 2017 Steve Strang
Announcement of his book *God and Donald Trump* release on November 7. The press release was on July 18. See Strang's Facebook posting.

"God and Donald Trump Generates Strong Early Response"
Charisma

July 20, 2017 Lance Wallnau
What is the Significance of the Year 5777?
Elijah List

Wallnau argues that Trump is the ultimate reset player over the history of the United States. Trump represents a "disruption of the global world order."

July 25, 2017 Mark Taylor
Scrambling the Enemies Radar [a prayer]
Sord Rescue

Father in the name of Jesus we ask that you would release your warrior angels and heavenly hosts. We decree and declare that they would take us off the enemies' radar and scramble the enemies' frequencies (airwaves). Your kingdom must come now, your will must be done right now as in the heavens also on the earth. Amen.

July 25, 2017 Rodney Howard-Browne
Pastor: Senior Republican Told Me of Plan to 'Take Out' Trump
Paul Joseph Watson at Alex Jones' InfoWars

Report on Howard-Browne's message from a Sunday morning worship service at The River Church in Tampa

July 25, 2017 Marc Brisebois
The Family is God's Weapon in Overcoming the Political Spirit
Elijah List

God has raised up Donald Trump. Yet, He has not only raised up Donald Trump, but the Trump family. It is a sign! Like the Kennedy family from years past, whose influence we know extended decades, God uses families. Today, like then, God is raising up a standard against the specter of political corruption, because He has His eye on a spirit. The Trump family points to a unity impervious to attacks able to destroy other structures.

July 28, 2017 Lance Wallnau
Urgent: Pray for the President and His Family
Elijah List

July 31, 2017 Ralph Drollinger
"Bible Studies at the White House: Who's at the Heart of This Spiritual Awakening?"
Jennifer Wishon at *Breaking Christian News*

Drollinger sees many similarities between Pence and biblical figures like Joseph, Mordecai, Samson, and Daniel.

"Mike Pence has respect for the office. He dresses right—like it says Joseph cleaned himself up before he went to stand before the Pharaoh ... Mike Pence has uncompromising Biblical tenacity and he has a loving tone about him that's not just a noisy gong or a clanging cymbal ... And then fourthly, he brings real value to the head of the nation."

July 31, 2017 Lance Wallnau
Prophetic Views Behind the News!
Facebook

Thoughts on why Trump picked Kelly for chief of staff: "He's the perfect trump card for doing what he's doing. And he has done for the Kingdom, things no other politician could do who is a Christian."

August 4, 2017 Sunnivie Brydum
"A President 'Anointed By God': POTUS Shield and Religious Right's Affair with Trump"
Sunnivie Brydum for *Religion Dispatches*

Brydum interacts with Peter Montgomery about his research for Right Wing Watch.

August 8, 2017 Steve Strang
The Left Finds New Way to Bash Trump: His Connection with Pentecostals
Strang Report

Strang reacts to the Brydum piece [August 4, see above] and Peter Montgomery's article for Right Wing Watch [March 14, see preceding]. Strang mentions his forthcoming book *God and Donald Trump* and includes a podcast with Frank Amedia.

August 8, 2017 Frank Amedia
The attack on POTUS Shield
StrangReport

August 8, 2017 Lance Wallnau
Jezebel is out to Take the Voice of the Prophetic
Facebook

Wallnau states that demonic attacks are behind the liberal revenge on Ailes, O'Reilly, and Hannity. [See Elijah List posting August 10.]

August 15, 2017 Johnny Enlow
Heaven is Shouting about the Great American Eclipse
Elijah List

We now enter into Reformation 2.0 where it is all about reformation of society—an entirely different genre of reformation. For 500 years, we primarily celebrated our access into Heaven, and now we will enter an era where we will celebrate Heaven breaking into society. We will go from being excessively future heavenly-minded to being champions of "on earth as it is in Heaven," thus embracing Jesus' original "Magna Carta" as stated in Matthew chapters 5 through 7.

It is not coincidental that essentially where the Elijah List is based from in Albany, Oregon, is where the eclipse will begin. Key cities in the path are Kansas City (essential nest of many of the prophets of our generation), Nashville and Charleston, and South Carolina where it all ends. Major prophetic windows will remain open over these cities (and the others in the pathway) from the day this reset takes place. The Elijah List will begin to release higher and higher levels of revelation into the nation and the world.

Nevertheless, I believe the Lord is about to release 50 "Lonnie Frisbee" mantles and these will operate again initially and primarily outside the four walls of the Church. These will be those new leaders who march to the beat of a different drum, love the unlovely, and burn with a passionate fire for God's Kingdom to be released on the earth.

Demons that have confused one's sexual identity will be cast out, and someone will immediately revert back to proper sexual identity. A lot of "one and done" is coming through the new demon-busting anointing being poured out.

Finally, let me report that another total solar eclipse will be visible in 7 years in America on April 8, 2024. This is essentially a rare back-to-back experience. As you can see this carries us through a projected Trump Presidency— should he also win the next election, which I believe he will do (according to how I have been shown vs. a political perspective).

August 18, 2017 Stephen Powell
Trump has God's Heart for North Korea
LionofFlight.org

The Lord says He's giving Trump his heart for North Korea. I believe the nature of God will be manifested through this man in this hour to deal with this situation according to God's love and justice for the North Korean people. I believe wisdom will be his, even supernatural intervention and assistance, because God's people are praying and have been praying for many years for God to move in that land. I believe those prayers have arisen and North Korea's time of deliverance is at hand. Kim Jong Un can either repent and agree with that word which is coming from heaven, or he can suffer the consequences of resisting the Lord at this hour when God is calling him to give an account of his actions and his ways.

August 18, 2017 Stephen Strang
Strang on Catholic Holy Man who prophesied about Trump
Strang Report

August 22, 2017 Paula White
"The True Story of Donald Trump"
Jim Bakker Show

Paula and her husband Jonathan on the *Jim Bakker Show*. Paula says she tries to go to the White House every week. "Our president loves prayer … He is a Christian."

Bakker: "And here is a woman who is from the bottom lands. But God has raised her up to the White House … She can now walk into the White House anytime she wants to."

August 23, 2017 Paula White
"'Raised up by God': Televangelist Paula White compares Trump to Queen Esther"
Colby Itkowitz at *The Washington Post*

[The article is built around White's appearance on the *Jim Bakker Show.*]

August 27, 2017 Mark Taylor with Sheila Zilinsky
"Are YOU Ready For What's COMING Next?"
YouTube

August 27, 2017 Lance Wallnau
"The eclipse and 40 days test, Donald Trump, Israel…"
Facebook

September 4, 2017 Mark Taylor with Greg Hunter
"Globalism vs. Patriotism, Evil vs. Good"
USA Watchdog

September 9, 2017 Paula White
"Trump Pastor Paula White: The President '100 percent is a Christian … a person of repentance'"
Michelle Boorstein at *The Washington Post*

[Article based on White's appearance at the Religious News Association annual meeting]

September 12, 2017 Hillary Clinton
Hillary Clinton releases *What Happened*, her memoir of her presidential run.

September 23, 2017 Joe Joe Dawson
Intercessors Arise! Strengthen the Hedge of Protection Around President Trump!
Elijah List

In the dream, it was as though I was seeing things from a heavenly realm and a higher perspective. The Lord showed me a live vision of President

Trump and a number of our national leaders. The national leaders were leaders of many different divisions and departments of America as well as the senators and governors from numerous states, Republicans and Democrats alike.

There was a hedge of protection around President Trump and the key leaders of America. It was as if an angelic host had created a sphere-like barrier around President Trump and the national leaders. Even though there was a huge demonic attack and presence surrounding these national leaders from every side and covering them, the hedge of protection was all around them and above them. They were completely protected from this demonic attack. It was as if they were enveloped in a huge bubble of divine protection.

September 24, 2017 Stephen Powell
Trump Standing in the Spirit War
LionofFlight.org

There is a battle raging which is light against darkness, Christ against antichrist, and this conflict is being revealed because of the power that is Donald J. Trump. Donald Trump is not God, but his power is not his own, and it comes from God. He has brought the fight back into the soul of this nation, and that is what this battle is for, the very soul of a nation; the future being created in light or darkness, in God's blueprint or the enemy's ... this is what the battle is over.

[This post is an update of an article from February 17, 2017.]

September 24, 2017 Mark Taylor with Mary Colbert
On Sid Roth, It's Supernatural

Taylor and Colbert, co-authors of *The Trump Prophecies*, are featured on Sid Roth's popular Christian show.

September 27, 2017 Stephen Powell
Trump is a Modern Day Churchill
LionofFlight.org

I strive not to exalt this man above measure, as the Bible tells us, but I must speak what the Lord gives me to say about this man. This is what he spoke to me as I was putting my children to bed recently.

The Lord says that Donald Trump is a modern day Winston Churchill, holding back a force of darkness which once overran Germany and threatened to overrun Great Britain. If not for that man, empowered by the prayers of intercessors like Reese Howells of the day, Great Britain most surely would have been overcome. And to think the devastation, the extent of that war, the change of the course of history that would have been affected. Make no mistake about it, that same spirit which overthrew Germany has grown in strength in America since abortion was legalized feeding the death culture, and it would have completely taken over this nation if not for this man, Donald Trump, which the Lord has raised up to stand in the gap.

October 1, 2017 Lance Wallnau
5778: Lead Gates! Find Out What 8 Means This Year!
Elijah List

Wallnau states again that Donald Trump is Cyrus. He also states that "the spirit of Antichrist is political."

October 1, 2017 Stephen Powell
Confronting the Power in the Tower
LionofFlight.org

We've been intent on huddling in church corners holding on til' Jesus returns so the devil can rule the world, while the enemy has been filling the gaps on top of the mountains left by the body of Christ. But this spirit is being challenged in a most remarkable way right now, and the Lord had to revive the Cyrus anointing, put it on a man which most would have thought to be inept and out of tune with God spiritually, but has proven to be more in touch with the heart of God for the nation than most Christians have been. That man is Donald J. Trump.

October 3, 2017 George Papadopoulos
Papadopoulos charged with lying to FBI. [Signs plea deal on October 5, 2017]

October 12, 2017 Chuck Pierce
Playing the Trump Card
Strang Report

November 1, 2017 Johnny Enlow
Greater Than 100 Revivals Is Here
Elijah List

In GOVERNMENT, it is quite obvious we are going through massive overhaul and yes, a "draining of the swamp." As it is playing out before us, it is evident that as many Republicans as Democrats are in the swamp, and so this is not a partisan thing taking place, but a rather a sweeping reform. President Trump is of course the catalyst for all this and he is only beginning. Explosive revelations such as who really was in "Russian collusion" are only going to increase. The FBI, the IRS, the Attorney General's office and the Intelligence Community have already been exposed for their duplicity and outright crookedness.

It is of no coincidence that as we have shifted into the new Hebraic year of 5778, that a very noteworthy shift towards women's justice matters has also taken place. Hugh Hefner, founder of Playboy, died September 27, and it meant something significant in the spirit realm. He is the man most responsible for pornography going mainstream and by extension, the one most responsible for women being objectified. It is no light thing.

November 5, 2017 Mark Taylor with Greg Hunter
"Mind Boggling Treasonous Acts Exposed and Punished"
USA Watchdog

November 7, 2017 Steve Strang
"Strang's *God and Donald Trump* released"
Charisma News

November 14, 2017, Paula White
"She led Trump to Christ: The rise of the televangelist who advises the White House"
Julia Duin profile on Paula White in *The Washington Post* magazine

Not all Christians, including evangelicals, are fans of the wealthy, thrice-married White, who has long been associated with the prosperity gospel, a set of beliefs that says God will reward faith, and very generous giving, with financial blessings. Detractors point to a congressional investigation of her former church's finances and accusations that she has taken advantage of her mostly African American parishioners through her fundraising. Southern Baptist leader Russell Moore has called her a "charlatan," conservative Christian writer Erick Erickson has said she's a "Trinity-denying heretic," and Christian rapper Shai Linne named her a "false teacher" in one of his songs.

But since the election, White's star has soared. She offered a prayer at Trump's inauguration (becoming the first clergywoman in history in such a role). She sat by the president at a private dinner for evangelical leaders on the eve of the National Day of Prayer. She has hovered close by during prayer sessions in the Oval Office.

"If I am not fresh with God, I might as well hang it up. You can't be a spiritual adviser and not pray," she says. She also explains that she pays her own way. "I've never received a dime from anything," she says of her work on the evangelical advisory council and trips to Washington. "I don't get paid at all. I feel it's part of my purpose. If God has given me this opportunity, it'd be irresponsible not to fulfill it. But I don't get a discount or special privileges."

November 15, 2017 Mark Taylor with Sheila Zilinsky
"UH-OH!! Mark Taylor Predicted This"
YouTube

November 20, 2017 Lance Wallnau
"Break Controlling Spirits Bible Study/Part 1"
YouTube

"The spirit of Antichrist is a political spirit."

December 1, 2017 Michael Flynn
Michael Flynn pleaded guilty to charge of lying.

December 4, 2017 Lance Wallnau
God Is Shaking Up the Leftist Media and Arts Mountain! Are We Ready?
Elijah List

"Trump doing great things … ignored by media."

December 6, 2017 Donald Trump, Israel
"Trump Recognizes Jerusalem As Israel's Capital"
Breaking Christian News

December 7, 2017 Steve Shultz
Israeli Prime Minister Benjamin Netanyahu: This is a Historic Day
Elijah List

Today, I feel like we are all feeling a new HIGH POINT or ZENITH of optimism as President Donald Trump kept YET ANOTHER of his many promises, unlike his many predecessors—becoming the very first president to OFFICIALLY recognize Jerusalem as the capital city of Israel, and well beyond that, he OFFICALLY LAUNCHED the process to move the US Embassy from Tel Aviv to Jerusalem.

This is a move that pleases God and will likely bring a GREAT DEAL OF FAVOR on both the land of Israel and yes, it will be healing to the LAND OF THE UNITED STATES OF AMERICA!

December 8, 2017 Steve Shultz
3 Prophets who Prophesied about Jerusalem, Israel and the USA!
Elijah List

[Kim Clement, Johnny Enlow, Charles Shamp]

December 9, 2017 Donald Trump
"Why I Can No Longer Call Myself an Evangelical Republican"
Peter Wehner at *The New York Times*

I consider Mr. Trump's Republican Party to be a threat to conservatism, and I have concluded that the term evangelical — despite its rich history of proclaiming the "good news" of Christ to a broken world — has been so distorted that it is now undermining the Christian witness.

But for now a solid majority of Republicans and self-described evangelicals are firmly aboard the Trump train, which is doing its utmost to give a seat of privilege to Mr. Moore. So for those of us who still think of ourselves as conservative and Christian, it's enough already.

December 14, 2017 Steve Strang
"Mark Joseph interviews Strang"
Huffington Post

December 14, 2017 Mark Taylor
Interview with Mark Taylor and report about him
CBN 700 Club, YouTube

December 16, 2017 Mark Taylor
"He Predicted Trump Would Be President Six Years Ago, Here's Why This Prophet Says Trump Is In For Two Terms"
CBN and Wendy Griffith on Mark Taylor

When asked whether Trump will win a second term, Taylor said, "Absolutely. I'm sure about that because when people see the good that the country is coming in to, the prosperity, the economy, the jobs—he's going to sail in to the second term."

[Griffith's written report duplicates much of the 700 Club video.]

December 19, 2017 Donald Trump
"Can Evangelicalism Survive Donald Trump and Roy Moore?"
Timothy Keller at *The New Yorker*

V. Second Year
2018

January-February 2018 Mike Pence
"God's Plan for Mike Pence"
McKay Coppins at *The Atlantic*

This is a thorough treatment of Pence's life, albeit mean at some points.

January 6, 2018 Johnny Enlow
2018: A Time of War and Victories
Elijah List

Trump is uniquely ordained and anointed BY GOD to lead the United States at this time. This I tell you not from a political perspective but from a purely prophetic perspective.

God spoke to me, "I chose Trump because I know some things that none of you know." Donald Trump was divinely chosen and placed in power by God, but because we cannot see "... the whole scope of God's work from beginning to end," (Ecclesiastes 3:11) many of us are presently confused or deceived.

You see, Trump has a similar call of God towards America's destiny as to what David had on behalf of Israel. Through Trump, God is drawing lines in the sand even for entire nations. The recent vote against the USA in the United Nations registered in Heaven. Most of the nations chose to condemn Trump and the USA for stating that we would recognize Jerusalem as Israel's capital—a fact already sanctioned in Congress over 20 years ago, but with no president that previously possessed the inner fortitude to stand up to the nations. Likewise, Trump's obedience to declare Jerusalem as Israel's eternal capital, as well as where we will now have our embassy located, resonated heavily in Heaven.

I was recently in South Korea and prophesied that I had seen that "NOW God" was about to intervene and take out Kim Jong-Un. I sensed it so strongly that I honestly felt the NOW would have already taken place. His NOW's always seem to have more elasticity than my NOW's, but I still believe this will happen soon.

January 15, 2018 Mark Taylor
Prophesies of Trump Revealed
Strang Report [19-minute interview]

January 16, 2018 Mark Taylor
The Evil Crew of 32
Sord Rescue

The Spirit of God says, "Who do you think you are, you who call yourselves Christians but further Satan's kingdom? Woe, Woe, Woe, to you leaders who stand in the way of my agenda but call yourself mine. You brood of vipers! My divine judgment is being poured out on the leaders of my United States of America and my Church. You leaders, who want open borders, attack and pray against my anointed men and women, sow division and strife among the people ... you hypocrites! Repent! My righteous judgment is falling now. You who indulge in the corrupt things of this world for power and greed. You who call yourselves leaders, America's leaders, yes even my church leaders, I will not only remove your authority and position, but some I will remove from the face of the earth. Repent! Before it's too late, for my righteous judgment is falling on those that have mocked, deceived, and led my people astray. For many are about to find out what the Spirit of the 'Fear of the Lord,' and who the one true God is."

The Spirit of God says, "Two will be taken and three will be shaken! For I will remove two from the evil crew of 32 and the other three shall be shaken to the core. The 32 years they have altogether served and empowered that entity called Baal, and the covenant they had holding up his house with the illuminati and the New World order, shall come crumbling down. For when the first one is taken, it will be a sign that the New World Order shall die. When the second one is taken, it will be sign that anyone calling himself Mine but comes against my Israel, sympathizing with her enemies, will not be tolerated. The three that will be shaken, will be a sign that no one is above the most high God, not even those that hold the highest office in the land. These among many others that have tried to exalt themselves above me and my law, will be exposed and imprisoned by me for the entire world to see. Righteousness and Justice are the foundation of my throne. Yes, even the Supreme Court will be shaken. Do not fear America when you see these things manifesting, for these things must come to pass. will clean up the darkness and it will usher in my light, for I have America in my hand."

The Spirit of God says, "Why are those that call themselves my people praying against my President? Why are you praying against my agenda for the United States of America? Repent! You pray against my agenda, therefore you are not for me but against me. You pray against my agenda, because you do not know your Father's business. You pray against my agenda because you do not know Me. Repent! Stop listening to Satan's frequency and tap into heavens frequency, then you will know the plans that I have for you."

January 18, 2018 Devon Nunes
"Devon Nunes Memo On FBI Abuse Of Surveillance"
Politico

The staff of House Intelligence Committee Chairman Devin Nunes issued a four-page memo to Majority Members that argued that the FBI abused its surveillance authority.

[Nunes was widely ridiculed and attacked after the Memo was released on February 2, 2018 but the Horowitz report from December 2019 confirmed its basic accuracy.]

January 19, 2018 Mark Taylor with Sheila Zilinsky
"2018 It Has Begun! Explosive Prediction"
YouTube

Taylor argues that "deep state" witchcraft is using the environment to attack God's people. Taylor predicts military tribunals for the enemies of Trump.

January 20, 2018 Steve Strang
The Importance of the 2016 Presidential Election
Strang Report

January 20, 2018 Jeremiah Johnson
2018: Cancer, Baby Boomers, Trump, and the Nations
JeremiahJohnson.tv

I truly believe God has and is using Trump as a type of trumpet in America, but he is like a bull in a china shop and his words must be sifted through in order to hear the truth He is speaking at times.

God said, "I have raised Donald Trump up for four years as a battering ram and trumpet in this nation, but without a serious sanctification and softening of his heart and words, there will be great trouble and danger that will mark his run for a second term. Even those who were once for him, will see the error of his ways and begin to cry out for his soul. Do not be deceived by the wealth and change that Donald has and will bring to America, for I am after far more than the gifts I have irrevocably given him, I must have his heart so that I can order His steps."

The following night after receiving this word, I had a prophetic dream where I saw Donald Trump crawling around on the White House lawn eating grass and acting like an animal. Immediately I cried out to the Lord in the dream and said, "God, shall Donald Trump become like Nebuchadnezzar? Shall he become so consumed with his success that he begins to credit his accomplishments to his own strength and power? Will you remove sovereignty from his life?"

God spoke to me and said, "Donald Trump is in great danger of becoming like Nebuchadnezzar in the years ahead. He will have great success, but the Church must pray for humility and the Daniel Company to arise. Just like Nebuchadnezzar, if Donald breaks away from his sins by doing righteously and showing mercy to the poor, I will prolong his prosperity." (Dan 4: 27)

I woke up from the prophetic dream with a tremendous burden upon my heart. To be honest, I could not believe what I just received. Could the prophetic narrative surrounding Donald Trump completely change without the prayers of the Church, the rise of the Daniel Company, and a repositioning of his own heart? Could Donald Trump have been raised up by God Himself like a Cyrus and bring necessary change to America, but through his own pride, arrogance, and forsaking of the poor end as a Nebuchadnezzar?

The answer is: ABSOLUTELY. Saints, this man desperately needs our prayers! God is prophetically warning us now in 2018 before its too late.

While I have not been given permission by God to directly prophesy into Trump's potential second term, I do sense strongly that there is potential great danger and trouble ahead for America if he is re-elected. He has currently been granted the "iron grip" that will run its course and fulfill its purpose, but Donald Trump may very well be a type of pioneer or trailblazer that must recognize when His mission is complete and it now becomes necessary to turn the nation over to another that can capitalize *on the momentum he helped to start, but do it in a much more wise and tactful way. We must keep praying for Donald Trump and for the purposes of God to be manifested through His life and presidency, but do not be surprised if Donald's grip and force becomes too much in the days ahead for many to bear. The attacks, plots, and plans against him will become more and more bizarre in the days ahead. I believe God is releasing a very clear prophetic narrative with Donald Trump so that the intercessors, watchmen, and prophets know how to pray and act in the days ahead.*

[This prophecy from Jeremiah Johnson shows a uniqueness about Johnson's prophetic ministry. As this guide shows, most prophets who endorse Trump do not give warnings to or about Trump. Johnson does so, along with positive words.]

January 23, 2018 Joe Biden
Foreign Affairs Issue Launch with Former Vice President Joe Biden
Joe Biden at Council on Foreign Relations

Richard Haass, president of Council on Foreign Relations, interviews Biden and Michael Carpenter, U.S. Deputy Assistant Secretary of Defense, 2015 to 2017. This is the meeting where Joe Biden bragged about threatening the withholding of aid to Ukraine unless they fire a state prosecutor. Biden recounted the meeting in Ukraine this way:

"I said, nah, I'm not going to—or, we're not going to give you the billion dollars. They said, you have no authority. You're not the president. The president said—I said, call him. [Laughter.] I said, I'm telling you, you're not getting the billion dollars. I said, you're not getting the billion. I'm going to be leaving here in, I think it was about six hours. I looked at them and said: I'm leaving in six hours. If the prosecutor is not fired, you're not getting the money. Well, son of a bitch. [Laughter.] He got fired."

The video of Biden's remarks from the CFR meeting circulated on Russian media the next day, January 24, 2018. The remark has been used against Biden since it is alleged that he wanted the state prosecutor fired in order to protect his son Hunter Biden, who was, at the time, a board member of Burisma, a Ukrainian energy company.

January 24, 2018 Mark Taylor
"Energy Now"
Sord Rescue

The Spirit of God says, "How do you capture a country? You capture it's energy. For too long, you evil globalists have controlled the energy and it stops now! It shall be exposed in one country after another who has been manipulating and controlling my earth through oil and energy. You evil globalists think you control the oil? Hah! I laugh at my enemies. The oil is not yours but mine and I the Lord God control it. I will release it to my righteous nations and I will cut it off from wicked ones, for I the Lord God own all the silver and gold including black gold."

The Spirit of God says, "The sign has been given that the energy boom is here now. This energy explosion will be the biggest in the history of my America and my Israel. New oil and energy will be discovered and released in the natural and will be a sign that new oil is being released in the spiritual over America and Israel. Other countries' economies will be affected. Russia and China, will be put in their place, your militaries shall be affected by this. Your planes will be seen sitting on the tarmac unable to fly for lack of parts. You will no longer be considered a threat or a superpower. When America announces she is energy independent, these things shall take place. The national debt will be dealt a death blow from what I am releasing in the natural and the spiritual. New energy, new energy is here now and these new discoveries will confound the wise, for it is those that think they are wise that have held all this energy captive, but no more, for I the Lord God am unleashing it now."

January 25, 2018 Mark Taylor
"All Roads Lead to Rome"
Sord Rescue

The Spirit of God says, "The Pope and the Vatican, that's right the Pope and the Vatican are not furthering my kingdom but are aiding the kingdom of darkness. Many are saying that this is the last Pope, but it's not for the reasons they think. This will be the last Pope, for what I the Lord God am about to do. I will expose this Pope and all those under his command for all the corruption he and the Vatican have been involved in for centuries."

The Spirit of God says, "There is a shaking and a quaking coming to this Pope and the Vatican, for I will split the Vatican and it's leadership wide open for the entire world to see the inner workings of this ancient beast. This Pope, the Vatican and all it's leadership, will come crumbling down. I will pull back the veil to show how deep and dark the deception has been. You whisper in your inner chambers 'we answer to no one. No one is above us; No one can hold us accountable.' I the Lord God see it all and the time has come when I will now hold you accountable for your darkness. This exposure will be of such magnitude that the people will say. 'What do we do now? Where do we go now? We want nothing to do with this. We have no religion now.' Millions will walk away from their religion, as this will affect other religions as well."

The Spirit of God says, "Is my Army ready? Are you ready to receive these people? Are you ready to receive my harvest that's going to take place from this exposure? Prepare yourselves for the tsunami of people that will be starving for me and have no place to turn. Prepare now! All roads lead to Rome."

The Spirit of God says, "There is a dig, an archeological find that is coming in an underground vault, which will be so cataclysmic that it will ROCK the Christian world. The answer lies between Jerusalem and Vatican city."

January 27, 2018 Stephen Strang
"Millions of Americans Believe God Made Trump President"
Amy Sullivan at *Politico*

[Based on Stephen Strang's work *God and Donald Trump*; Sullivan is appreciative of the book.]

January 28, 2018 Mark Taylor
"Nuclear Bomb Memo Is About to Explode"
USA Watchdog

January 30, 2018 Donald Trump
State of the Union address.

January 31, 2018 Mark Taylor
"Largest Turnover in Midterm History"
YouTube

February 2, 2018 Devin Nunes
Devin Nunes Memo from January 18 on FBI abuses released.

The president allowed the memo to be released. His legal counsel Donald McGahn II wrote Nunes on the matter.

February 7, 2018 Johnnie Moore
"Evangelicals, Having Backed Trump, Find White House 'Front Door Is Open'"
Noah Weiland at *New York Times*

Focus on Rev. Johnnie Moore

February 13, 2018 Mark Taylor
Mark Taylor … False Prophet?
YouTube

An attack on Mark Taylor and argument that Trump is run by Israel.

February 15, 2018 FBI Investigation
"The Media Stopped Reporting The Russia Collusion Story Because They Helped Create It"
Lee Smith at *The Federalist*

"So let us have the truth. I suspect we will be as unimpressed by Mr. Comey's Russian intelligence as we have been by the Steele dossier. Its provenance will be nothing anyone should have respected—a flimsy basis for actions hugely consequential in our democracy. The real fabricators will turn out to be the U.S. intelligence community agents who, as they did with the Steele dossier, fabricated a significance for an apocryphal document that it didn't merit. They will have done so as an excuse for ill-conceived and improper acts that roiled our politics and undermined domestic harmony. The public campaign of Messrs. Comey, Brennan and

Clapper, after Nov. 8, 2016, to paint Mr. Trump as a Russian agent will appear in a far more cynical and sinister light. And the disgrace of the U.S. mainstream media will be complete."

February 16, 2018 FBI Investigation
Three Russian companies and thirteen Russians charged in indictment.

February 21, 2018 Billy Graham
Death

February 22, 2018 Kat Kerr
Interview with Steve Shultz
Elijah List

Months before the 2016 election Kerr states that God told her, "I've chosen Trump and people won't like it and they won't understand it but that doesn't matter right now because I'm going to change America and I need him. He's an all-American boy that is all for America and he is smart, he can't be bought, he can't be moved, and he cannot be controlled."
Kerr also states that God said that Trump "will know me and he will hear my voice ... From the time he sits in the White House America will not have a boring day."
God also stated, "You don't need a pastor in the White House right now" and that Trump will win two terms; Pence will go two terms.
According to Kerr, God also said that "Trump is raw ... really raw but I will temper him, Pence will temper him..."
There will be amazing new inventions, according to Kerr, and there will be miscarriages and aborted babies in heaven, restored for parents.

[January 11 is the day of the interview but it was released on February 22.]

February 23, 2018 Rick Gates
Gates changed plea to guilty.

February 27, 2018 Jeremiah Johnson
Facebook

Johnson mentions prophecy from January and then writes about The Daniel Company. The Facebook post duplicates some of the words given in a January 2018 posting (see preceding).

I'm convinced through prayer that Donald Trump desperately needs a Daniel Company to arise in the United States that will faithfully give him the word of the Lord and advise him with Godly counsel at strategic times during his Presidency. Donald Trump has and will even appoint some of those in the Daniel Company. God has revealed to me that Sarah Huckabee and Mike Pence are specifically carrying this anointing and have undoubtedly been placed around Trump for such a time as this. On Inauguration Day (January 20, 2017), I gave the following public prophecy in Merritt Island, FL: "Mike Pence will not bow down to Donald Trump, but rather will stand up to him. I am giving Mike Pence a backbone like never before and he will faithfully deliver the truth to Donald Trump again and again" says the Lord. Then God said "I myself will stand up in the midst of the UN council. Those who oppose Israel, I will oppose. Those who defend Israel, I will defend" says God.

February 28, 2018 Donald Trump, Billy Graham
Speaks at Billy Graham memorial service [Washington].

March 3, 2018 Benjamin Netanyahu
In a visit to the White House Israeli Prime Minister Netanyahu compared Trump to Cyrus of Persia.
WhiteHouse.gov

March 5, 2018 Donald Trump
"The Biblical Story The Christian Right Uses To Defend Trump"
Tara Isabella Burton at *Vox*

March 15, 2018 Charles Shamp
God is Calling Us to Pray for North Korea's Dictator Kim Jong-un and His Sister
Elijah List

Shamp has a dream on March 5, 2018, about the North Korean leader and his sister and explains prophetic significance.

March 18, 2018 Mark Taylor with Greg Hunter
"Not a Time to Walk in Fear"
USA Watchdog

March 21, 2018 Mark Taylor
"Liberty University Is Making A Movie About Trump-Loving 'Firefighter Prophet' Mark Taylor"
Kyle Mantyla at Right Wing Watch

April 9, 2018 Michael Cohen
Michael D. Cohen's hotel and office raided.

April 19, 2018 Donald Trump
"Why Evangelical Leaders Opposed to Trump Speak for More Evangelicals Than You Think"
Napp Nazworth at *The Christian Post*

April 21, 2018 Kanye West
West tweets appreciation for Candace Owens, the conservative political commentator.
Twitter

"I love the way Candace Owens thinks."

May 9, 2018 Donald Trump
President tweets appreciation for Candace Owens.
Twitter

"Candace Owens of Turning Point USA is having a big impact on politics in our Country. She represents an ever expanding group of very smart 'thinkers,' and it is wonderful to watch and hear the dialogue going on … so good for our Country!"

May 9, 2018 Lance Wallnau
You Must Go Up and Go Through! The Door is Open, the Voice is Calling—the Timing is Now!
Elijah List

May 12, 2018 Angela Greenig
Passover into Pentecost: We Are Living in Historical Times!
Elijah List

As we approach the celebration of Israel's 70th year of Independence, I sit back and reflect on how God the Father has strategically positioned President Trump to become the President of the United States of America, and how I feel this connects to Israel. It is not happenstance or chance that God has had His hand on President Trump, or that he would win the Presidential election ... These next few years are going to bring forth the greatest revival the world has seen; so great that we can't begin to describe the fullness of it, because I believe God's people have never encountered any revival like it ever before."

May 14, 2018 Johnnie Moore
Moore participates in a panel on "Role of Religion in the Republican Party" at Georgetown University.

Here are some of the words of Moore, quoted in Samuel Smith's May 20 report at *The Christian Post* on the Georgetown event:

Although the evangelical leaders have established a "genuine relationship" with the president, Moore suggested that the leaders have not been afraid to voice their disagreements or concerns. "By the way, it is not that this community doesn't criticize him," Moore said. "The Bible tells me that 'Faithful are the words of a friend.' That doesn't say that it has to be in bold 32-point font on the front page of the New York Times." "I think that this is a community that has ... in a particular environment in a particular time in series of circumstances, created an unlikely alliance," he continued. "There was a lot of pessimism about how that alliance would play itself out. But what has happened is we found that again and again and again, there is this strange politician that generally has kept his promises to our community, which is an unusual characteristic for a politician."

May 14, 2018 David Brody
"An Evangelical Journalist Finds His Calling at the White House"
Elizabeth Dias at *The New York Times*

Article on David Brody of Christian Broadcasting Network [Brody interviewed Trump eight times during campaign.]

May 14, 2018 Donald Trump, Israel
Opening of US Embassy in Jerusalem

Benjamin Netanyahu: "What a glorious day. Remember this moment. This is history. President Trump, by recognizing history, you have made history."

May 16, 2018 Donald Trump, Israel
Trump Fulfills a 'Biblical Prophecy'—by Moving US Embassy to Jerusalem
Elijah List

[CBN News reports on Judge Jeanine Pirro calling Trump a Cyrus figure. Dore Gold, former Israeli ambassador to the UN, also made a link between Trump and Cyrus.]

May 18, 2018 Mark Taylor
How God Will Remove Obama
YouTube

Taylor claims Obama will go to prison and repeats prophecy about Pope Francis being removed from office.

May 27, 2018 Mark Taylor with Greg Hunter
"Time is Up for Those Corrupt"
USA Watchdog

May 31, 2018 Mark Taylor
"Did Trump fulfill a divine prophecy? What to expect from a new Liberty University film"
Lauren Markoe at *The Washington Post*

A balanced piece about upcoming Mark Taylor film

June 1, 2018 Donald Trump
"The Amazing 'Words of Faith' Spoken by President Trump"
Aimee Herd at *Breaking Christian News*

Trump's words during National Day of Prayer, May 3, 2018.

June 1, 2018 Mark Taylor
Taylor on Sheila Zilinsky
Sheila Media, YouTube

Movie about Mark Taylor is announced. Taylor says that the UK monarchy "may come down."

June 5, 2018 Donald Trump
"How Statements On Trump Tower Meeting Have Changed"
CBS News

June 14, 2018 Charles Shamp
A Tsunami Wave Over the Nation! Trees Planted and Uprooted in the White House!
Elijah List

I heard the Lord speak, "I have extended an olive branch of peace to the United States of America and will extend Donald Trump's presidency into a second term by the power of My right hand. What I have done in the White House will happen with every 'branch' of government in the United States for I will pull out corruption and plant trees of righteousness that will bear much fruit."

The Lord spoke to me again, "As a sure sign of these things coming to pass, there will be a wave of conservatives elected during the midterm election in November 2018. It will be Breaking News. They will carry the House and the Senate and I will uproot, replant and rebuild the nation.

"I will tie the three branches of government together; for a person standing alone can be attacked and defeated, but two can stand back-to-back and conquer. Three are even better, for a triple-braided cord is not easily broken. I will no longer allow your president to stand on his own. Even now, I have called others to come alongside and help bring the nation back from the dead and they will take their seats in the coming days."

I saw the House of Representatives stay in the hands of the Republicans and will move much more to a conservative position. I could see into the Senate and saw the Republicans gain nine seats. Those that took their place were considerably more conservative then those who had previously been there. I heard the Lord say, "Yes, nine will be a sign—a sign that righteousness has been birthed in the nation and earth." I saw three more constitutional conservatives were appointed to the Supreme Court by President Trump before 2020.

June 15, 2018 Shawn Bolz
The Angel Over Korea and God's End-Time Plan
Elijah List

An angel of Korea appeared to me and said, "Behold, I am strong, and I shall do a mighty work, even in preparing Israel for the return of Jesus."

Korea was never on the map of my heart or mind. Then one day, very randomly, an angel appeared in my room in a physical form. He said, "Behold, I am from Korea." (Photo: Angels Among Us from Jennifer Page)

I asked him, "From North or South?" and he almost yelled at me, "I am from Korea." And I realized there is no North or South Korea in God's heart. He never designed it to be separated. I didn't dare speak again.

I prophesy now that the economy will become one of the largest in the world when the unification happens, because the technologies and resources that God wants to entrust to Koreans are some of the most valuable in the world markets because He knows what they will do with them.

June 29, 2018 John Fea
Kristin Kobes Du Mez at *Christianity Today*
Review of Fea's book *Believe Me*

July 2, 2018 Lou Engle
A Crucial Turning Point for America
Elijah List

Thankfully we have come to a profound moment of opportunity, but we must not take it for granted. While President Trump is consulting with his advisors to consider his choice of nominees, we must set ourselves to prayer on his behalf and on behalf of the person whom God has chosen to fill this vital position in our nation's highest court.

Amy Coney Barrett is on President Trump's short list of potential nominees. In the natural, this judge from Indiana who was confirmed last year to the 7th Circuit Court of Appeals, is everything we would hope for in a judicial candidate for the Supreme Court. Yet, even more than having the professional credentials and reputation of someone who would make a great justice, we believe Barrett has the endorsement of Heaven behind her. Matt's dream is one of several prophetic indicators that have repeatedly brought her to our attention.

July 6, 2018 Chuck Pierce
Pierce On Importance of Supporting Israel
Strang Report

July 11, 2018 Mark Taylor
The Trump Prophecies and SCOTUS
YouTube of Taylor on SkyWatch TV

July 23, 2018 Eddie Hyatt
"5 Reasons I Changed My Mind About Donald Trump"
Charisma News

August 1, 2018 Donald Trump
"Meeting With Inner City Pastors And Faith Leaders At White House"
NBC

Darrell Scott, Alveda King, Paula White, and John Gray were among attendees. Scott said, "this is probably going to be… the most pro-black president I've seen in my lifetime." President Trump thanked Scott for his support.

August 2, 2018 Mark Taylor
Taylor on SkyWatch about upcoming movie The Trump Prophecy
YouTube

August 7, 2018 Lou Engle with Matt Lockett
An Esther Moment! A Call to Fast and Pray for the US Supreme Court
Elijah List

Even though the president did not select Judge Barrett for the current vacancy on the court, it is our conviction that she must not be forgotten. Perhaps she will be raised up in the days ahead as a replacement for Ginsburg or someone else. We will continue to stand in faith and declare to the spiritual realm over the president, the senate, and all involved, "Remember the name Amy Barrett!"

Immediately following Justice Kennedy's retirement announcement, something quite revealing began to take place—something you won't hear about in the news. Sources revealed that witches began making phone calls to senators' offices to curse them with brazen witchcraft in an effort to exert a demonic influence over the process. Make no mistake—this is a spiritual battle of the highest order.

August 10, 2018 Alveda King
'President Trump Turns Out to Be a Samson!' Alveda King Asks for Prayer after 'Hot Meeting' in the White House
Elijah List

Success or failure? Which one will we choose? While I've often said that I don't care what people say or think about me, that's not entirely true. If your hatred for me prevents your being able to receive truth and light, I do care.

"Have I now become your enemy by telling you the truth?" Galatians 4:16

[The preceding link is to the Elijah List. King blogs directly at her blog Civil Rights for the Unborn.]

August 10, 2018 Peter Strzok
Peter Strzok, FBI agent, fired. Strzok became famous over his anti-Trump tweets.

August 13, 2018 Alveda King
"Evangelist Alveda King Responds to Controversial Omarosa Book"
Charisma News

August 14, 2018 Omarosa Manigault Newman
Former White House aide and one-time friend to President, Omarosa Newman, releases *Unhinged*.

August 15, 2018 Donald Trump, John Brennan
President removes security clearance of John Brennan, former CIA director.

August 17, 2018 Kat Kerr
God Bless America and Planet Earth—Another Incredible Suddenly!
Elijah List

God has assured me that He will continue to support and encourage Trump and his plans to make America great again. God chose him because he was a good businessman, not a pastor. You vote where life is honored and protected and where evil is exposed

God has assured me, like you saw during the 2016 election time when he won the presidency, that the masses will vote for life and not darkness. We will all see an amazing, incredible "suddenly" on behalf of Trump and Pence.

Trump was chosen before he was born and cannot escape being great and will continue to recognize God as the creator of all things. God trusts him and we must trust him also. Get ready for many exciting days in America and on this earth.

We are entering into the days of greater glory and the manifested sons and daughters of God who will shock and stun this world, doing greater works like raising the dead who were cremated or raising the dead en masse—even at the scene of accidents that would've brought great trauma to many people but instead they will rejoice at the power of our God.

August 19, 2018 John Kilpatrick
Kilpatrick issues prophetic warning in morning worship against a Jezebel spirit of witchcraft that will be released against President Trump
YouTube video of morning service is at Church of His Presence.

Kilpatrick said that God told him the previous evening that "there is "about to be a shift and the deep state is about to manifest and it's going to be a showdown like you can't believe…"
Kilpatrick also said that God told him about an attempt to take the president out of power.

August 20, 2018 Mark Taylor
"God's About To Bring All The Corruption Down And Judge The Deep State"
Taylor on The Mc Files [PSCP TV]

August 21, 2018 Paul Manafort, Michael Cohen
"Paul Manafort, Former Trump Aide, Convicted."
New York Times

"Michael Cohen, former Trump lawyer and personal assistant, pleads guilty to campaign-finance violations and other charges."
CNBC

Mainstream media focused on Cohen's allegation that Trump directed him to pay hush money to two women who have claimed to have had an affair with the president.

August 21, 2018 Steve Strang
Announcement of Strang's *Trump Aftershock* [scheduled to be released November 6, 2018]

August 23, 2018 Steve Strang
"Omarosa, Loyalty and Donald Trump"
Charisma News

August 23, 2018 John Kilpatrick
"Famed AG Preacher John Kilpatrick Calls Out Spirit of Jezebel, Witchcraft Attacking Trump"
Charisma

August 23, 2018 John Kilpatrick
"Pastor Prays For Trump To Defeat Deep State 'Witchcraft,' Speaks in Tongues"
Benjamin Fearnow in *Newsweek*

August 23, 2018 Jo Ellen Stevens
Pray for the Trump Family! The Shaking of the Tower of David
Elijah List

I want people to know up front that I believe God has placed Donald Trump in office and that he will be there until God says so. When God began to show me this, I was a bit taken back and didn't want to bring it forth, but I feel it is necessary for prayers' sake. In the spirit, I saw Trump on top of David's Tower as if he were David looking down on Bathsheba on that building. I was then impressed by the Lord that as Trump is being accused of these things with these women, God is working on his humility and he is about to have a bit of a shaking that will turn around for his good and bring much repentance and restoration to him. He is going to encounter God at a heart-level like He has never known.

The Lord said that the "Ivory Tower" that he lived in before the presidency is slowly coming down and being placed with God's Strong Tower! He is finding Him (the Lord) to be his only "Strong Tower" in the midst of the shaking that he is encountering. God is saying that the shaking which is happening now will seem high on the Richter scale, but it will not do any permanent damage! He said that as President Trump is going through this, we are to pray, pray, pray that no principalities or powers can have their way!

It is going to look a bit rough for a while, but the president will come forth and do all which God has called him to do! In fact, this is going to solidify his calling even more!

Very important prayer right now: I also heard the Lord say to pray for President Trump's son BARRON TRUMP very specifically. Pray in the spirit (in tongues) as you pray for Barron too!

But even as the Lord forgave David and called him "a man after His own heart," so He will do and has done for this president and will cause him to stand before the people in His (God's righteousness). This is not of his own, and who are we to call something unclean that God has cleansed?

August 25, 2018 Michael Brown

"Did a Leading Pastor Give a Prophetic Warning About Trump's Monday from Hell?"
God TV

Brown is speaking of Kilpatrick's prophecy and his warning about the Jezebel attack on Trump. Brown explains the Old Testament context:

For those unfamiliar with biblical imagery, Ahab and Jezebel were notorious leaders in ancient Israel, Ahab the king and Jezebel the queen. But it was Jezebel who was more sinister, the driving force behind her husband's sins.

It was Jezebel who killed Israel's prophets, recognizing them as a direct threat to her authority, since she herself was a non-Israelite idol worshiper. And it is this Jezebel-type influence that John Kilpatrick calls "witchcraft."

This is the biblical imagery used by Pastor Kilpatrick, who spoke of a new wave of attacks coming against the president as he sought to drain the swamp.

August 25, 2018 John McCain

Death of Senator John McCain.

August 27, 2018 Donald Trump

President Hosts Dinner At White House For Evangelical Leaders
Whitehouse.gov

Trump: "I want to say a special thank you to Paula White, Alveda King, Franklin Graham, Jerry Falwell, Darrell Scott, Robert Jeffress, Ralph Reed, Tony Perkins, Lester Warner, and everyone here tonight. So many great, great leaders. Incredible leaders. I know you, I watch you, I see you. Yours are the words we want to hear."

Mainstream media claim that Trump said violence would result if Democrats win at mid-terms and that Trump urged evangelical leaders to get out the vote. Various evangelical leaders said they were not alarmed by the president's talk.

At dinner Trump made this comment: "Also, our hearts and prayers are going to the family of Senator John McCain. There's going to be a lot of activity over the next number of days. And we very much appreciate everything that Senator McCain has done for our country."

August 29, 2018 Johnny Enlow
The Lord is Coming—Riding on a Red Horse
Elijah List

In our color template for the 7 mountains, red is also the color associated with the mountain of media, and this has been the mountain of huge focus this year. Media has been overrun by the demonic and by those who unwittingly serve the demonic. This all changes now.

The word I give here is not to be seen as a pro-Republican word, as they are under judgment as well, but it is related to the assignment Donald Trump carries and he is represented by the color red, which he frequently carries on his tie and on his hat. His political entrance was ordained to be through the Republican red. Now, I know many minorities in America are greatly bothered by the prophetic words that validate or support President Trump, but a message from God has to be spoken no matter who it is popular with. One of the "great awakenings" of this season is and will be minorities realizing how horribly they have been manipulated and played by the Democratic party "elite." It is going to be a shocking eye opener. It is not that the Republicans have been righteous, only that the Democrats have been particularly manipulative and insidious while having made nothing better. There is no point arguing about it now, but it will all become clear very soon.

Signs from 5 sports events...

#1 Washington Caps Win NHL Championship: A Russian is Series MVP

Prophetically it is finally time for patriotic celebration in DC and it will be related to the winning of the team in red. To the surprise of many the cleansing that is coming to DC will end up proving not only that there was no collusion between Russia and Trump but that a Russian component will have been very key to a good and righteous thing. Watch and see on this one.

#2 Alabama Crimson Tide Win the National Championship: A Red Wave in Midterms

I believe that this football result "prophesies" an upcoming "crimson tide/red wave" in the upcoming midterm elections. Many will believe it not possible, but it will be not just a win but a historic "red wave" coming in. The man riding a red horse will come in on this red wave. It will be a victory for the American people and will be part of a great cleansing.

#3 Philadelphia Eagles Defeat N.E. Patriots: Prophets and Intercessors are Winning

God is working more with His intercessors and His prophetic voices (symbolic of Eagles) than with patriotism. The coming victory is not dependent on Patriots, and so this should be encouraging to those who worry about that.

#4 Golden State Warriors Win NBA Finals: #35 Kevin Durant MVP Again

A main message from the NBA Finals is the fact that #35 Kevin Durant won the series MVP award for the second consecutive year. Isaiah 35 tells about "a highway of holiness" that would be central, and this is key. Last year's very rare total solar eclipse went from the West Coast to the East Coast and the path of totality was 35 miles wide. These 35s are not coincidental. On a map the stripe across the USA looked like a seat belt. There were 7 different cities named Salem that were in that path of totality. Salem means "peace." Yes, it draws our attention to Jerusalem as well, which has been big in the news since Trump declared she would be our embassy base, but it also has prophesied what is coming over America as we go through this justice wave.

A "highway of holiness" is going to suddenly open from sea to shining sea and it is what will be a seat belt of protection for us. 7 is also an ongoing key number that speaks both of God and His 7 spirits, but also of the 7 mountains of society that are about to come under a new order of Salem/

Shalom. Not coincidentally, Kevin Durant is 7 feet tall. Kevin means "handsome" and Durant means "enduring." This will be a beautiful awakening to righteousness and it will be an enduring theme.

#5 Man O'War, Secretariat and Justify: The Ride of the Red Horses

There is an unmistakable message for us today from the Lord saying He is coming to us as the Man riding a red horse. These are arguably the three greatest racing horses in history and you can see the Trinity representation showing up through them. Man O'War as the Father, Secretariat as the Holy Spirit (he raced when the Charismatic movement ignited), and now Justify speaking of the Son, and reminding us that it is the Blood of Jesus that sets the agenda for everything else.

August 30, 2018 Lance Wallnau

Wallnau refers to August 27 meeting at White House and calls it Trump's "prophetic warning to Christian leaders."

YouTube [18 minutes]

Wallnau calls for renewed zeal to support Trump.

August 30, 2018 Mike Pence

VP Pence tells *CBN News* that mainstream media have "met their match" in Trump.

CBN

"Well, all I know is for a lot of the liberals in the national media, they met their match in President Donald Trump. He understands that look, the American people elected this man because he had a right vision for this country but also because he's a fighter. He's willing to fight every day to move this country forward to see jobs created, to see us reaffirm our commitment to the timeless principles in the Constitution, to see our military standing tall again, to see America respected in the world again, and to be able to take on his critics, one after another, and the only thing I know for sure is that President Trump is going to keep on fighting and we're going to keep on winning for the American people."

August 31, 2018 Mike Pence

"Is it God's Plan for Mike Pence to be President?"

Connie Schultz at *The Washington Post*

August 31, 2018 Michael Horton
"What Are Evangelicals Afraid of Losing?"
Christianity Today on August 27 White House meeting

And yet, swinging from triumphalism to seething despair, many pastors are conveying to the wider, watching public a faith in political power that stands in sharp opposition to everything we say we believe in. To many of our neighbors, the court chaplains appear more like jesters.

Something tremendous is at stake here: whether evangelical Christians place their faith more in Caesar and his kingdom than in Christ and his reign. On that one, we do have everything to lose—this November and every other election cycle. When we seek special political favors for the church, we communicate to the masses that Christ's kingdom is just another demographic in the US electorate.

September 2018 James Beverley
"Evangelical Support for Donald Trump"
Faith Today

September 1, 2018 Mike Evans
"Donald Trump and Holy Ground"
Charisma News

Evans attended an August 27 dinner at the White House and says mainstream media reports about the event are "fake news."

September 4–7, 2018 Brett Kavanaugh
Nomination hearings for Brett Kavanaugh to the Supreme Court

September 5, 2018 Donald Trump
"I Am Part of the Resistance Inside the Trump Administration"
New York Times

This anonymous opinion piece created enormous interest, praise, and condemnation. President Trump suggested that the Justice Department should find out who wrote the piece.

September 6, 2018 Hank Kunneman
A Call to Prayer and Intercession for the Month of September: Who will Stand on the Lord's Side for Such a Time as This?
Elijah List [from a prophecy on August 12, 2018, at The Lord of Hosts Church in Omaha, Nebraska]

So I speak to you now as there are storms in August, forming and stirring to counter what I am doing. Look to September, for the enemy has said, "We shall cause September to be violent. We shall cause September to be chaotic and cause September to be filled with rage and with storms."

September 7, 2018 Barack Obama
"Obama Lashes Trump in Debut 2018 Speech"
Peter Baker at *New York Times*

September 7, 2018 Donald Trump
"A Cheer for Trump's Outreach to the Taliban"
Douglas Lute and Denis McDonough at *New York Times*

September 11, 2018 Bob Woodward
Release of Bob Woodward's book *Fear*

September 11, 2018 Franklin Graham
"Franklin Graham's Uneasy Alliance with Donald Trump"
Eliza Griswold at *The New Yorker*

September 13, 2018 Charles Shamp
Prophet and Revivalist, President of Destiny Encounters International
Elijah List [Shamp interview with Steve Shultz]

Parallel to his June 14, 2018, prediction, Shamp predicts a red tsunami in the mid-term elections.

September 16, 2018 Lisa Page
"Lisa Page Bombshell: FBI Couldn't Prove Trump-Russia Collusion Before Mueller Appointment"
John Solomon at *The Hill*

"It's a reflection of us still not knowing," Page told Rep. John Ratcliffe (R-Texas) when questioned about texts she and Strzok exchanged in May 2017 as Robert Mueller was being named special counsel to take over the Russia investigation.

With that statement, Page acknowledged a momentous fact: After nine months of using some of the most awesome surveillance powers afforded to U.S. intelligence, the FBI still had not made a case connecting Trump or his campaign to Russia's election meddling.

Page's comments also mean FBI and Justice officials likely leaked a barrage of media stories just before and after Mueller's appointment that made the evidence of collusion look far stronger than the frontline investigators knew it to be. Text messages show contacts between key FBI and DOJ players and The Washington Post, The Associated Press and The New York Times during the ramp-up to Mueller's probe. And that means the news media — perhaps longing to find a new Watergate, to revive sagging fortunes — were far too willing to be manipulated by players in a case that began as a political opposition research project funded by Clinton's campaign and led by a former British intelligence agent, Christopher Steele, who despised Trump.

Finally, Page's statement signals that the nation's premier intelligence court may not have been given a complete picture of the evidence — or lack thereof — as it approved an extraordinary surveillance intrusion into an American presidential nominee's campaign just weeks before Election Day. There was no fault to the FBI checking whether Trump was compromised by Russia; that is a classic counterintelligence responsibility. The real fault lies in those leaders who allowed a secret investigation to mushroom into a media maelstrom driven by leaks that created a story that far exceeded the evidence, and then used that false narrative to set a special counsel flying downhill ahead of his skis.

[Solomon is referencing an interview Page gave during a congressional interview in the summer of 2018.]

September 21, 2018 Johnny Enlow
5779: A Great Day of Deliverance (Trump, Justice, Elections, Israel, Church and the Economy)
Elijah List

In the year 5777 on the Jewish calendar, a man named Donald Trump shocked these same global "elitists" by winning the United States election. He won by 77 electoral votes. Trump was 70 years old, 7 months, and 7 days on his first full day as President. What are the odds this many 7s could be coincidental?

The Church has fallen asleep as a result of rapture-minded "end-times-itis" and its ensuing abandonment of the 7 Mountains mandate (being salt and light in society, not just in Church) giving the enemy extended time to become embedded in power. God is now moving with those who are awake, knowing the greater awakening is ensuing.

I see "a strong east wind" sent by God, coming through the November midterm elections. They are going to be key in ultimately unleashing a "Red Sea" wave that will position the man God has chosen to lead the United States with a supporting cast in the Congress, the Senate, and ultimately the Supreme Court. It is not that God is "Republican red" in general, it's just that who God chose He happened to orchestrate through this party.

Trump will succeed in his assignment to drain the "Red Sea" swamp because he is on assignment from God and empowered by God for that assignment. Forthcoming will be the complicity of the truly "fake news" with the embedded corruption, and it will be even more clear why Trump had to point them out. There is a Great Awakening ahead, but as I have said before it might be preceded by a rude awakening for many.

Those who "leap over the threshold" are associated with the worship of Dagon. Dagon was the Philistine deity who was the father of Baal. Part of what will be coming out in 5779 is the proof that many of the corrupt ones being disempowered are actual worshipers of Baal, Molech, Dagon, and satan himself. Some of the most abominable practices imaginable will come to light and it will be initially hard to believe because it will be so evil—and so widespread among certain evil elite.

September 25, 2018 Dutch Sheets
America's Destiny is at Stake: A Call to Pray for Judge Kavanaugh and Midterm Elections
Elijah List

First, the level of spiritual warfare was extraordinary. Never have I been more convinced that a war of historical proportions is underway for the soul of our nation, a war that will have worldwide implications. Like Israel, America's role on the earth is extremely significant. Israel was chosen to bring forth the Messiah, the Savior of the world; America was chosen to be the foremost messenger of this "good news."

Regarding the recent allegations against Judge Kavanaugh, no compassionate person would ever belittle the pain and trauma of a person who has suffered a sexual assault. But whatever occurred to his accuser, I don't believe it was perpetuated by Judge Kavanaugh. I believe he is an honorable man and a competent judge. More importantly, I am 1000% certain that neither guilt nor innocence can ever be proven in this case. I am also certain that, in such a situation, it is completely inappropriate for a person's reputation, family, and career to be destroyed. This unacceptable treatment of him contradicts every tenet of law and justice America was built on. And the manner in which this accusation has been handled by the left makes clear that their actions are nothing but a Democrat smear campaign.

Also, ask God to give us the breakthrough in the Supreme Court we have been requesting for decades—a majority of Justices who are Constitutionalists, literalists (meaning they believe the Constitution is to be taken literally, exactly as it is written) and who are pro-life. Let's also boldly ask Him for another vacancy on the Court soon—I feel strongly in my spirit another is coming quickly. We should be offensive in our prayers, not just defensive and reactionary.

President Trump, though imperfect, is doing a good job. Make no mistake about it, the vile hatred of him by the left is not because of his immoral past. Hollywood—the heroes and partners of those on the left—glorifies immoral lifestyles on a daily basis. They hate President Trump because he is helping turn around the antichrist agenda they love, and because he is halting their transformation of America into something other than what was intended by God and our Founders.

September 28, 2018 Jerry Falwell, Jr.
Tweet from President of Liberty University

"Conservatives & Christians need to stop electing "nice guys." They might make great Christian leaders but the US needs street fighters like @realDonaldTrump at every level of government b/c the liberal fascists Dems are playing for keeps & many Repub leaders are a bunch of wimps!"

October 2, 2018 James Dobson, Brett Kavanaugh
Dr. James Dobson Calls for Urgent Prayer Over Brett Kavanaugh's "Wounded Family": Mrs. Kavanaugh Asks for Psalm 40 Prayer
Elijah List

We're asking the Lord during the day and into the night to defeat the schemes of those who clearly want to destroy this great nation. I'm not accusing Dr. Ford of anything. She might remember the ghosts of her past, though the facts appear to contradict her description of them. But something else is going on here. At its core, this isn't just another political conflict. Swirling around us is a life and death struggle for the soul of America. It is a profound spiritual battle that touches something deep within me. We are left with an agonized prayer: "God, please help us."

October 2 and 4, 2018 Mark Taylor
The Trump Prophecy movie plays in 1200 theatres across USA.

October 3, 2018 Donald Trump
"The Cruelty Is the Point"
Adam Serwer at *The Atlantic*

President Trump and his supporters find community by rejoicing in the suffering of those they hate and fear.

Only the president and his allies, his supporters, and their anointed are entitled to the rights and protections of the law, and if necessary, immunity from it. The rest of us are entitled only to cruelty, by their whim. This is how the powerful have ever kept the powerless divided and in their place, and enriched themselves in the process.

Trump's only true skill is the con; his only fundamental belief is that the United States is the birthright of straight, white, Christian men, and his only real, authentic pleasure is in cruelty. It is that cruelty, and the delight it brings them, that binds his most ardent supporters to him, in shared scorn for those they hate and fear: immigrants, black voters, feminists, and treasonous white men who empathize with any of those who would steal their birthright. The president's ability to execute that cruelty through word and deed makes them euphoric. It makes them feel good, it makes them feel proud, it makes them feel happy, it makes them feel united.

And as long as he makes them feel that way, they will let him get away with anything, no matter what it costs them.

October 4, 2018 Mark Taylor
"'The Trump Prophecy' Is a Horrifying Window Onto Evangelicalism"
Emily Pothast at *Medium*

"Every American who values democracy should be alarmed by the fact that this film exists at all."

October 6, 2018 Donald Trump, Brett Kavanaugh
Senate confirms Brett Kavanaugh to Supreme Court and he is sworn in.

October 8, 2018 Mark Taylor
"Christian Nationalism, Explained Through One Pro-Trump Propaganda Film"
Tara Isabella Burton at *Vox*

A very negative response to the film about Mark Taylor.

October 11, 2018 Conor Ryan
"The 45th President"
Ryan at *Christian Today*

I was distracted, my mind was full of mental clutter. Another spiritual battle but I was determined to push through.

I sat down at my desk and there it was again. The number 45. This time on an empty coke bottle on my desk.

Suddenly the clutter was gone and I had clarity as the realization came to me 'hold on, isn't Donald Trump the 45th US president?' I quickly googled 'what number president is Donald Trump?'

Sure enough the answer was he is the 45th president. The previously dormant information had been there in my head but now jumped out at me as it took on specific relevance.

Discovering that Trump is the 45th president only brought weight to the sense that God is saying something prophetically about the significance of his purpose.

I realize that many find Trump distasteful and it may sound ludicrous and far-fetched that he may have some special role in God's plans for the world today. Whether or not God is highlighting a parallel between Cyrus and Trump that is worthy of consideration is for the reader to discern.

There is, of course, many things to criticize about Donald Trump and he should be held accountable like any other powerful leader. But I am also convinced that the unusual presidency of Donald Trump has a deeper meaning that is worth pursuing.

October 11, 2018 Kanye West
Kanye West meets Trump in Oval Office, wears a MAGA hat, and supports Trump.
CNN

"I love this guy," Kanye states about Trump.

October 19, 2018 Mark Taylor
"The Christian Conspiracies That Keep Evangelicals On Trump's Side"
Leah Payne and Brian Doak at *The Washington Post*

This is an analysis of "The Trump Prophecy" movie about Mark Taylor.

October 22, 2018 Donald Trump
"Mail Pipe Bomb Cases and Arrest On 26th of Cesar Sayoc"
Huffington Post

October 22, 2018 George Soros
"George Soros and His 'Rented Evangelicals' Outed by Christian Leaders"
Cheryl Chumley at *The Washington Times*

October 23, 2018 Michael Brown
Brown releases his book *Donald Trump is Not My Savior* (Destiny Image). Brown tracks his opposition to Trump as a Republican candidate then support for Trump over Clinton and his balanced appraisal for Trump and Evangelicals.

October 24, 2018 Michael Brown
"Evangelicals Should Support Trump but Publicly Criticize His Sins, Michael Brown Says in New Book"
Napp Nazworth at *Christian Post*

October 24, 2018 Mark Taylor
Taylor releases many videos of his interviews on his new official YouTube site (launched October 23). The videos published on the 24th are from prior engagements, mainly with Sheila Zilinsky.

October 27, 2018 Donald Trump
"Killings In Synagogue In Pittsburgh"
Campbell Robertson, Christopher Mele and Sabrina Tavernise at *New York Times*, CBS News

The racially motivated murders at a synagogue led to Trump's visit to Pittsburgh and controversies over his trip.

October 30, 2018 Donald Trump
"President Trump Visits Pittsburgh"
Alex Leary and Kris Maher at *Wall Street Journal*

October 31, 2018 Mark Taylor
"The Deep State within the Church"
YouTube of Taylor on The Mc Files with Christopher McDonald

October 31, 2018 Hank Kunneman
YouTube

Kunneman prophesies that there will be an acceleration of God's work as of mid-term elections. He also prophesies that there will be medical miracles involving cures for cancer, diabetes, and Alzheimer's.

November 1, 2018 Donald Trump
"For Trump's Evangelicals, the Inconvenient Teachings of Christ"
Jonathan Beasley and Dudley Rose at *Harvard Religion Beat*

November 5, 2018 Mark Taylor
The Church's Alignment with Wickedness
YouTube of Taylor on The Mc Files

November 6, 2018 Steve Strang
Release of *Trump Aftershock*

November 6, 2018 Donald Trump
Mid-term elections: Democrats gain in House, Republicans in Senate.

November 7, 2018 Mark Taylor, Brett Kavanaugh
The Spiritual War over Brett Kavanaugh
YouTube of Taylor on The Mc Files

November 7, 2018 Steve Shultz, Charles Shamp
What Happens When Prophets MISS an ELECTION PROPHECY?
Elijah List

Shultz publishes his communication with Charles Shamp, who admits he was wrong about the mid-term election results.

Last night the elections finally happened, and while it is good that the Senate was held (so that future judges can still be appointed by President Trump), it honestly was not the "RED TSUNAMI" that several prophets prophesied.

In order for us to have integrity, we must be willing to say "we got it wrong" or "we missed it" or "at least on the surface, what was prophesied does not appear to have happened at all."

False prophets lead people intentionally away from God. NONE of our prophets do that. NONE of them. But sometimes a prophet we publish will miss it on certain words. Most of these misses are small, even tiny. Several prophets had stated that God would turn the map red again during this election, and rather than being a blue wave, they said it was going to be a "RED TSUNAMI."

There is not any level where a "Red Tsunami" was apparent. Control of the House was lost. This is not an inconvenience to God! NOTHING is impossible for God. It's an inconvenience for President Trump but NOT FOR GOD!

Charlie tells Steve,

"In fact, I believe it is important as this could also be a test to where we are headed in the prophetic. Can God trust us to have purity and integrity when it comes to the prophetic? To whom much is given, much is required. We celebrate when the word comes to pass and we must make corrections, adjustments and have humility when it does not. God has challenged me not to be vague in prophetic words, but to be exact when it comes to words for nations because the Church isn't just looking, but those in the world are looking as well."

November 10, 2018 Dutch Sheets
My Midterm Election Response
Elijah List

Sheets is disappointed in the results but not discouraged and was very encouraged by the wins in the Senate: "We are weaker in the House but much stronger in the Senate, where the most important cause of our day can still be accomplished: the shifting of the Supreme Court."

November 20, 2018 Donald Trump, FBI Investigation
Trump submits written answers to Mueller inquiry.

November 21, 2018 Johnny Enlow
The Greatest Thanksgiving Ever
Elijah List

Resist the urge to want to curse and bash California and realize that it is on the front lines for kingdoms clashing. Darkness has embedded itself deeper in California. Know that as it gets exposed and cleared up here, it will have national and worldwide repercussions. The embedded evil at the top of all the 7 mountains (media, family, economy, government, education, arts, religion) has been worse than we thought.

November 27, 2018 Charlie Shamp
America is not Sodom and Gomorrah, but Nineveh
Elijah List

They have said, 'Impeachment is at hand, impeachment is our plan, impeach the man in God's hand.' They cry, 'The prophets are false, there was no tsunami wave,' but I say, 'Is there not stillness before the great wave comes ashore? Is there not silence before it breaks and crashes in? Do not the waters recede so that all that is hidden may be exposed?'

"Some have proclaimed, 'The prophets are wrong, those that speak that America will arise, they only tell lies to the people. They do not hear from Heaven.' They shout, 'The prophets are exposed, exposed, exposed. America will fall, it's under judgment, this is the final call.' They shout, 'America, your economy, it will crash, it will crash. The Stock Market will crash, recession will come.'

"But I say to America, 'You will not fall or fail! A crash, yes it will come upon you, but it will be a crash of My mercy, My redemption, My revival! My prophets prophesied My perfect plan and it will come to pass, for My prophetic word will never return to Me without accomplishing My will in the world."

"The witches have cursed My prophets in the night. They have cast spells in hopes that many would come to death, but have I not said, 'Suffer not a witch to live'? Have I not declared, 'You will reap what you have sown'? Have I not told you, 'My Word will never fail'? Have I not said, 'Touch not My anointed and do My prophets no harm'?

"My prophets have suffered greatly in this last season, but in the new year they will see My salvation and redemption for the nation."

[Shamp's prophecy is duplicated in a post on The Elijah List on September 27, 2019.]

December 18, 2018, Lana Vawser
Miracles and Divine Alignments in Bodies as We Magnify the Lord!
Elijah List

"There is a MAJOR MOVE of My Spirit taking place right now where I am supernaturally restoring bodies, breaking fear and releasing Kingdom keys for divine health. Stand against the lies and KNOW that these are smokescreen symptoms and lies. Physical restoration is upon you."

December 26, 2018 Frank Amedia
Discourse on the Real Truth Heading into 2019
YouTube

December 31, 2018 Donald Trump
"Why Trump Reigns as King Cyrus"
Katherine Stewart in *The New York Times*

We still buy the line that the hard core of the Christian right is just an interest group working to protect its values. But what we don't get is that Mr. Trump's supposedly anti-Christian attributes and anti-democratic attributes are a vital part of his attraction.

Today's Christian nationalists talk a good game about respecting the Constitution and America's founders, but at bottom they sound as if they prefer autocrats to democrats.

And while I have heard plenty of comments casting doubt on the more questionable aspects of Mr. Trump's character, the gist of the proceedings almost always comes down to the belief that he is a miracle sent straight from heaven to bring the nation back to the Lord. I have also learned that resistance to Mr. Trump is tantamount to resistance to God.

This isn't the religious right we thought we knew. The Christian nationalist movement today is authoritarian, paranoid and patriarchal at its core. They aren't fighting a culture war. They're making a direct attack on democracy itself.

They want it all. And in Mr. Trump, they have found a man who does not merely serve their cause, but also satisfies their craving for a certain kind of political leadership.

VI. Third Year
2019

January 1, 2019 Jerry Falwell Jr.
"Jerry Falwell Jr. Can't Imagine Trump 'Doing Anything That's Not Good For The Country'"
Joe Heim at *The Washington Post*

"What earns him my support is his business acumen. Our country was so deep in debt and so mismanaged by career politicians that we needed someone who was not a career politician, but someone who'd been successful in business to run the country like a business. That's the reason I supported him.... I know that he only wants what's best for this country, and I know anything he does, it may not be ideologically "conservative," but it's going to be what's best for this country, and I can't imagine him doing anything that's not good for the country."

January 2, 2019 Steele Dossier
"New Documents Suggest the Steele Dossier Was A Deliberate Setup For Trump"
Lee Smith at *The Federalist*

January 15, 2019 Donald Trump
The president issued a proclamation that January 16, 2020, is Religious Freedom Day. He stated, "On this Religious Freedom Day, we reaffirm our commitment to protecting the precious and fundamental right of religious freedom, both at home and abroad. Our Founders entrusted the American people with a responsibility to protect religious liberty so that our Nation may stand as a bright beacon for the rest of the world. Today, we remain committed to that sacred endeavor and strive to support those around the world who still struggle under oppressive regimes that impose restrictions on freedom of religion."

January 16, 2019 Mark Taylor
First Interview of 2019
YouTube of Taylor on The Mc Files

January 18, 2019 Johnny Enlow
2019: A Year of Extreme Revelation
Elijah List

We have entered into perhaps the most revelatory year since the birth of Jesus and because of it, none of us will ever be the same. A day of so much disclosure is now upon us and by this time next year, we will be amazed at how different our world actually is from what we thought."

One of the areas of profound blindness right now for many Christians is understanding the role of President Donald Trump. As 45th president of the United States he carries an Isaiah 45 "Cyrus anointing" to break down the "double, bronze and iron gates of Babylon" (Isaiah 45:1–2). This is an assignment to dislodge and eliminate embedded and syndicated evil in government. The tentacles are at the tops of all the 7 mountains of society (media, economy, education, family, arts/entertainment, religion and government) and the tops of all the mountains are going to have their evil "gatekeepers" removed.

It is a historic moment for the Kingdom of God. Because of it, in 2019 Trump is not going to tone down and weaken his approach. He is going to become stronger and his voice will become louder and louder. He is not going to fail in his assignment and it will be a testament not to his greatness, but to the greatness of God.

Despite Trump's billions, his friends and his influence, he is far too limited to take on what he has been called to take on. It is God's anointing on him for the assignment that covers and emboldens him. Our nation will be known as "before Trump" and "after Trump." The Lord also clearly spoke to me that the whole world will be known as "before Trump" and "after Trump." I am neither a Trump fan, nor a Republican fan, nor even a Conservative fan. I am a God fan. Trump is God's idea, and though God is patient, the sooner you recognize that truth the sooner it will be evidence of your seeing being anointed. Once you begin to discover the level of evil against him, you will no longer ask the irrelevant question of, "How could God pick such an imperfect man?" What he lacks in holiness he makes up for in courage, and ultimately his courage is going to lead him into holiness.

President Donald Trump is an emissary of the justice of God, and I believe God is quite pleased with how well he has done since being elected president. His courage is seen as heroic in Heaven because they see what he is up against. This year enough of that gets revealed to the Body of Christ so that we stop the finger pointing. President Trump was not called to be your pastor so let's quit putting that standard on him.

January 20, 2019 Johnnie Moore
"Trump Insider Says Evangelical Advisers 'Don't Stand Up For Morality'; Johnnie Moore Responds"
Michael Gryboski at *The Christian Post* reports on Cliff Simms' book *Team of Vipers: My 500 Extraordinary Days in the Trump White House.*

January 2019 Jeremiah Johnson
Release of Jeremiah Johnson's *Trump, 2019, & Beyond* (Lakeland: Jeremiah Johnson Ministries, 2019)

February 1, 2019 Mark Taylor
Bringing Down The Prophetic Thunder On The Deep State Church!
YouTube of Taylor on The Mc Files

February 7, 2019 Donald Trump
Speaks at National Prayer breakfast

February 13, 2019 Steve Shultz
I Couldn't Believe it. I Was in the Same BIG Room with President Trump and Vice President Pence!!
Elijah List

February 14, 2019 William Barr
"William Barr Sworn In As Attorney General"
Alex Pappas and Brooke Singman at *Fox News*

February 27, 2019 Steve Shultz
Reporting to You from the D.C. Presidential Prayer Breakfast
Elijah List

February 28, 2019 Donald Trump
Meets with North Korean leader Kim Jong-un

March 5, 2019 Victor Davis Hanson
The Case for Trump (Basic Books) by Victor Davis Hanson released.

[Hanson did an interview on April 1 with Peter Robinson at the Hoover Institution about his book.]

March 15, 2019 Jonathan Cahn
"#MAGA Church: The Doomsday Prophet Who Says the Bible Predicted Trump"
Sam Kestenbaum in *The New York Times*

March 21, 2019 Donald Trump, Israel
President Donald Trump tweets, "After 52 years it is time for the United States to fully recognize Israel's Sovereignty over the Golan Heights, which is of critical strategic and security importance to the State of Israel and Regional Stability!"

March 22, 2019 FBI Investigation
The Mueller investigation is concluded.

March 25, 2019 Donald Trump, Israel
Trump issues proclamation recognizing Israel's sovereignty over Golan Heights.

"NOW, THEREFORE, I, DONALD J. TRUMP, President of the United States of America, by virtue of the authority vested in me by the Constitution and the laws of the United States, do hereby proclaim that, the United States recognizes that the Golan Heights are part of the State of Israel."

March 26, 2019 Lance Wallnau
The Cyrus Anointing, President Trump and America
Elijah List

Wallnau comments on prophesying about Donald Trump being God's choice in a time when Evangelicals were in favour of Ted Cruz or Marco Rubio. Wallnau was supposed to be in a meeting with Kim Clement when Clement had a stroke. This was the context for Lance hearing from God that Trump was a wrecking ball to a spirit of political correctness.

Later, Wallnau hears from God that the next president will be an Isaiah 45 president. He then gets an invitation to a meeting at Trump Tower. Lance told Trump about the Isaiah 45 word.

March 26, 2019 Tony Cavener
The Enemy's Plans are Being Exposed and Overturned!
Elijah List

Cavener lists the injustices that God has exposed:
• The Deep State attempting to destroy our "Cyrus," Donald J. Trump.
• The godless seeking to destroy our nation—Antifa, etc.
• Evil plotting against God's anointed, the "Ekklesia," the Church.
• The Senate not protecting live birth abortion survivors."

With Donald Trump as the (Isaiah 45) 45th president, he has a "Cyrus" mandate from the Lord to subdue nations, break open the gates of bronze, and rebuild what Babylon has torn down. The entire world is shifting and shaking since he took office. He will not fail because God is fighting for him and through him just as He did with Cyrus.

March 27, 2019 Paula White
"Paula White: The Pastor Who Helps Trump Hear 'What God Has To Say'"
Jessica Glenza in *The Guardian*

April 1, 2019 Robert Henderson
Praying for President Trump from the Courts of Heaven
Elijah List

After Trump's inauguration Henderson was told by God that Trump would need two terms to fulfill all that God wants to do through Trump.

"Lord, we thank You that You have set President Donald J. Trump. He is firmly established as the one You have chosen. We ask, as Your Church, that all efforts to unseat him come to nothing. We ask that what You have decreed will be the final word concerning President Donald J. Trump. We thank You that he will complete this first term and be re-elected for the second term. The heathen will rage, but Your will will be done."

April 2, 2019 Steve Cioccolanti
Prophetic Word for Donald Trump | Election 2020
YouTube

He claims God told him Trump would win in 2016; Trump will win the 2020 election if he follows path of justice and will win both House and Senate.

April 12, 2019 Mark Taylor
A Great Power Transfer Is Coming
YouTube interview by Tiffany FitzHenry

April 13, 2019 Michele Bachmann
"Drowning in Deep State Delusion" (Part 1)
One Place with Jan Markell

April 16, 2019 Michele Bachmann
"Michele Bachmann Claimed That Donald Trump Is 'Highly Biblical.' So … "
CNN

Cillizza: "But every visible sign—from the language he uses to his personal life to his seeming lack of familiarity with the Bible—suggest that Bachmann and her fellow evangelicals are faking it until Trump makes it on religion. He has shown little interest in the basic elements of his faith—whether in politics or in his private life. And even if Trump does have a private faith that he never talks about, the idea of him as "highly biblical' seems like a massive stretch."

[Cillizza is referencing Bachmann's April 13 radio interview.]

April 17, 2019 Mark Taylor
Prophetic Thunderings and Rumblings Across America and the World
YouTube of Taylor on The Mc Files

April 20, 2019 Michele Bachmann
"Living in Prophesied Times" (Part 2)
One Place with Jan Markell

April 28, 2019 Joe Biden, Steele Dossier
"Joe Biden and the Framing of Trump: He Was in the Room"
Al Perrotta at *The Stream*

Argument that Joe Biden knew about the Steele Dossier and that it was used by Hillary Clinton. Biden was in the Oval Office when the Intelligence officials told about the material. "They did not make the President-elect of the United States aware that a lurid dossier set to go public accusing him of conspiring with Russia — of being, in essence a traitor — was the work of Clinton and the DNC. Why? Because if they told Trump the truth, the Steele Dossier would be a one-day story. Or at best the collusion narrative would be immediately exposed as an anti-Trump concoction."

April 29, 2019 Mark Taylor
Taylor releases second edition of *The Trump Prophecies* (Defender Publishing). This edition contains new prophecies from Taylor since the first edition was released in 2017.

[In a surprising development, the second edition contains no references to Don and Mary Colbert, the medical doctor and his wife who were central in the first edition and in the promotion of Taylor, the book, and the film.]

April 30, 2019 Mark Taylor
False Shepherds, False Unities and Covenants with Hell
YouTube of Taylor on The Mc Files

May 2019 Mark Taylor
"The Trump Prophecy"
David Gushee at *Sojourners*

"In the Trump era, we again witness a conservative Christian flirtation with authoritarianism. These conservative Christians compare Donald Trump to Cyrus of Persia—both authoritarian rulers, both 'friendly' to but not part of God's people, both supposedly used by God—and Trump is lauded as the president of divine providence in shlock films such as Liberty U.'s *The Trump Prophecy*."

May 5, 2019 Paula White
White announces resignation as senior pastor at New Destiny. Son Brad Knight and wife become senior pastors.

May 7, 2019 Mark Taylor
The Church Must Divorce Baal and Remarry God
YouTube of Taylor on The Mc Files

May 28, 2019 James Comey
"No 'Treason.' No Coup. Just Lies — And Dumb Lies At That"
James Comey at *The Washington Post*

"But go ahead, investigate the investigators, if you must. When those investigations are over, you will find the work was done appropriately and focused only on discerning the truth of very serious allegations. There was no corruption. There was no treason. There was no attempted coup. Those are lies, and dumb lies at that. There were just good people trying to figure out what was true, under unprecedented circumstances."

June 13, 2019 Lance Wallnau
Why Preachers Aren't Enough to Defeat the Spirit of the Antichrist
Elijah List

For Kingdom transformation to take place on a cultural level, the Church mountain needs to stop trying to replicate preachers to expand the Church mountain and, instead, start sending men and women with the mind of Christ into the mountains of culture that are presently under the influence of false messages and demonized messengers. We need a few more anointed educators, school administrators, journalists, filmmakers, mayors, lawyers, and entrepreneurs and fewer Sunday sermon critics.

[Mention of Ed Delph and David Lake's *Refining Rhema*.]

June 15, 2019 Curt Landry
The Golan Heights: President Trump's Bold Move
Elijah List

Landry responds to President Trump's tweet on March 21, 2019 ("After 52 years it is time for the United States to fully recognize Israel's Sovereignty over the Golan Heights, which is of critical strategic and security importance to the State of Israel and Regional Stability!").

Until the borders of Israel align with what God has commanded, turmoil will continue ... As a nation, we are used to slow governmental changes that block political and Biblical alignment. But President Trump, who is believed to carry the Cyrus anointing, is known for making bold moves and statements.

This is exactly what this nation needs—a strong leader who is not afraid to stand with God's people and align our land with Israel's ... President Trump's bold move to proclaim Golan Heights as part of Israel is not just a political move but a God move. God is aligning the nations. He is positioning His people for what is to come.

June 16, 2019 Carter Page
"The Carter Page FISA: A timeline"
Jerry Dunleavy at *Washington Examiner*

June 18, 2019 Mark Taylor
Obama's Third Term, Hydrogen Healing, Justice Served on a Cold Plate
YouTube of Taylor on The Mc Files

June 25, 2019 Mark Taylor
The Shame of the SBC, Judgement on the Church System Continues
YouTube of Taylor on The Mc Files

June 28, 2019 Jimmy Carter
"Jimmy Carter Suggests Trump Is an Illegitimate President"
CNN

June 30, 2019 Mark Taylor
What can we expect next?
YouTube

July 1, 2019 Hunter Biden
"Will Hunter Biden Jeopardize His Father's Campaign?"
Adam Entous at *The New Yorker*

This is a long article that profiles Hunter Biden, the controversial son of Joe Biden.

July 4, 2019 Rodney Howard-Browne
We Are In A Last Minute Reprieve
Jim Bakker Show

July 8, 2019 Jeremiah Johnson
Trump, 2019 & Beyond
Interview by Daniel Kolenda on Christ for All Nations TV

July 9, 2019 Mark Taylor
The Prophetic and Spiritual Shaking over America
YouTube of Taylor on The Mc Files

July 11, 2019 Mark Taylor
It's Happening. The Storm Is upon Us
YouTube of Taylor on Up Front in the Prophetic

July 14, 2019 Donald Trump
President tweets that progressive Democratic congresswomen should "go back and help fix the totally broken and crime infested places from which they came."

July 17, 2019 Donald Trump
President meets with survivors of persecution with Sam Brownback, ambassador at large for international religious freedom.

July 17, 2019 Mark Taylor
Spiritual Entities Coming Across-Border Destroying America
YouTube of Taylor on The Mc Files

July 18, 2019 Faith Marie Baczko
The Breaker is Here! He Says, 'Ready or Not, Here I Come.'
Elijah List

Moves of God are never neat and tidy, and the One who is coming, who will release the billion soul harvest or possibly much more, will certainly come as a mighty, potent tidal wave that sparks and ignites war, as the rulers of darkness vie to retain power over their prey.

In Donald Trump's great speech on D-Day, he honored the soldiers who fought that day on the shores of Normandy as the greatest generation ever. Now, however, another of the greatest and most significant generations ever to live is being made ready for notable battles ahead.

July 23, 2019 Mark Taylor
The Spirit Realm is A Blazing
YouTube of Taylor on The Mc Files

July 24, 2019 FBI Investigation
Mueller testifies before two House committees.

July 25, 2019 Donald Trump
President Trump calls President Zelensky of Ukraine. This is the call that created the whistleblower complaint and decision by Democrats to start impeachment proceedings.

August 2019 Miguel A. De La Torre
"Christianity and the Cult of Trump"
Utne

This is an excerpt from the author's book *Burying White Privilege*:

The problem with white Christianity is that most Christian moral reasoning is done from the sectarian realm of abstractions. Christianity has a problem with "what you do" because of its focus on "how you believe." A mental decision to accept Jesus Christ as one's Lord and savior trumps using Jesus Christ as the paradigm for how to live one's life.

Through this sleight of hand, white Christians can profess their belief in Jesus while refusing to "be Jesus" and create a more just social order, or worse, can engage in activities diametrically opposed to Jesus's life and teachings.

August 1, 2019 Mark Taylor
The Obama Legacy Will Be Stripped and Destroyed
YouTube of Taylor on The Mc Files

August 6, 2019 Mark Taylor
Prophetic Warnings from This Weekend's Shootings
YouTube of Taylor on The Mc Files

August 6, 2019 Michael Brown
Brown releases his book *Jezebel's War with America* (Lake Mary: FrontLine, 2019).

August 12, 2019 Donald Trump
An anonymous person writes a whistleblower report about Trump's conversation with Ukraine president.

August 13, 2019 Lance Wallnau
BE BOLD for What You Stand for and Discerning About What You Fall for
Elijah List

Is God speaking in this shaking? Are we being reminded that the hour of divine mercy, under the era of Trump's presidency, is dependent on a response to this mercy? If that response does not become manifest, should we not be concerned that time is running out?

Trump's enemies have become so focused and energized, and his defenders so intimidated and silenced, that one can only wonder if 2020 can be won. It is at best a 50–50 proposition.

Many Believers anticipated a different result in the mid-terms, a "red wave." I didn't. I said, "We are a house divided," and that is what this will look like. I was correct. We are operating as a nation under a reprieve and that suspension of judgment is not subject to our election cycle. The point is—we do not know how long this mercy will last.

For too long the Church and many name-recognized ministries have been focused on their own business. They say that they are doing what

God called them to do, but in truth, they are self-absorbed. And when I say "they" I include myself in this examination. We have tried to ignore the storm and avoid stormy topics. We have been building our house while God's project, the nation, His House, is coming apart.

August 13, 2019 Mark Taylor
The Jeffrey Epstein Death
YouTube of Taylor on The Mc Files

August 13, 2019 Donald Trump
"'He Gets It': Evangelicals Aren't Turned Off By Trump's First Term"
Julie Zauzmer at *The Washington Post*

August 14, 2019 Donald Trump
"In God's Country"
Elizabeth Bruenig in *The Washington Post*

"That the thrice-wed, dirty-talking, sex-scandal-plagued businessman actually managed to win the steadfast moral support of America's values voters, as expressed in routinely high approval ratings, posed an even stranger question: What happened?"

Bruenig focuses on Robert Jeffress, pastor of First Baptist Church, Dallas, Texas, and parishioners in other parts of Texas.

In some sense it seemed that Trump is able, by being less Christian than your average Christian, to protect Christians who fear incursions from a hostile dominant culture. But that paradox also supplies a handy solution to the question of whether Christians should direct their efforts to worldly politics or turn inward, shunning political life for spiritual pursuits. By voting for Trump — even over more identifiably Christian candidates — evangelicals seem to have found a way to outsource their fears and instead reserve a strictly spiritual space for themselves inside politics without placing evangelical politicians themselves in power. In that sense, they can be both active political agents and a semi-cloistered religious minority, both of the world and removed from it, advancing their values while retreating to their own societies.

And will the evangelical politics of the post-Bush era continue to favor the rise of figures such as Trump, who are willing to dispense with any hint of personal Christian virtue while promising to pause the decline of evangelical fortunes — whatever it takes? And if hostilities can't be reduced and a detente can't be reached, are the evangelicals who foretell the apocalypse really wrong?"

[Bruenig decides to avoid putting her own family's views into the article.]

August 15, 2019 Mark Taylor
It's Getting Hot up in Here!
YouTube of Taylor on Up Front in the Prophetic

August 15, 2019 Donald Trump
"For White Evangelicals, It's Not About Fear"
John Stoehr at *The Editorial Board*

"But trust me when I say white evangelical Christians are presuming the worst in normal people—in you. Have you accepted Jesus Christ as your personal Lord and Savior? No? You are therefore not one among God's Chosen. This is their moral compass, which is not a moral compass at all, and as such, Trump-voting white evangelical Christians do not have the ability to reason their way out of fear. And because they don't, they will choose sadism. Why? Sadism feels good."

August 19, 2019 Mark Taylor
Mark Taylor's Most Shocking Prediction of 2019
YouTube of The Sheila Zilinsky Show

August 20, 2019 Mark Taylor
Speaking Life over America and Exposing the Darkness
YouTube of Taylor on The Mc Files

August 20, 2019 Donald Trump
"President Trump Targets Jewish People In America Who Support The Democratic Party"
Julie Hirschfeld Davis at *The New York Times*

August 20, 2019 Francis Myles
Three Reasons Why God Chose Donald Trump
The Jim Bakker Show

God enabled him to be part of elite.
He fulfills the prophetic template of generational disruptors.
He will have the spirit of Jehu to confront the Jezebel spirit.

August 20, 2019 Donald Trump
"Trump: Jewish People That Vote For A Democrat Show Great Disloyalty"
Ian Schwartz report at *Real Clear Politics*

Trump issues a critique of Democrats in relation to controversies over Israel and Reps. Ilhan Omar and Rashida Tlaib: "Where has the Democratic Party gone? Where have they gone where they are defending these two people over the state of Israel? I think any Jewish people that vote for a Democrat, I think it shows either a total lack of knowledge or great disloyalty."

August 20, 2019 Donald Trump
"Conservative Evangelicals Aren't Hypocrites, They're Sadists"
Daniel Schultz Religion Dispatches at Rewire. News

August 21, 2019 Wayne Allyn Root
In a series of tweets, Trump thanks talk-show host Wayne Allyn Root for his commendation of Trump.

Here are Root's words: "President Trump is the greatest President for Jews and for Israel in the history of the world, not just America, he is the best President for Israel in the history of the world... and the Jewish people in Israel love him like he's the King of Israel. They love him like he is the second coming of God ... But American Jews don't know him or like him. They don't even know what they're doing or saying anymore. It makes no sense! But that's OK, if he keeps doing what he's doing, he's good for all Jews, Blacks, Gays, everyone. And importantly, he's good for everyone in America who wants a job."

Trump noted at end of last tweet: "Wow!"

August 21, 2019 Donald Trump
"I am the Chosen One"
BBC

In an interview President Trump said he was "the chosen one" as he looked to heaven. He was referencing his trade war with China.
His remark led to lots of media coverage and nastiness. Trump said in a tweet that he was joking.

For a sober Christian perspective on Trump's comment, see David Brody on CNN Anderson Cooper.

August 21, 2019 Donald Trump
"Trump Goes Godly"
Gail Collins at *The New York Times*

Do you blame God for Donald Trump? "I am the chosen one," Trump announced on Wednesday. O.K., he was talking about fighting his trade war with China, not ascending into heaven. It was all a joke, sort of. But we've been so far down the megalomania road with this president that it would not be a total surprise to discover he had delusions of divinity.

August 22, 2019 Wayne Allyn Root
"Who is Wayne Allyn Root, the man who crowned Trump 'King of Israel'?"
Ron Kampeas at *The Jerusalem Post*

August 22, 2019 Jonathan Cahn
Cahn on Sid Roth's *It's Supernatural* about Cahn's new book *The Oracle*

[Sid Roth also features an hour-long video with Cahn.]

August 22, 2019 Donald Trump
"Evangelicals Told Trump He Was 'Chosen' By God. Now He Says It Himself."
Amanda Marcotte at *Salon*

August 22, 2019 Donald Trump
"Trump Is Either Trolling Everyone Or Thinks He's Like A God"
Zachary B. Wolf at CNN

August 22, 2019 Stephen Powell
Todd Bentley, Rick Joyner & Issues in the Church
Facebook

Powell calls for discipline of Todd Bentley and accuses him of great sin. Powell also accuses Rick Joyner, a major Trump supporter, and other Christian leaders of being too lenient with Todd. Joyner posted two Facebook videos in response.

First Joyner video in response: August 23
Second Joyner video in response: August 27

[Note: In early January 2020 other major leaders, including Michael Brown, said that Trump was unfit for ministry.]

August 23, 2019 Donald Trump
"Trump and the Politics of the Messiah"
Emily McFarlan Miller, Jack Jenkins, and Yonat Shimron at *National Catholic Reporter*

Explanations about Trump's August 21 statement that he was "the chosen one"

August 24, 2019 Wayne Allyn Root
"What It's Like To Be Caught In The Middle Of A Media Firestorm"
Review Journal

Root comments on media response to his comments about Trump being king of Israel.

It all comes down to this for liberals: 1) If you can't beat your opposition, make it personal. Destroy, malign, slander and demonize. 2) The truth to liberals is like a Christian cross to a vampire. So if someone exposes the truth, by any and all means, use "weapons of mass distraction." Change the subject.

I'm a witness to their ruthless strategy. From that moment on, all hell broke loose. The whole media world exploded with rage. At me.

August 28, 2019 Donald Trump
Dilemma 2020
Joe Betz at *World*

If most of us American evangelicals are still flummoxed by the ethical dilemmas of the 2016 presidential election, we should be studying hard and getting ready. Things could be even more challenging in 2020.

My personal prayer is that a brand-new person might take the presidency a year and a half from now. That might be someone who hasn't won the nation's attention yet—from some unknown political background, or maybe an independent. But it could also be Trump himself, humbled and renewed by a sovereign God.

August 28, 2019 Rick Joyner
"Trumpkin Pastor: Revival Leader's Accusers Have 'Spiritual Rabies'"
Darrell Lucus at RDT Daily

Critique of Rick Joyner

August 29, 2019 Rick Joyner
"Trump-Worshiping Pastor and Prophet Has A History of Coddling Sleazeballs And Perverts"
DailyKos.com

Joyner is accused of blindly supporting controversial charismatic leaders Todd Bentley, Bob Jones, and Paul Cain.

September 2, 2019 Jonathan Cahn

"The Oracle Unveiled: Jonathan Cahn Reveals a Stunning End-Times Secret"

Charisma News

The sense that things are spinning out of control is shared by believers throughout the world—and not just by believers, but by unbelievers as well. But what if there was a master plan behind the key events of our times—past, present, future, America, Israel, the world, end-time prophecy and, yes, even Donald Trump? This is the revelation that came to me concerning The Oracle.

Is it possible that the events unfolding in the world right now are following the exact parameters of a 3,000-year old mystery? Is it possible that this mystery has determined the past, the present and will determine the future? Could this mystery have even ordained the outcome of American elections and the secret of a modern American president?

The article is based on Cahn's new book, which is about seven doors that reveal events, past, present, and future.

September 9, 2019 Donald Trump

"Trump Is Not Well"

Peter Wehner at *The Atlantic*

"The office is too powerful, and the consequences are too dangerous, to allow a person to become president who views morality only through the prism of whether an action advances his own narrow interests, his own distorted desires, his own twisted impulses. When an individual comes to believe his interests and those of the nation he leads are one and the same, it opens the door to all sorts of moral and constitutional devilry. Whether or not his disorders are diagnosable, the president's psychological flaws are all too apparent. They were alarming when he took the oath of office; they are worse now. Every day Donald Trump is president is a day of disgrace. And a day of danger."

September 16, 2019 James Robison
Make America Great
YouTube

I believe the positive things that are happening are an answer to prayer, and I believe the willingness of this man to stand up against all the assault and keep trying to do what he believes is best is a miracle of God.

I believe if we keep praying, [God] will hear and he will have people sitting in front of [the president] who will so speak the truth with conviction, convincingly and with wisdom, and I believe he will respond. I think we can witness the greatest spiritual awakening in history and one of the least likely people, many of you would say, will be used by God to accomplish God's will for the blessing and benefit of this nation.

September 23, 2019 Donald Trump
"In UN Speech, Trump Announces New Religious Freedom Initiatives"
Jayson Casper at *Christianity Today*

September 24, 2019 Impeachment
Nancy Pelosi announces beginning of formal impeachment inquiry into Trump.

September 25, 2019 Impeachment
Justice Department releases five-page summary of phone conversation between President Trump and Ukraine President.

September 25, 2019 Jeremiah Johnson
"Prophetic Dream: Donald Trump, Justin Bieber and Kanye West To Be God's Wrecking Balls"
Charisma

"God has chosen these three men to be incredible wrecking balls to American religious and political beliefs and ideologies."

In his dream Johnson is with a large audience listening to Trump and West onstage who are then joined by Bieber. All three are hurt by nasty crowd reaction and Johnson goes to the front to prophesy to each.

"Kanye, just as the Lord raised up Donald Trump to be a wrecking ball to this nation, so God has raised you up as another wrecking ball for such a time as this. Trump has wrecked the political landscape in America, but you shall wreck the religious one. You both will not say and do many things that the church will demand, but heaven has designed it this way. There is a spiritual father, a pastor that will take you underneath his wing and protect you from the masses. For the brood of vipers will seek to crucify you ahead your time."

"Justin, how long will you waver between two opinions? How long will you run from Jezebel? For the spirit of Elijah is resting upon you, son, to turn the hearts of fathers back to their sons. Out of your own brokenness and pain, there shall be a fresh anointing flowing through you that will heal many. You shall be a wrecking ball to the mainstream media as you introduce them to the heart of the Father."

"Donald, I have given you Kanye and Justin as gifts to help bring a greater influence that you will need heading into the 2020 elections. Keep your eyes on Israel and China, as I will continue to give you great wisdom that will bring tremendous increase and protection in the days ahead. Like King Josiah, you must not fight battles that are not yours to fight. Allow me to fight the deception taking place in the political arena in America. For I am moving in the media and the church even now," says the Lord.

September 26, 2019 Donald Trump
Release of whistleblower complaint

September 27, 2019 Steve Shultz
What God's Prophets are Saying about President Trump, Impeachment and America's Future
Elijah List

Steve Shultz posts earlier prophecies about impeachment from Charlie Shamp, Hank Kunneman, Kim Clement, and Johnny Enlow.

September 27, 2019 Hank Kunneman
An Elijah List Exclusive: Prophecy Decoders—Impeachment, Boomerang, Exoneration
Elijah List

This is the introduction to the first of a series called Prophecy Decoders.

A formal impeachment inquiry into President Trump has been launched and we are seeing the uproar play out in the news. Rather than rushing to find out what CNN, FOX NEWS and MSNBC pundits have to say, we need to seek the prophetic perspective.

I've got good news for you! Prophetic voices have released insight in advance, thereby giving us clarity as to how we should pray and intercede prophetically.

After this introduction, an earlier prophecy by Hank Kunneman is given from May 22, 2019:

"They shall say through the 90 days of summer, 'We are now ready to bring articles of impeachment.' Ha! What you seek to take out by your impeachment shall lead to your own demise and in the fall of 2020 there shall be a great fall," says the Spirit of God.

"I speak a double meaning that you will understand when that moment arises upon this land. For there is jealousy and where there is strife, I speak to your house, to your congress—there is confusion and there is every evil work. It is written and it shall be seen if you bite and devour, you will be consumed by one another.

"This I speak—listen to the warning that I give to you," says the Spirit of God, "stop or you shall fall. Stop or you and your party will be consumed—for you are kicking against the pricks.

"What do I speak? You are speaking against and working against My plan! This is not a political thing, even though you may say that it is. You are working against My hand, therefore you will see your foolishness cause a boomerang upon your own party and there is an exoneration that shall come to this house and to this land."

[The prophecy from May 22, 2019, is distinct from the Kunneman prophecy of March 19, 2017, given on the Elijah List and then repeated on September 27, 2019, along with earlier prophecies from Charlie Shamp (November 27, 2018), Kim Clement (February 22, 2014), and Johnny Enlow (May 18, 2017). In other words, the Elijah List provided five prophecies about impeachment on September 27, four in the regular format and one through Prophecy Decoders.]

September 30, 2019 Impeachment
"Bring on the Biggest Nothingburger of Them All"
Conrad Black at *American Greatness*

"There has not in modern American history been such a preposterous excuse for a threat to the presidency as the Ukraine affair. This Ukraine allegation has all the earmarks of a Democratic hit-job, and the whistle-blower's chances of retaining anonymity for the hearsay-based complaint that was lodged, are, and deserve to be, zero. The idea that a U.S. president can be shaken in his legitimacy by anonymous unsubstantiated charges that, even if true, don't add up to a real impropriety, is the destruction of constitutional democracy."

October 4, 2019 Joe Biden
"Ukraine to Review Investigations Into Firm Linked to Biden's Son"
Thomas Grove and Georgi Kantchev at *Wall Street Journal*

October 5, 2019 Joe Biden
"Joe Biden's Advisers Knew In 2018 His Comments About Ukraine Would Be A Problem"
Miriam Elder at *BuzzFeed News*

[For Biden's comments, see entry on January 23, 2018.]

October 7, 2019 Donald Trump
"Why Evangelicals Support Donald Trump"
Francis Fitzgerald in *New York Times Book Review*

Assessment of Thomas S. Kidd's *Who is an Evangelical* (Yale) and Ben Howe's *Why Evangelicals Chose Political Value over Christian Values* (Broadside) [Fitzgerald is author of *The Evangelicals: The Struggle to Shape America* (Simon & Schuster).]

October 7, 2019 Donald Trump
"Donald Trump's Lesson for Mitt Romney"
Miranda Devine at Fox News

"The American people chose a barbarian for president because they knew only a barbarian could drain the Washington swamp. If the swamp gets in his way, Trump bulldozes over it. Supreme Court, tick. Taxes cut, tick. Regulations slashed, tick. Jobs up, tick. Military rebuilt, tick. ISIS stopped, tick. Globalism challenged, tick. Paris climate treaty scrapped, tick. Borders strengthened, tick. Wall built, half-tick."

October 9, 2019 Joe Biden
"Biden Calls for Trump Impeachment for First Time"
Jonathan Martin in *The New York Times*

"To preserve our Constitution, our democracy, our basic integrity, he should be impeached. He's afraid about just how badly I will beat him next November."

October 9, 2019 Steven Hassan
"Fake Enemies, Loaded Language, Grandiosity, Belittling Critics: Cults Expert Claims Donald Trump's Tactics Are Taken Straight From Playbook of Sun Myung Moon, David Koresh and Jim Jones"
Caroline Howe at *Daily Mail*

Based on Hassan's forthcoming book *The Cult of Trump*

October 10, 2019 Donald Trump
"'Shame on Him': Evangelicals Call Out Trump on Syria"
Elizabeth Dias in *The New York Times*

Pat Robertson, founder of the Christian Broadcasting Network, said he was "appalled" by the president's decision, and added that "the president of the United States is in great danger of losing the mandate of heaven if he permits this to happen." Senator Lindsey Graham, who rarely breaks with the president, said it could be "the biggest mistake of his presidency."

October 11, 2019 Michael R. Pompeo
"Being a Christian Leader" [Secretary of State gives address at American Association of Christian Counselors]
State.gov

I've found this in life—truth telling isn't just a matter of private conversations for me. It's what I try to do publicly as we lay down President Trump's foreign policy to keep Americans safe and secure.

This administration has spoken to the truth in many ways that previous administrations haven't done. (Applause.) For example, on China's rule-breaking and authoritarianism; for example, on why the Islamic Republic of Iran is an aggressor, not a victim; for why, in fact, we know in our hearts that America is a force for good in the world. (Applause.)

And I'm especially telling the truth about the dire condition of religious freedom around the world. America has a proud history of religious freedom, and we want jealously to guard it here. But around the world, more than 80% of mankind lives in areas where religious freedom is suppressed or denied in its entirety.

October 11, 2019 William Barr

Attorney General William Barr gives address at Notre Dame
Justice.gov

No society can exist without some means for restraining individual rapacity.

But, if you rely on the coercive power of government to impose restraints, this will inevitably lead to a government that is too controlling, and you will end up with no liberty, just tyranny.

On the other hand, unless you have some effective restraint, you end up with something equally dangerous—licentiousness—the unbridled pursuit of personal appetites at the expense of the common good. This is just another form of tyranny—where the individual is enslaved by his appetites, and the possibility of any healthy community life crumbles.

I think we all recognize that over the past 50 years religion has been under increasing attack.

On the one hand, we have seen the steady erosion of our traditional Judeo-Christian moral system and a comprehensive effort to drive it from the public square.

On the other hand, we see the growing ascendancy of secularism and the doctrine of moral relativism.

By any honest assessment, the consequences of this moral upheaval have been grim.

Virtually every measure of social pathology continues to gain ground.

In 1965, the illegitimacy rate was eight percent. In 1992, when I was last Attorney General, it was 25 percent. Today it is over 40 percent. In many of our large urban areas, it is around 70 percent.

Along with the wreckage of the family, we are seeing record levels of depression and mental illness, dispirited young people, soaring suicide rates, increasing numbers of angry and alienated young males, an increase in senseless violence, and a deadly drug epidemic.

Because this Administration firmly supports accommodation of religion, the battleground has shifted to the states. Some state governments are now attempting to compel religious individuals and entities to subscribe to practices, or to espouse viewpoints, that are incompatible with their religion.

Ground zero for these attacks on religion are the schools. To me, this is the most serious challenge to religious liberty.

For anyone who has a religious faith, by far the most important part of exercising that faith is the teaching of that religion to our children. The passing on of the faith. There is no greater gift we can give our children and no greater expression of love.

For the government to interfere in that process is a monstrous invasion of religious liberty.

October 12, 2019 Donald Trump
Value Voters Summit
WhiteHouse.gov

Trump gives a long address and covers many topics about his presidency, his major achievements, and the attacks on him.

And as we have seen in the last three years, the extreme left has absolutely no respect for the will of the American people. They are determined to stop our movement and impose their agenda by any means necessary. It makes no difference to them.

First, it was the Russia hoax. It was a total hoax — made up. Then there was the outrageous smearing of Justice Kavanaugh — that goes on. They want him impeached, even when the woman said, "I don't know that anything happened. Nothing happened." They said, "Let's impeach him anyway." And the whole thing was phony. So phony. He's a good man. What he's gone through, I don't know if anyone's ever gone through anything like that."

In every generation, the faith of our people has spurred our nation to overcome every challenge to our values and to our way of life. It has inspired us to face down the worst evils, unlock the greatest mysteries, and achieve what no one thought was ever possible.

Now, powered by those same historic values that have always defined our nation, we will reach new heights, make new breakthroughs, and we will strengthen the bonds of love and loyalty that unite us all as citizens, as neighbors, as patriots, as Christians, as people of faith.

As one people, one nation, and one United States of America, we will stand as a light of liberty, a land of courage, and a home for proud people of faith. (Applause.)

Forever and always, Americans will believe in the cause of freedom, the power of prayer, and the eternal glory of God. Thank you. God bless you. And God bless America. Thank you very much. [Applause.]

October 13, 2019 Steven Hassan
"Take It From a Former Moonie: Trump Is a Cult Leader"
Steven Hassan at *The Daily Beast*

October 17, 2019 William Barr
"William Barr's Wild Misreading of the First Amendment"
Jeffrey Toobin at *The New Yorker*

Perhaps the most galling part of Barr's speech, under current circumstances, is its hymn to the pious life. He denounces "moral chaos" and "irresponsible personal conduct," as well as "licentiousness—the unbridled pursuit of personal appetites at the expense of the common good." By contrast, "religion helps teach, train, and habituate people to want what is good." Throughout this lecture, one can only wonder if William Barr has ever actually met Donald Trump.

October 17, 2019 Paula White
"Paula White On How She Became Trump's Spiritual Adviser and Why He'll Carry Evangelical Vote In 2020"
Caleb Parke at Fox News

The report is based around White's new book *Something Greater*. She states, "As much as I know God has sent me into Donald Trump's life to pray for him and his family and be a person who wants nothing from him but to show him God, I am beginning to realize that he is being used in my life to help restore my confidence after some pretty shaky years."

October 18, 2019 Eric Metaxas
"What Changed Eric Metaxas' Mind About Trump"
Katrina Trinko at *The Daily Signal*

Trinko asks Metaxas what he likes about Trump.

I like almost everything about him. He's, I would say, a very refreshing figure in American politics. And of course, that's what makes him a disruptor. I guess his ability to see things slightly differently is what's most refreshing, his ability to look at an issue and say, "Why don't we do this?" And everybody says, "Well, you can't do that." And he says, "Well, why not?" He has that side to him, and I think it served him very well in a number of ways.

For me, basic conservative values, you know, low regulation, low taxes, the life issue, the unborn, freedom generally, those are things that I think are very quickly being pushed away because we have a culture [where] we've been so blessed with these things that we don't really know what they are.

If you really want to know why a lot of Christians have supported him, [it's] because to lose religious Liberty in America is not simply to lose rights. It's not about Christians are going to lose Christian rights. That's nonsense. It's about losing something so foundational, so central to the republic that you will eventually lose everything. It's like pulling a thread and it's going to unravel the whole thing.

But I'll tell you, I used to really despise this president. I was horrified by him culturally. I just thought that this is a man who is contributing to the vulgarization of the culture. And to some extent, I think that that was true. But when he was in the primaries, I began to listen to him on the stump.

A friend of mine kind of rebuked me and said, "Hey, you need to give him a listen. I think you're missing something. He's like a folk hero." And I began to listen...

October 20, 2019 Donald Trump

Fractured Nation: Widening Partisan Polarization and Key Issues in 2020 Presidential Elections

Public Religion Research Institute

October 21, 2019 William Barr, Mike Pompeo

"Barr and Pompeo Speeches Show Why Evangelical Warriors Won't Abandon the President"

Bradley Onishi, Religion Dispatches at Rewire News

Trump is the barbarian-king leading white evangelicals in their war against all those they deem God's enemies. For evangelicals, his authoritarian rhetoric is an asset; his cruelty is a mark of determination; his unwillingness to compromise is a welcome change from "softer" evangelical politicians.

The question we should be asking is not when white evangelicals will finally have had enough. It's how the rest of us are going to stop a corrupt president and his most loyal supporters from destroying the country and the world order.

October 22, 2019 Paula White

"Paula White-Cain's Evangelical Support Squad Isn't as Surprising as It Seems"

Leah Payne and Aaron Griffith at *Christianity Today*

This is a comprehensive online piece that documents White's style of evangelicalism and how it relates to mainline Evangelicals, the African Black community, and the impact that her connection with Trump has on evangelical leaders.

In the end, what is significant about Paula White-Cain's endorsement is not the fact that conservative white evangelicals are crossing theological lines to extend friendship to her. Similar lines have been crossed many times in the past and will be crossed again in the future. What is new in this scenario is White-Cain's proximity to the president. Unlike Franklin Graham, Jack Graham, and Jeffress, she is not from the "respectable" institutions or networks that have birthed powerful evangelical political operatives in previous generations. She does not present herself to the president as a symbol of American conservatism. Like the president under her pastoral care, White-Cain is a flamboyant, controversial celebrity who operates outside the traditional halls of power.

October 24, 2019 Donald Trump
"10 Questions To Ask About Trump's Removal Of Troops From Syria"
Lee Smith at *The Federalist*

October 24, 2019 Impeachment
"The Democrats' Impeachment Inquiry Is a Doomed and Desperate Time-Buying Ploy"
Roger Kimball at *Spectator USA*

October 24, 2019 Impeachment
"Quid Pro Quo In Ukraine? No, Not Yet"
Sharyl Attkisson at *The Hill*

"All things considered, it begins to look like the quid pro quo accusations are an extension of the strategy that sought to keep President Trump from providing typical direction to the Justice Department for the better part of two years ... because his critics cried that it would be obstruction of justice or interfering with the Mueller probe. With that investigation closed, Trump's enemies appear to be trying to keep him from digging into dark, uncomfortable places about how it all came about and who was behind it, from Washington, D.C., to Kyiv, Ukraine."

October 25, 2019 Kanye West
West, an outspoken Trump supporter, releases Gospel album *Jesus Is King* and Imax film with same title.

[See Ben Sisario's report "Kanye West's 'Jesus Is King' Is No. 1" at *The New York Times*]

October 25, 2019 Impeachment
"This Impeachment Subverts the Constitution"
David B. Rivkin Jr. and Elizabeth Price Foley in *Wall Street Journal*

October 25, 2019 William Barr
"Bill Barr's Point About Religion Is Underscored by His Critics"
Editorial of *The New York Sun*

"The attorney general's remarks at Notre Dame are one of the most important statements of support that religious Americans have had at a time when a campaign is underway to cast religion as a cover for bigotry. We are in a time when the left seeks to intimidate those who would cast religion as an inherently good thing for America."

October 26, 2019 William Barr
"Who is Bill Barr?"
Emily Bazelon at *The New York Times*

The article contains extensive material about Barr's background and offers a critique of his work under President Trump.

October 26, 2019 Paula White
"Donald Trump Is 'Not At All Impulsive': Presidential Pastor Paula White"
Doree Lewak at *New York Post*

"He does not by any means think he's the perfect person," said White of Trump, adding that he can be surprisingly vulnerable."
    She even admitted that Trump has felt regret over certain things he's tweeted: "We've all said and done things we ... wish we'd done differently. He is no different." Still, the pastor added, "He's in total control. He's not at all impulsive — he's so far ahead of everyone, very much a strategic thinker."
    White conceded that the impeachment inquiry "wears on him ... But he's not going anywhere. He's not a quitter."
As for the 2020 elections, the pastor — who had a hand in securing the Evangelical vote for Trump in 2016 — isn't sweating it. "I've never seen the base more energized than it is now."

October 27, 2019 Donald Trump
The president announced that on October 26, US forces raided an ISIS compound and killed Abu Bakr al-Baghdadi, the founder and leader of the Islamic State.

New York Times Transcript of President's message
Video on YouTube of Trump announcement
Announcement from the White House

"Last night, the United States brought the world's No. 1 terrorist leader to justice. Abu Bakr al-Baghdadi is dead. He was the founder and leader of ISIS, the most ruthless and violent terror organization anywhere in the world. The United States has been searching for Baghdadi for many years. Capturing or killing Baghdadi has been the top national security priority of my administration. U.S. Special Operations forces executed a dangerous and daring nighttime raid in northwestern Syria and accomplished their mission in grand style."

[*The Washington Post* was widely criticized for referring to al-Baghdadi as an "austere religious scholar" in its obituary notice. The wording was changed to "extremist leader of Islamic State."]

October 28, 2019 Lee Smith
"How the Obama Administration Set In Motion Democrats' Coup Against Trump"
Lee Smith at *The Federalist*

October 29, 2019 Lee Smith
Smith releases his work *The Plot Against the President* (New York: Hachette). Smith's book centers on the work of Congressman Devin Nunes to expose the campaign by major U.S. leaders to destroy Trump's presidency.

October 29, 2019 Steven Hassan
"The Cult of Trump? What 'Cult Rhetoric' Actually Reveals"
Ben Zeller at *Religion and Politics*

Zeller critiques using the "cult" concept in general but on Trump in particular. Zeller also targets Steven Hassan and his forthcoming book *The Cult of Trump*.

"Scholars of new religious movements have shown that the mythology of cultic mind-control is more rhetoric than reality. It is easy to understand why critics of the president dismiss him as a cult leader, and his political followers as brainwashed. But it says a lot more about the power of the language than it does the president himself."

[Jon Atack, a specialist on undue influence, has written a major critique of Zeller's dismissal of Hassan and also defends the view that some groups deserve the cult label.]

October 29, 2019 Donald Trump
"Faith Leaders Pray With Trump At White House"
Michael Gryboski at *Christian Post*

"Participants at the meeting included: Paula White Cain; former Republican Congresswoman Michelle Bachmann; American Values President Gary Bauer; Dr. James Dobson; Free Chapel Senior Pastor Jentezen Franklin; Prestonwood Baptist Church Senior Pastor Jack Graham; First Baptist Dallas Senior Pastor Robert Jeffress; Harvest Christian Fellowship Senior Pastor Greg Laurie; National Hispanic Christian Leadership Conference President, the Rev. Samuel Rodriguez; and Family Research Council President Tony Perkins, among others."

October 31, 2019 Impeachment
House of Representatives approved an impeachment inquiry by a vote of 232 to 196. All Republicans were opposed, along with two Democrats.

President Trump noted on Twitter, "The Greatest Witch Hunt in American History!"

November 1, 2019 Paula White
"Paula White, Trump's Personal Pastor, Joins the White House"
Jeremy W. Peters and Maggie Haberman at *New York Times*

White is to work in the Office of Public Liaison and advise the Faith and Opportunity Initiative.

November 2, 2019 Paula White
"Paula White, Newest White House Aide, Is a Uniquely Trumpian Pastor"
Jeremy W. Peters and Elizabeth Dias at *New York Times*

November 4, 2019 Paula White
White is interviewed by Shannon Bream at Fox News.

Below is some of the text of the interview. It is provided in Media Matters
by Madeline Peltz in her critique of the Bream interview.

SHANNON BREAM (HOST): Well, now, President Trump's longtime
personal pastor is taking a new role inside the Trump administration,
advising the Faith and Opportunity Initiative, working to keep the
president's strong evangelical base in 2020. But the announcement was
not without controversy as some question her theology. So, joining me now
to answer those critics, President Trump's newest White House adviser,
Paula White-Cain, also the author of the brand-new book Something
Greater. Paula, great to have you with us tonight.
PAULA WHITE-CAIN: It's great to be with you, Shannon, and with
everyone.
BREAM: OK, so listen, the president has talked a lot about religious
freedom. He's taken a lot of steps that he said to that end. And of course,
his critics say, especially with the move last week dealing with LGBT
issues and religious freedom and the intersection — they say that what
he's doing is legalizing discrimination but pinning it on religious liberty.
How do you answer that? [...]
BREAM: Well, there are those who, including Joshua Harris, famous
pastor who's now left Christianity and says it's not how he chooses to
identify himself anymore. But he's got this warning, he says evangelical
support for President Trump, quote, "incredibly damaging to the gospel."
He says, "I don't think it's going to end well." How do you respond?
WHITE-CAIN: You know, people are going to say some pretty ridiculous
things all the time. I think this is ending very, very well as we see that
evangelicals support President Trump at an all-time historical high. The
base is stronger than ever. [...]
BREAM: Now, you like the president. You all have bonded, as you've
talked about over the years, and there's some really interesting tidbits in
your book as well. But both of you are used to coming under criticism. So,

I want to read a little bit for you, which is obviously being revved up now that you're in this new position as well.

Jeremy Peters, writing this in The New York Times, says, "Among Christians, Ms. White is a divisive figure. Her association with the belief that God wants followers to find wealth and health commonly called prosperity gospel is highly unorthodox in the faith and considered heretical by many." I mean, you've been a faith leader for a long time. What do you make of that critique of you?

WHITE-CAIN: I've been in ministry for 35 years and I've heard just about everything said. First off, I do not believe that, in this — what you would say, like, you give to get, and that is what they try to label it as prosperity. I believe that God's and his only begotten son, Jesus Christ. I've had to defend the trinity, of all things, that God the Father; God, the Son; God, the Holy Spirit. I think most of this is a political ploy just to hurt our president, to hurt the great faith agenda that he continues to advance. Anyone that's ever listened to my message knows very well, that I believe in very solid biblical beliefs. So, this is not anything new.

BREAM: Well, you all now continue your partnership. It goes into a new phase, and we will watch with the faith efforts, we know they're going to be key moving into 2020 as well. Paula White-Cain, thank you.

November 5, 2019 Donald Trump
"Donald Trump, Anointed Of God — Seriously?"
Neil Macdonald at *CBC News*

This is a nasty article arguing that Evangelicals who support Trump are basically white and racist.

"Unsurprisingly, the demarcation line for Trump where evangelicals are concerned is racial. Eighty-six per cent of black evangelicals surveyed by PPRI said they disapprove of Trump. So did 72 per cent of Hispanic Catholics, many of whom are evangelical. Now why would that be? Because he's white evangelical America's man."

November 6, 2019 Stephen Strang
Will Trump Be a Two-Term President? Hear the Prophesy Made Before He Ever Entered the Race
Strang at *The Stream*

"The number of prophecies about Donald Trump, many of which have gone viral, is one of the reasons Trump received so much support from the Christian community, especially charismatics and Pentecostals. Not only is Trump a champion of religious freedom who is keeping his promises, but there is also a sense that somehow, some way, God is behind this unlikely builder from Queens."

Strang highlights two prophecies from Kim Clement, the famous prophet from South Africa. Strang states: "But to me it's interesting that between these two prophecies he touched on most of the significant issues at stake during Trump's presidency, and he uttered specific words about Trump that have come true."

The article is excerpted from Strang's book *God, Trump, and the 2020 Election*.

November 6, 2019 Shawn Bolz with Lance and Annabelle Wallnau
Interview on Exploring the Prophetic (39 minutes)

Lance Wallnau recounts the beginning of his more public ministry and his first prophecy about Trump in 2015. He and his wife also share personal stories about each other. Lance talks about the separation of church and state. In Annabelle's family, there has been deep division over Trump. Lance says in the last days you have "the Ahab of passivity and the Jezebel of intimidation, seduction and domination." Lance says God is raising up Cyrus figures in various parts of the world.

November 8, 2019 Paula White
"Paula White: Trump's televangelist in the White House"
Jeremy Diamond at CNN

Diamond quotes Erick Erickson:

There are lots of evangelicals who have been skeptical of him all along. And seeing a prosperity gospel minister most of these people look at as a heretic in charge of faith-based outreach ... sends a signal that maybe he's not taking it as seriously as some people think," Erickson said. "Even some of the evangelical movement leaders who are standing shoulder to shoulder with her privately recognize that she is not of the orthodox Christianity and the faith they proclaim in the pulpit on Sundays."

But right now, she's a means to an end with the President and they're focusing on their power through him.

November 11, 2019 Pete Buttigieg
"Why Pete Buttigieg Is The Most Destructive Candidate For Christianity"
Kylee Zempel at *The Federalist*

November 11, 2019 Michael Brown
The Trump Prophecies
Ask Dr. Brown podcast

Brown mentions prophecies by Mark Taylor and Lance Wallnau and focuses on Kim Clement's words from 2007. Brown states that his vote is not based on prophecies but on principles and policies.

November 11, 2019 Johnny Enlow
The Big World Series Message
Elijah List

Realizing that the mountain of media is where the frontline battle is taking place, President Trump has taken unprecedented and exhaustive measures to get communication to the people. Never has a president made more of an effort to communicate with his nation—and never has it been more intentionally suppressed and distorted.

Our President Trump trumps a message of patriotism and nationalism. It is "America First," SO THAT the nations of the world may be blessed as they align with values of liberty and justice for all. America is not the kingdom, BUT the United States of America is a gift of God to the nations to lead them out of their hopelessly unending cycles of war and devastation.

Without the United States we would all be Third World nations, or worse. The socialist agenda that is rampant today, masquerading as egalitarian, planet sensitive, and compassionate is actually a Trojan Horse for the three exact opposite realities—despotism, planetary devastation, and a ruthless, anti-humanity agenda. This agenda was about to enslave the last remaining nation capable of heading it off—BUT GOD!

November 11, 2019 Stephen Strang
Strang promotes a new book on Trump scheduled to be released January 2020: *God, Trump and the 2020 Election*.

November 12, 2019 Impeachment
"Ten Reasons Impeachment Is Illegitimate"
Victor David Hanson, author of *The Case for Trump*, at *National Review*

November 12, 2019 Impeachment
"Republicans Have No Convincing Argument Against Impeachment"
Max Book at *The Washington Post* replies to Hanson's same-day *National Review* piece.

"If even the great historian Victor Davis Hanson can't make a single convincing argument against impeachment, I am forced to conclude that no such argument exists. All that is left is the tribal loyalty that Republicans, including Republican intellectuals, feel toward a Republican president."

November 12, 2019 Paula White
"Trump's Pastor Paula White 'Wrong' to Hawk Religious Products While Working for the White House, Says Ex-Obama Adviser"
Shane Croucher at *Newsweek*

The article features criticism of White by Melissa Rogers, former advisor under President Obama.

November 13, 2019 Paula White
"Bush Ethics Lawyer Suggests Trump's Spiritual Adviser Paula White Committing 'Fraud,' and Running a 'Ponzi Scheme'"
Jason Lemon at *Newsweek*

Richard Painter attacks White.

November 13, 2019 Mark Galli, James Beverley
Pentecostals and the President: Why their prophets exalt Trump and Paula White pastors him
Christianity Today "Quick to Listen" podcast

November 14, 2019 Frank Amedia
Were These Pushed Impeachment Hearings Prophesied?
Strang Report podcast with Stephen Strang

November 14, 2019 Michael Brown
"What If The Trump Prophecies Are True?"
The Christian Post

Brown mentions Kim Clement and links to Mark Taylor's book *The Trump Prophecies.*

"As for how we vote, we make our decisions based on policies and positions, not prophecies. That means that, when it comes to 2020, if it is Trump vs. a radical leftist, I will cast my vote for Trump, not because of prophecy, but because of principle. And so, my vote will not be intended to help bring a prophecy to fulfillment. It will simply be a vote. And if Trump is reelected in accordance with these prophecies, that will simply mean that God foreknew the results. Simple."

November 14–16, 2019 Global Prophetic Summit
Hosted by Cindy and Mike Jacobs, co-founders of Generals International

November 15, 2019 Michael Brown
Are Demonic Spirits Influencing the Trump Impeachment Process?
Strang Report podcast with Stephen Strang

November 15, 2019 William Barr
Attorney General speaks at Federalist Society National Lawyers Convention
Justice.gov

"In this partisan age, we should take special care not to allow the passions of the moment to cause us to permanently disfigure the genius of our Constitutional structure. As we look back over the sweep of American history, it has been the American Presidency that has best fulfilled the vision of the Founders. It has brought to our Republic a dynamism and effectiveness that other democracies have lacked."

November 16, 2019 Jeremiah Johnson
Facebook post on a dream:

"I had such an alarming dream last night where Washington D.C. had turned into a HUGE jungle and it was absolutely INFESTED with snakes. I found Donald Trump and his wife Melanie forced down into a bunker of some sorts. I somehow knew exactly where to find them. They told me they were forced to go underground because they could no longer discern who their true friends and enemies were. I tried to encourage him that the Church was praying for them but it was to no avail. He was simply too emotionally and physically exhausted to listen."

November 19, 2019 Frank Amedia
How a Prophetic Word Propelled Trump to Fulfill His God-Given Israel Assignment
Strang Report podcast with Stephen Strang

Amedia recalls prophetic words given to Trump in 2016.

November 19, 2019 Mark Taylor
Countdown Till the Exposure of Corruption
YouTube of Taylor on the McFiles

November 20, 2019 Impeachment
"From Impeachment to the Debates—and Back Again"
Victor Davis Hanson at *National Review*

November 21, 2019 Franklin Graham
Graham tells Eric Metaxas that opposition to Trump is "demonic."
YouTube

[Metaxas tweeted later that he and Graham were not calling those who oppose Trump demonic but were saying that the forces behind Trump opposition might be demonic.]

November 21, 2019 Peggy Noonan
"Trump's Defenders Have No Defense"
Peggy Noonan at *Wall Street Journal*

As to impeachment itself, the case has been so clearly made you wonder what exactly the Senate will be left doing. How will they hold a lengthy trial with a case this clear? Who exactly will be the president's witnesses, those who'd testify he didn't do what he appears to have done, and would never do it?

Procedures, rules and definitions aren't fully worked out in the Senate. But we are approaching December and the clock is ticking. A full-blown trial on charges most everyone will believe are true, and with an election in less than a year, will seem absurd to all but diehards and do the country no good.

So the reasonable guess is Republican senators will call to let the people decide. In a divided country this is the right call. But they should take seriously the idea of censuring him for abuse of power.

November 21, 2019 Donald Trump
"Explaining The Bond Between Trump And White Evangelicals"
Matthew Avery Sutton at *The Washington Post*

Sutton draws a parallel between fundamentalist Christian support of President Harding and modern evangelical support of Donald Trump. Despite some valuable insights he is nasty on Evangelicals and offers simplistic judgments. "Although evangelicals preach family values and often claim moral superiority, history reveals that they are most interested in exercising political power and identifying politicians who help them do it." This hardly fits with the realities of Evangelicals often missing from the public square. Likewise, Sutton is way over the top in suggesting that Evangelicals "ignore, downplay or embrace" Trump's immorality. This ignores the anguish that many Evangelicals had in choosing Trump. One can understand Sutton's argument that Evangelicals downplay Trump's failings or ignore them. To suggest they embrace them is ridiculous.

November 22, 2019 Donald Trump
Trump calls into "Fox and Friends" and talks for an hour amid impeachment probe.

November 24, 2019 Jeremiah Johnson
Johnson announces his new book *Trump and the Future of America* scheduled to be released on January 1, 2020.
Facebook

November 24, 2019 Steven Hassan
Cult Expert Turns His Attention to Trump
CNN video of Brian Stelter interviewing Steven Hassan.

November 25, 2019 Donald Trump
"Brian Stelter Pushes 'Trump Cult' Narrative, Asks About 'Mind Control' By The President"
Scott Boyd at *NOQ Report*

"There aren't many occasions when CNN's Brian Stelter can stoop lower than he normally does. His 'Reliable Sources' show is a complete and total joke. But he took it to a new level of lunacy and lack of self-awareness today by calling President Trump a cult leader who uses mind control over his devoted followers."

November 25, 2019 Steven Hassan
"CNN guest equates President Trump to a 'cult leader'"
Yahoo News

Along with guest Scott Adams (creator of Dilbert), Tucker Carlson mocks Hassan's interview on CNN. [Tucker Carlson is a famous talk show host on Fox News.]

November 25, 2019 Donald Trump
"Trump Backers Aren't a Cult ... But We Are the Outsiders"
Steve Cortes at *Real Clear Politics*

The message here is clear on two fronts. First, in this present media landscape, a cult could roughly be defined as groupings of people despicable enough to hold views contrary to those of New York newsrooms and Ivy League faculty lounges. The second message also seems self-evident. Rather than debate policy, disparagement becomes the default narrative of the president's detractors. This new "cult" criticism seems to flow directly from the inability, so far, of the Democrats to damage the president in the impeachment imbroglio.

Consequently, as his Capitol Hill opponents lose momentum on impeachment, and minorities increasingly rally to the president's growth agenda, the sadly predictable default posture of the Democrats and their media allies is to embrace a dehumanizing castigation of our movement. We are, according to their aspersions, a giant basket full of "deplorables": racists and other irredeemables. Now, it seems, we are also cult members.

November 26, 2019 Donald Trump
"What a Witch Hunt Really Looks Like"
Stace Schiff at *The New York Times*

Drawing on her knowledge of the Salem witch trials of 1692, Schiff, a non-fiction author, argues that it is President Trump who is carrying on a witch hunt.

By definition you do not qualify as the victim of a witch hunt if you are the most powerful man on the planet. You do, however, incite a witch hunt when you spew malignant allegations and reckless insinuations, when you broadcast a fictitious narrative, attack those who resist it and charge your critics with a shadowy, sinister plot to destroy you. (Witness intimidation can sound strangely like a witchcraft accusation. Did someone really tweet that everything a middle-aged woman touched during her diplomatic career tended to sour?)

There are 53 Republican senators. Might one of them care to rise above the paranoid imaginings, the mad rants, the noxious conspiracy theories, the cruel, crazy character assassinations? Anyone?

November 26, 2019 FBI Investigation
"Who Will Turn Over the 2016 Rocks?"
Holman Jenkins at *The Wall Street Journal*

Jenkins offers analysis on background to forthcoming reports by the Inspector General and John Durham about matters related to the Trump-Russia saga. Jenkins argues that "we're left with the possibility that Mr.

Comey's actions in response to dubious Russian danglings accidentally elected Donald Trump. The Obama administration, after Mrs. Clinton's defeat, shifted overnight from downplaying Russian meddling to highlighting it. We're left with the possibility that the collusion canard was deliberately promoted to distract from what otherwise would have been the story of the century—the FBI's harebrained intervention in a presidential election."

November 26, 2019 William Barr
"The Post-Christian Culture Wars"
Ezra Klein at *Vox*

Analysis of two speeches from William Barr

November 27, 2019 Michael Brown
Is Opposition to Trump Demonic?
Line of Fire TV

November 27, 2019 Donald Trump
"Trump Signs Hong Kong Democracy Legislation, Angering China"
Emily Cochrane, Edward Wong, and Keith Bradsher at *New York Times*

November 27, 2019 Donald Trump
"Conservatives at the Maginot Line"
Rod Dreher at *The American Conservative*

Dreher argues that conservatives have largely lost the cultural wars in America.

November 29, 2019 Donald Trump
"Christian Trump Supporters Don't Have A 'Branding Problem,' The Left Has A Lying Problem"
Kylee Zempel at *The Federalist*

If the religious right wanted a president who was overtly Christian, we would have elected Mike Pence. We didn't elect Trump to lure millennials and Gen Zers to Christianity. We didn't elect him for his doctrine or because we thought he would be the most tolerant or the most bipartisan.

We elected him because we wanted the option to send our kids to religious schools that uphold the values we believe, because we wanted to see our grandchildren compete in fair athletic competitions, because we didn't want to see small businesses exploited and Twitter-destroyed by transgender religious bigots.

Trump is the man for that job. He's no saint. But no milquetoast Mitt Romney was going to get it done. Trump's is precisely the "personal brand" we needed, personal life aside.

December 1, 2019 Lisa Page
"Lisa Page Speaks: 'There's No Fathomable Way I Have Committed Any Crime at All'"
Molly Jong-Fast at *The Daily Beast*

Lisa Page explains her emotions and views as she has gone through media attention, scandal, and attacks from President Trump and Republicans.

December 2, 2019 Donald Trump
"Is the Democratic Party the Real Cult?"
Frank Miele at *Real Clear Politics*

Yes, Trump has demonstrated the power to persuade voters to rethink their entire political philosophy, using harsh truth and direct talk to convince Americans to take an honest look at what their "dear leaders" have been telling them for years. That's why Democrats are so frightened. In 2016, Trump peeled away mostly white blue-collar voters from the Democratic Party and thus secured his victory. If the polls are correct, and blacks and Latinos are now trending toward Trump, then it's game over for the Democrats' ability to exercise near total control over those communities.

Trump isn't a cult leader; he's a deprogrammer.

December 2, 2019 Donald Trump
"False Idol — Why the Christian Right Worships Donald Trump"
Alex Morris at *Rolling Stone*

Morris writes a long piece about the roots of support for Trump among Evangelicals. He also narrates his own faith journey.

December 4, 2019 Donald Trump
The Pulpit, Power & Politics: Evangelicalism's thumbprint on America
CBC radio program [Episode produced by Greg Kelly; guests for show: Jemar Tisby (director of *The Witness: A Black Christian Collective*), John Fea (professor, Messiah College) and Molly Worthen (University of North Carolina, Chapel Hill)]

December 4, 2019 Chris Thurman
"You Foolish Evangelicals, Trump Has Bewitched You"
Chris Thurman at *The Christian Post*

Thurman mentions "the four evangelical enablers of the Trumpocalypse:" Ralph Reed, Jerry Falwell, Jr. , Franklin Graham, and Mike Pence.

Ralph, Jerry, Franklin, and Mike, my brothers in Christ, I believe you are being blind and foolish to support Trump. From my perspective, you are significantly misaligned with what Scripture says about how we as Christians are supposed to deal with someone like our current president. You got "bewitched" by an exploitative, pathologically lying snake oil salesman, and your unrestrained support of Trump has not only turned off untold numbers of non-believers to the cause of Christ but brought great dishonor on Christianity.

I also believe Trump is so malignantly narcissistic that he claimed to be a Christian simply to get evangelicals to vote for him in 2016. Evangelicals foolishly drank the Trump Kool-Aid and got conned into voting for him. Trump was cunning and conniving enough to know that without evangelical support he wouldn't win the 2016 election, and he was more than willing to misrepresent himself as a follower of Christ in order to gain the presidency for his own personal glory and enrichment.

While only God knows who His "sheep" are, I believe Trump is no more Christian in how he lives his life than I'm a Nobel Prize winning physicist. God expressly commands His followers to have nothing to do with someone like Trump, and yet, millions of evangelicals continue to enthusiastically support him.

In supporting Trump, evangelicals have called him good when he is evil, light when he is darkness. This is especially disconcerting given that Christians have the Holy Spirit inside of them, part of whose function is to guide us to truth and convict us of sin. We, of all people, should be the most discerning about a wolf in sheep's clothing like Trump. Trump-supporting evangelicals would be wise to ask themselves why so many secular mental health professionals who are not indwelt by the Holy Spirit see Trump as an evil, malignant narcissist while so many Christians keep sticking their head in the sand denying it all.

December 6, 2019 Michael Brown
"Are Evangelicals Who Support Trump 'Fools'?"
Michael Brown at *The Christian Post*

This is Brown's reply to Chris Thurman's December 4 article.

My response to Thurman's article is that he is just as guilty as the evangelicals he accuses, except from the opposite perspective. In short, while some evangelicals seem blind to his failings and his potential to hurt America deeply, Thurman seems blind to Trump's strengths and his potential to help America greatly.

Never before in my memory have we seen the depths of the DC swamp. Or the bias and even dishonesty of the media (on both sides, actually, but especially on the left). Or the blood-thirsty nature of the pro-abortion camp. Or the extreme radicality of the left (including the new push for socialism and the attempt to silence opposing ideas, even violently). Or the danger of the internet giants suppressing conservative voices and influencing elections. This is what Trump is fighting, and as flawed as he is, those of us who support him recognize that very few men would be able to withstand all this pressure without caving and compromising along the way.

December 6, 2019 Donald Trump
"Christian Doomsayers Have Lost It"
Peter Wehner at *The New York Times*

To my fellow Christians, then, a friendly reminder from a conservative who shares many of your concerns: We are not living in Nero's Rome. In world history, there are very few nations that have been as accommodating to Christianity as the United States is today; and America is hardly on the edge of a moral abyss.

This apocalyptic moral mind-set has led to an alliance with a shockingly unethical figure, who embodies a mobster's mentality and an anti-Christian ethic. Mr. Trump, a skilled demagogue, has taken full advantage of this. There appears to be almost nothing he can say or do to break the bond that has developed, and virtually nothing that many of his Christian supporters will not excuse.

December 7, 2019 Donald Trump
Why Did Evangelicals Vote for Trump?
Frank Turek at Cross Examined

A lengthy explanation of support for Trump

December 8, 2019 Donald Trump
"Understanding 'The Strange Case of Donald Trump'"
Dinesh Sharma interviews Dan McAdams at *Psychology Today.*

December 9, 2019 FBI Investigation
Release of Inspector General report on FBI Crossfire Hurricane Investigation
Justice.gov

Michael Horowitz and his team studied FBI scrutiny of the alleged Trump-Russia collusion. The report said there was no political bias in the FBI in relation to their investigation about Trump and Russia. Horowitz also claimed that there were reasonable grounds to do an investigation, even though there were significant errors in the process.

Here is one of the conclusions of the report:

"We are deeply concerned that so many basic and fundamental errors were made by three separate, hand-picked investigative teams; on one of the most sensitive FBI investigations; after the matter had been briefed to the highest levels within the FBI; even though the information sought through use of FISA authority related so closely to an ongoing presidential campaign; and even though those involved with the investigation knew that their actions were likely to be subjected to close scrutiny. We believe this circumstance reflects a failure not just by those who prepared the FISA applications, but also by the managers and supervisors in the [investigation's] chain of command, including FBI senior officials who were briefed as the investigation progressed."

December 9, 2019 William Barr

Statement by Attorney General William P. Barr on the Inspector General's Report of the Review of Four FISA Applications and Other Aspects of the FBI's Crossfire Hurricane Investigation
Justice.org

William Barr, U.S. Attorney General, critiqued some of the Inspector General's findings. Barr stated, "The Inspector General's report now makes clear that the FBI launched an intrusive investigation of a U.S. presidential campaign on the thinnest of suspicions that, in my view, were insufficient to justify the steps taken. It is also clear that, from its inception, the evidence produced by the investigation was consistently exculpatory. Nevertheless, the investigation and surveillance was pushed forward for the duration of the campaign and deep into President Trump's administration. In the rush to obtain and maintain FISA surveillance of Trump campaign associates, FBI officials misled the FISA court, omitted critical exculpatory facts from their filings, and suppressed or ignored information negating the reliability of their principal source."

John Durham (Attorney General, Connecticut) also issued some criticism of Horowitz's report: "I have the utmost respect for the mission of the Office of Inspector General and the comprehensive work that went into the report prepared by Mr. Horowitz and his staff. However, our investigation is not limited to developing information from within component parts of the Justice Department. Our investigation has included developing information from other persons and entities, both in the U.S. and outside of the U.S. Based on the evidence collected to date, and while our investigation is ongoing, last month we advised the Inspector General that we do not agree with some of the report's conclusions as to predication and how the FBI case was opened."

December 9, 2019 James Comey
"The Truth Is Finally Out. The FBI Fulfilled Its Mission"
James Comey at *The Washington Post*

On Monday, we learned from a report by the Justice Department's inspector general, Michael Horowitz, that the allegation of a criminal conspiracy was nonsense. There was no illegal wiretapping, there were no informants inserted into the campaign, there was no "spying" on the Trump campaign. Although it took two years, the truth is finally out.

As the leader of an institution that is supposed to be devoted to truth, Barr needs to stop acting like a Trump spokesperson. In the words of the nation's Founders, the Justice Department's inspector general has "Let Facts be submitted to a candid world." The FBI fulfilled its mission — protecting the American people and upholding the U.S. Constitution. Now those who attacked the FBI for two years should admit they were wrong.

Comey's opinion piece was posted at 4.25 p.m. At 4:30 p.m. Comey tweeted, "So it was all lies. No treason. No spying on the campaign. No tapping Trump's wires. It was just good people trying to protect America."

December 9, 2019 James Comey
"The 'Vindication' of James Comey"
William McGurn at *The Wall Street Journal*

After applying heavy sarcasm in the title, McGurn provides a listing of Comey's faults as noted in the I.G. report and overlooked in Comey's *Washington Post* opinion piece.

December 9, 2019 William Barr
"Barr Rejects Watchdog Finding That FBI Was Justified in Opening Trump Probe"
Sadie Gurman at *The Wall Street Journal*

December 10, 2019 Chris Thurman
"Yes, Evangelicals, It Is Foolish To Support Trump"
Chris Thurman at *The Christian Post*

This is Thurman's reply to Michael Brown's critique of his views.

"I'm not blind to Trump's strengths. I don't believe he has any … If Trump is a malignant narcissist as many of us believe, he is an *evil person* and has no redeeming qualities … I would like to challenge Brown and the others who criticized the op-ed I wrote to come up with *one* positive character trait Trump possesses … Is it possible that Trump ended up in the Oval Office empowered by spiritual forces of darkness and that God *permitted* him to be president but didn't *desire* it?"

December 10, 2019 Impeachment
Democrats issue two articles of impeachment against Trump.

December 10, 2019 Impeachment
"Impeach Trump, Save America"
Thomas Friedman at *The New York Times*

"It is the only thing to do if our country's democracy is to survive."

December 10, 2019 James Comey
"Misfired 'Hurricane': Comey's team abused Carter Page and the FBI"
Kevin Brock at *The Hill*

The IG can assess that the investigation was technically justified, but in tradition and common counterintelligence practice it was not — particularly, and especially, since it involved the incredibly sensitive specter of investigating a presidential campaign. It was overkill on very lightweight assertions by a team of individuals in leadership positions who appeared to be driven by personal agendas, rather than normal protocols and practices.

The abuse of Carter Page by this team at the top of the FBI is unconscionable. The report is troubling to read for anyone who has been part of that storied institution. May it spur all appropriate reforms that will help restore confidence in the FBI's vital objectivity and unbiased mandate.

December 10, 2019 William Barr
"Barr thinks FBI may have acted in 'bad faith' in probing Trump campaign's links to Russia"
Ken Dilanian interviews Pete Williams, *NBC News* [Full interview on YouTube]

Barr: "I think our nation was turned on its head for three years based on a completely bogus narrative that was largely fanned and hyped by a completely irresponsible press. I think there were gross abuses … and inexplicable behavior that is intolerable in the FBI. I think that leaves open the possibility that there was bad faith."

NBC issued the report by Dilanian at 1:16 pm. It contained a brief clip from the interview with Barr, along with Dilanian's news report.

December 10, 2019 William Barr
"Attorney General Barr Calls FBI's Trump Probe 'Travesty'"
Sadie Gurman at *The Wall Street Journal*

December 10, 2019 FBI Investigation
"The Horowitz Horror Show"
Holman W. Jenkins, Jr. at *The Wall Street Journal*

"Whatever his legitimate complaints about his treatment at the hands of the FBI, Mr. Trump managed to win in 2016. Hillary Clinton fans are the ones still contending that improper FBI actions cost her the election. We can only wonder when Democrats and their media supporters will find their way out of their own fog and start demanding an unsparing examination of the FBI's role in the 2016 race."

December 10, 2019 Steele Dossier
"It's Official: The Dossier Was Malarkey"
Byron York at *The Washington Examiner*

The new report from Justice Department Inspector General Michael Horowitz is an absolutely damning indictment of the Steele dossier. The dossier, compiled by the former British spy Christopher Steele during the 2016 campaign, was a collection of damaging and unfounded rumors about candidate Donald Trump. It was paid for by the Democratic National Committee and the Hillary Clinton campaign and overseen by the opposition research firm Fusion GPS. It was never verified, and some of it was laughably far-fetched from the very beginning.

Still, the dossier's tales were taken seriously by officials in the highest ranks of the FBI — then-director James Comey and top deputy Andrew McCabe. In January 2017, Comey briefed President-elect Trump on the dossier's most sensational allegations. The briefing provided a hook for some news organizations to tell the public of the dossier's existence, and then, days later, publish the entire document.

The reporting did terrible damage to a new president as he took office. And now, the Horowitz report definitively shows that it was all garbage.

December 10, 2019 Steele Dossier
"'Corroboration Zero': An Inspector General's Report Reveals the Steele Dossier Was Always a Joke"
Matt Taibbi at *Rolling Stone*

"If the report released Monday by Justice Department Inspector General Michael Horowitz constitutes a "clearing" of the FBI, never clear me of anything. Holy God, what a clown show the Trump-Russia investigation was."

[It should be noted that the testimony of Horowitz on December 11 shows him very open to the view that the errors in the FBI investigation were not accidental.]

December 11, 2019 Brian Houston
"Brian Houston, Christian Worship Leaders Pray for Trump, Visit Oval Office"
Samuel Smith at *The Christian Post*

Smith highlights the December 6 visit by Houston (famous Hillsong Church founder) and others, including Sean Feucht.

December 11, 2019 Michael Brown
"When A Christian Psychologist Makes Trump Into A Monster"
The Christian Post

Brown presents four positive characteristics of Donald Trump, in reply to Chris Thurman's December 10 post.

"First, he has kept his word to evangelical leaders, showing consistency and faithfulness. Second, despite his playboy past and his narcissistic ways, he seems devoted to his wife and children. Third, he is determined to do everything in his power as president to 'rescue the perishing,' to borrow a phrase from Proverbs 24, applied here to the unborn. Fourth, his heart for prison reform and rehabilitating our inner-cities also seems genuine."

December 11, 2019 FBI Investigation
Inspector General testifies at Senate Judiciary Committee hearing
Prepared statement from Michael Horowitz, U.S. Department of Justice

December 11, 2019 FBI Investigation
"Of Course the FBI Spied On the Trump Campaign"
Byron York at *The Washington Examiner*

December 11, 2019 Carter Page
"Unraveling the Criminal Web at Comey's FBI and Beyond"
Charles Lipson at *Real Clear Politics*

The FISA court was told Carter Page was a foreign agent when the FBI, DoJ, and CIA knew he was not. The court was told Russians had offered Page billions of dollars in an oil-and-gas deal to pay for his help. The FBI, DoJ, and CIA knew there was no such offer.

The same officials pulled the same trick with the Steele dossier. They knew it was based on unreliable gossip and rumors — they had that evidence in writing — and they hid it from the courts. The Horowitz Report says so definitively. They not only hid it; they told the court the exact opposite.

These are serious crimes, not only against Carter Page but against the true target of the spying, Donald Trump's campaign and presidency — and ultimately against the American people. Those who committed the crimes must be held to account. The rule of law must apply to government officials, not just the unwashed masses. In addition, we need to restore confidence in our counterintelligence tools, which are essential for national security.

December 11, 2019 William Barr
"William Barr is Unfit to be Attorney General"
Eric Holder, former attorney general, at *The Washington Post*

December 11, 2019 William Barr
"Barr's focus on abuses by the FBI is entirely warranted"
Hugh Hewitt at *The Washington Post*

Hewitt's opinion piece is related to Barr's interviews about Horowitz's report.

There isn't a single factual argument to be made against Barr's assertions on Tuesday. Transcripts of both full interviews should be studied in detail in constitutional law courses, as well as within the FBI, the Justice Department and the intelligence community. A surveillance state unchecked by internal controls is deeply sinister.

Lots of suspected wrongdoers and allies of suspected wrongdoers were out on cable news proclaiming vindication after the inspector general's report came out, and many had willing media accomplices. But their declarations of innocence, filled with false, indeed almost palpable bravado, certainly will not work on Barr, nor should they. Barr takes seriously his No. 1 job, as he described it, which is to protect the governed from those with law enforcement powers that can be abused.

December 11, 2019 FBI Investigation
"The FBI's Corrupt Cops"
Kevin Williamson at *National Review*

Williamson targets Horowitz for not seeing that there was bias in the FBI, not just "basic and fundamental errors."

December 11, 2019 FBI Investigation
Graham sends warning to FBI officials responsible for FISA abuse
Lindsay Graham on Sean Hannity show on Fox News

December 11, 2019 FBI Investigation, Page, Strzok
"IG Report Shows Russia Hoax A Coup Attempt"
Miranda Devine at *New York Post*

Inspector General Michael Horowitz finally damned the FBI during his testimony Wednesday when he said he would be "skeptical" that there was anything accidental in the egregious catalog of errors the bureau committed in its spying operation on Donald Trump's presidential campaign.

Devine notes that Lindsay Graham in his opening statement at the hearing read text messages between FBI agent Peter Strzok and lawyer Lisa Page as proof of bias against Trump. The texts read,

March 3, 2016, Page: "God, Trump is a loathsome human."
Strzok: "OMG, he's an idiot."
July 16, Page: "Wow, Donald Trump is an enormous douche."
July 19, Stzrok: "Trump is a disaster."
August 8, Page: "He's not ever going to become president, right?"
Strzok: "No. No, he won't. We'll stop it."
August 15, Strzok: "I want to believe the path you threw out in [their then-boss Andrew McCabe's] office — that there's no way he gets elected — but I'm afraid we can't take the risk. It's like an insurance policy in the unlikely event you die before you're 40."
August 26, Strzok: "Just went to a southern Virginia Walmart. I could smell the Trump supporters."

Strzok was fired on August 10, 2018, but has appealed his firing.

December 11, 2019 FBI Investigation
"We Just Got a Rare Look at National Security Surveillance. It Was Ugly."
Charlie Savage at *The New York Times*

"The Justice Department's independent inspector general, Michael E. Horowitz, and his team uncovered a staggeringly dysfunctional and error-ridden process in how the F.B.I. went about obtaining and renewing court permission under the Foreign Intelligence Surveillance Act, or FISA, to wiretap Carter Page, a former Trump campaign adviser."

December 12, 2019 William Barr
"Summary of William Barr's Reaction To Horowitz Report"
Sharyl Attkinson at *The Epoch Times*

Contrary to much reporting, Horowitz didn't rule out improper motive; he didn't find documentary or testimonial evidence of improper motive. Those are two different things.

Instead of talking to the Trump campaign, the FBI secretly "wired up" sources and had them talk to four people affiliated with the Trump campaign, in August, September, and October 2016.

December 12, 2019 FBI Investigation
"Horowitz Report Finally Unmasks Adam Schiff. Who's Going To Call Him Out On His Lies?"
John Kass at *Chicago Tribune*

"Now that the Horowitz report is out, revealing all those lies told by the FBI as it worked to hamstring a presidency with a debunked Russia collusion theory, here's a question: Where do U.S. Rep. Adam Schiff — the Inspector Javert of Trump Impeachment Theater — and Schiff's eager handmaidens of the Washington Democratic Media Complex go now to get their reputations back? Nowhere. There is no place for them to go … Schiff is a dissembler, a prevaricator, a distortionist, a spreader of falsehoods. In Chicago we use the short word: liar."

December 12, 2019 Donald Trump
"Media Attack on John Solomon Is an Attack on the Free Press"
C. Boyden Gray at *Real Clear Politics*

Gray defends Solomon's journalistic integrity against what he calls "an unprecedented, coordinated hit job by his fellow journalists."

John Solomon is one of the major reporters who often defends Trump. As a result, Solomon is frequently attacked in mainstream media.

December 12, 2019 FBI Investigation
"The Inspector General's Report on 2016 FBI Spying Reveals a Scandal of Historic Magnitude: Not Only for the FBI but Also the U.S. Media"
Glenn Greenwald at *The Intercept*

There is simply no way for anyone of good faith to read this IG Report and reach any conclusion other than that this is yet another instance of the FBI abusing its power in severe ways to subvert and undermine U.S. democracy. If you don't care about that, what do you care about?

But the revelations of the IG Report are not merely a massive FBI scandal. They are also a massive media scandal, because they reveal that so much of what the U.S. media has authoritatively claimed about all of these matters for more than two years is completely false.

Perhaps these revelations will finally lead to a realization about how rogue, and dangerous, these police state agencies have become, and how urgently needed is serious reform. But if nothing else, it must serve as a tonic to the three years of unrelenting media propaganda that has deceived and misled millions of Americans into believing things that are simply untrue.

None of these journalists have acknowledged an iota of error in the wake of this report because they know that lying is not just permitted but encouraged as long as it pleases and vindicates the political beliefs of their audiences. Until that stops, credibility and faith in journalism will never be restored, and—despite how toxic it is to have a media that has no claim on credibility—that despised status will be fully deserved.

December 12, 2019 Carter Page
"The Carter Page/Ukraine Lie That Kept on Lying for Mueller and the FBI"
Paul Sperry at *Real Clear Investigations*

December 13, 2019 Katie Barker
America, You Will Be Known Again As 'One Nation Under God'
Elijah List

I am calling My people to cover the path to the presidential election in prayer and intercession, beginning now. Great will be the spiritual battle leading up to this election, but My people will see the one I have chosen re-elected as they partner with Me in intercession.

Much will be accomplished in advancing My plans on the earth in the following years through this administration. There is a need to be diligent and intentional in this assignment and to press on with purpose, right up to the day of the election. You have already seen change on the earth through decisions made by this administration, but much greater change will be seen in the following term.

I am calling the people of the United States to see My hand is on this administration; I am using them to advance My plans and purposes. Don't look to the man I have chosen but instead trust in Me and look to all I desire to do through him. Realize My thoughts are higher and My ways are higher.

The United States has led the world in recognizing the importance of Israel, and due to their stance, more nations will follow in the years to come.

Katie Barker and her husband, Aaron, run Bring the Fire Ministries. They are based in the Tweed Coast of Australia.

December 14, 2019 Carter Page
"An Apology to Carter Page"
Jonathan Turley at *The Hill*

At what point does someone apologize to Page? He is, in fact, the victim of this criminal referral. He is the victim of what Horowitz describes as a "misleading" basis presented to the FISA court. He is a victim of media "groupthink" that portrayed him as the sinister link proving collusion with Russia, an allegation rejected by the FBI, by the inspector general, and by the special counsel. Of course, Washington does not work this way. Page served his purpose and the trashing of his reputation was a cost of doing business with the federal government for many members of Congress and the media.

December 15, 2019 James Comey
James Comey with Chris Wallace at *Fox News Sunday*

Wallace grilled Comey in a 15-minute segment. Here is some of the conversation:

Comey: *"As the director you're not kept informed on the details of an investigation. So no, in general I didn't know what they'd learned from the sub-source, I didn't know the particulars of the investigation,"*

Wallace: *"But this isn't some investigation, sir. This is an investigation of the campaign of the man who is the president of the United States,"* Wallace said. *"You had just been through a firestorm investigating Hillary Clinton. I would think if I had been in your position I would have been on that like a junk yard dog."*

Comey: *"That's not the way it works, though. As a director sitting on top of an organization with 38,000 people, you can't run an investigation that's seven layers below you."*

December 16, 2019 Chris Thurman
"To President Trump, Evangelicals Who Support Him, and Michael Brown: An Apology and a Challenge"
Chris Thurman at *The Christian Post*

I want to apologize to evangelicals for the way I have expressed my opinion about your support of the President. Throughout my walk with the Lord, I have had a sinful tendency to say things in too harsh of a manner and paint with too dark of a brush. Second, I want to apologize for getting into an argument with my brother in Christ, Michael Brown. Finally, and I never anticipated this happening in a million years, President Trump, I want to apologize to you. Calling you evil and saying that you have no redeemable qualities was out of line and inappropriate… .

Now, my challenge.

President Trump, I challenge you to get a psychiatric evaluation.

Evangelicals who support Trump, I challenge you to spend time between now and the 2020 election reading and viewing other *sources of input on the President than what you turn to on a regular basis.*

Thurman recommends Bandy Lee's edited volume *The Dangerous Case of Donald Trump* and the writings of Peter Wehner and concludes,

I am a Christian and a conservative. As both, I am going to go to my grave convinced that Donald Trump is, objectively, a severely mentally and morally disturbed individual, unfit to hold the office of the presidency, only going to get worse over time, and that we must remove him from office by any legal means possible — the 25th Amendment, articles of impeachment, or the general election — and find another Republican candidate to run in 2020.

[An acceptance of Thurman's apology by Michael Brown is added at the end.]

December 16, 2019 James Comey
"Devastating: Chris Wallace Grills, Dismantles Comey on IG Report"
Guy Benson at *Townhall*

"If Comey intended to strut his way through a triumphant 'vindication' end zone dance on Fox News, he had another thing coming. He ran into the buzzsaw of Chris Wallace."

December 17, 2019 FBI Investigation
"Five Questions Still Remaining After the Release of the Horowitz Report"
Matt Taibbi at *Rolling Stone*

Yet reporters kept taking the bait on the key idea that Steele was an in-the-know superspy whose conspiracy/blackmail claims were taken seriously by investigators. Credulous reports originating from this premise — about Comey's "bombshell" delivery of Steele's compromise claims to Trump, or news that a court found "probable cause" to believe Page was a foreign agent, or even in hagiographic portraits of Steele as a real-life George Smiley — now look like fruit from a poisoned tree. Was it eaten knowingly or unknowingly?

If reporters were burned, they should be angry, and corrections should be forthcoming. If there isn't an effort to reverse the wrong coverage, it will look like certain outlets (particularly cable channels) were complicit in knowingly giving oceans of airtime to shaky stories. It's a bad look either way, but door number two is worse.

December 17, 2019 Impeachment
President sends six-page letter to Nancy Pelosi against impeachment.

Part of the letter reads,

After three years of unfair and unwarranted investigations, 45 million dollars spent, 18 angry Democrat prosecutors, the entire force of the FBI, headed by leadership now proven to be totally incompetent and corrupt, you have found NOTHING! Few people in high position could have endured or passed this test. You do not know, nor do you care, the great damage and hurt you have inflicted upon wonderful and loving members of my family. You conducted a fake investigation upon the democratically elected President of the United States, and you are doing it yet again.

Since the moment I won the election, the Democrat Party has been possessed by Impeachment Fever. There is no reticence. This is not a somber affair. You are making a mockery of impeachment and you are scarcely concealing your hatred of me, of the Republican Party, and tens of millions of patriotic Americans. The voters are wise, and they are seeing straight through this empty, hollow, and dangerous game you are playing.

I have no doubt the American people will hold you and the Democrats fully responsible in the upcoming 2020 election. They will not soon forgive your perversion of justice and abuse of power.

December 18, 2019 Donald Trump
"Trump Impeached"
Nicholas Fandos and Michael D. Shear at *The New York Times*

Trump is impeached on two counts: abuse of power and obstruction of congress. The vote was basically partisan, except two Democrats joined the Republicans in voting no on the first article while three Democrats joined on the second article.

December 18, 2019 James Comey
"Comey's Dishonest Spin is Going Nowhere"
Joseph DiGenova at *The Epoch Times*

It's hard to say which of those two possibilities ought to frighten Americans more. Either Comey's FBI was plagued by "gross incompetence," while exercising extraordinary powers over U.S. citizens, or corrupt actors within the bureau's leadership successfully targeted domestic political rivals with manipulated evidence. Either scenario would represent a disaster for the FBI and a damning indictment of Comey's tenure as director.

But Comey didn't seem to see the problem, telling Wallace that he wouldn't have resigned in response to the Horowitz report if he were still director.

That's the preening, self-righteous Comey we've gotten to know over the past three years. His act is getting harder and harder to believe, the more we learn about the extent of the FBI's malfeasance during his tenure. Three years ago, after he illegally exonerated Hillary Clinton, I called Comey a dirty cop. He's even dirtier today.

[DiGenova is writing in context of Comey's interview on *Fox News Sunday*.]

December 19, 2019 Donald Trump
"Samuel Rodriguez After House Impeaches Trump: Dems 'Impeached Millions of God-Fearing Americans'"
Jenny Rose Spaudo at *Charisma News*

"The Democrats in the House impeached millions of God-fearing, family-loving and patriotic Americans from the Democrat and Republican parties."
"They impeached millions of Americans—Democrat and Republican—who believe in one nation under God, indivisible with liberty and justice for all, including the president of the United States."
"They impeached millions of Americans—Democrat and Republican—who believe in due process, the rule of law and in the primacy of our free elections in determining our political leadership."

[The statement was also signed by Johnnie Moore.]

December 19, 2019 Kat Kerr
What the Maker of Heaven and Earth Has to Say on the Impeachment
Elijah List [The video of Kat Kerr's message is on her Facebook page.]

"The souls of the left are being exposed. God hears every word we speak but He also sees within the layers of our souls. Nothing can be hidden from Him, and He said the liberals are not just fighting against Trump but they are fighting against HIM and that is why they will never win. If you want a show, He will give one that proves He is for Trump, for life, for justice, for liberty, for righteousness and for His plan."

She states in the video that God will use the impeachment for his purposes. Democrats will fail miserably. Here are some direct quotes:
"You're sore losers."
"Trump is winning. Get over it."
"So, roll up your little impeachment scrolls and stick them away for another time. And get you some color books and crayons. You'll do better for our country."

On her Facebook page, she writes in the comments section, "We NULLIFY every word spoken against our President and God's plan for America. We DECLARE God's Will, God's Way be done in Jesus name. We command the Hosts of Heaven to go and pull down every spiritual stronghold against Trump and his family and his campaign for 2020. SO BE IT!!"

December 19, 2019 Michael Brown
"A Reality Check for Christian Supporters of President Trump"
The Stream

This is a call to Trump supporters to object to the president's statement about deceased Democrat John Dingell: "Maybe he's looking up. I don't know. ... But let's assume he's looking down."

December 19, 2019 William Barr, Eric Holder
"Von Spakovsky, Fund: Barr Not 'Unfit' To Be Attorney General—Here's The Man Who Deserves That Title"
Hans A. von Spakovsky and John Fund at *Fox News*

The authors argue that Eric Holder was a "nakedly partisan" attorney general under Obama.

December 19, 2019 Victor Davis Hanson
"Former Intelligence Chiefs Fit Perfectly Into Media Advocacy Culture"
Real Clear Politics

*The most powerful intelligence chiefs of the Obama administration —
Brennan, Clapper, Comey and McCabe — have routinely offered the
nation their own warped theories about wrongdoing in high places that
are as self-serving as they are contradicted by facts.*

*The conclusions of both the Mueller investigation and the Horowitz
report are damning to the past analyses of all four. In the advocacy culture
of our new media, ex-government officials such as Brennan, Clapper and
McCabe can be paid to appear on news programs to analyze (or vindicate)
their own unethical behavior.*

*As employees of the media, they sell their checkered government
service to exonerate themselves while confirming the anti-Trump biases
of their paying hosts.*

December 19, 2019 Devin Nunes
"Devin Nunes Is Owed An Apology"
The Washington Times editorial

December 19, 2019 Mark Galli
"Trump Should Be Removed from Office"
Christianity Today

*Whether Mr. Trump should be removed from office by the Senate or by
popular vote next election—that is a matter of prudential judgment. That
he should be removed, we believe, is not a matter of partisan loyalties but
loyalty to the Creator of the Ten Commandments.*

*To the many evangelicals who continue to support Mr. Trump in
spite of his blackened moral record, we might say this: Remember who
you are and whom you serve. Consider how your justification of Mr.
Trump influences your witness to your Lord and Savior. Consider what
an unbelieving world will say if you continue to brush off Mr. Trump's
immoral words and behavior in the cause of political expediency. If we
don't reverse course now, will anyone take anything we say about justice
and righteousness with any seriousness for decades to come? Can we say
with a straight face that abortion is a great evil that cannot be tolerated*

and, with the same straight face, say that the bent and broken character of our nation's leader doesn't really matter in the end?

We have reserved judgment on Mr. Trump for years now. Some have criticized us for our reserve. But when it comes to condemning the behavior of another, patient charity must come first. So we have done our best to give evangelical Trump supporters their due, to try to understand their point of view, to see the prudential nature of so many political decisions they have made regarding Mr. Trump. To use an old cliché, it's time to call a spade a spade, to say that no matter how many hands we win in this political poker game, we are playing with a stacked deck of gross immorality and ethical incompetence. And just when we think it's time to push all our chips to the center of the table, that's when the whole game will come crashing down. It will crash down on the reputation of evangelical religion and on the world's understanding of the gospel. And it will come crashing down on a nation of men and women whose welfare is also our concern.

December 19, 2019 Mark Galli
"How Trump Lost an Evangelical Stalwart"
Emma Green at *The Atlantic*

Interview with Mark Galli about his editorial against Trump

December 19, 2019 Mark Galli
"Evangelical Magazine Christianity Today Calls for Trump's Removal"
Elizabeth Dias at *New York Times*

[The article was updated on the 20th at 9.28 a.m.]

December 20, 2019 Franklin Graham
Franklin Graham issues blistering critique of Galli editorial.
Facebook

Yes, my father Billy Graham founded Christianity Today; but no, he would not agree with their opinion piece. In fact, he would be very disappointed. I have not previously shared who my father voted for in the past election, but because of this article, I feel it is necessary to share it now. My father knew Donald Trump, he believed in Donald Trump, and he voted for

Donald Trump. He believed that Donald J. Trump was the man for this hour in history for our nation.

For Christianity Today *to side with the Democrat Party in a totally partisan attack on the President of the United States is unfathomable.*

Christianity Today *said it's time to call a spade a spade. The spade is this*—Christianity Today *has been used by the left for their political agenda. It's obvious that* Christianity Today *has moved to the left and is representing the elitist liberal wing of evangelicalism.*

December 20, 2019 Donald Trump, Mark Galli
Trump tweets response to Galli editorial

7:12 A.M.
"A far left magazine, or very "progressive," as some would call it, which has been doing poorly and hasn't been involved with the Billy Graham family for many years, Christianity Today, knows nothing about reading a perfect transcript of a routine phone call and would rather... ..

7:12 A.M
... have a Radical Left nonbeliever, who wants to take your religion & your guns, than Donald Trump as your President. No President has done more for the Evangelical community, and it's not even close. You'll not get anything from those Dems on stage. I won't be reading ET again!

[ET is probably a typo.]

December 20, 2019 Mark Galli
Mark Galli responds to Trump Tweets
CNN New Day

December 20, 2019 Mark Galli
"Christianity Today, An Influential Evangelical Magazine, Says Trump 'Should Be Removed From Office'"
Sarah Pulliam Bailey at *Washington Post*

December 31, 2019 Nancy LeTourneau
"The Seeds Of Theocratic Authoritarianism Are Being Planted"
AlterNet

VII. Fourth Year
2020

January 2020 Jeremiah Johnson
Release of Jeremiah Johnson's book *Trump and the Future of America* (Jeremiah Johnson Ministries, 2020)

"I believe Donald Trump will win the 2020 election, but he cannot do it without supernatural intervention. For Donald Trump to win the 2020 election, the Baby Boomers must arise in America and take a stand. The future of America belongs to this generation in this season."

January 2, 2020 Michael Brown
Call for removal of Todd Bentley from ministry
Brown and five other leaders issued a Facebook statement.

January 2, 2020 Lance Wallnau
2020 Prophetic Window
Facebook video [30 minutes]

Wallnau makes a lot of different observations. He refers to *Christianity Today*'s "apocalyptic declaration" from the December 19 editorial by Mark Galli. He states that the church needs deliverance from the "Jezebel witchcraft" of always halting between two opinions. Wallnau believes that the false prophet of the end times is the media and that the Hebrew year 5780 [2020] is significant as a symbol. Wallnau also states that prophecy has become cheap, but he also affirms his 2015 declaration that "Trump is God's Cyrus." Wallnau states that Republicans need one million new voters for the November election. "It's not because we just prophesied Donald Trump is gonna win and then we're going decree it. Let's be delivered from that kind of adolescence."

January 2, 2020 Mark Galli
"Christianity Today Editor Laments 'Ethical Naïveté' of Trump Backers"
Nicholas Bogel-Burroughs at *The New York Times*

January 2, 2020 Donald Trump
"U.S. Strike in Iraq Kills Qassim Suleimani, Commander of Iranian Forces"
Michael Crowley, Falih Hassan, and Eric Schmitt at *The New York Times*

[The strike was on January 3rd on Iraq time.]

January 2, 2020 Guillermo Maldonado
"Evangelicals for Trump Host Says God Raised Up Trump as Part of Plan for End Times, Second Coming"
Peter Montgomery at *Right Wing Watch*

Article on Guillermo Maldonado, founder of King Jesus International Ministry

January 2, 2020 Donald Trump
King Jesus International Ministry issues statement on Evangelicals for Trump.

January 3, 2020 Mark Galli
"Trump To Rally Evangelicals After Critical Christianity Today Editorial"
Morgan Chalfant and Brett Samuels at *The Hill*

[Miami rally at Maldonado church]

January 3, 2020 Donald Trump
"Democrats Prebut Donald Trump's Miami Evangelical Event"
Phil Ammann at *Florida Politics*

January 3, 2020 Donald Trump
Trump speaks at Evangelical coalition event in Miami.

January 3, 2020 Donald Trump
"In Miami Speech, Trump Tells Evangelical Base: God Is 'on Our Side'"
Jennifer Medina and Maggie Haberman at *The New York Times*

January 6, 2020 Stephen Strang
What Really Happened at Friday's 'Evangelicals for Trump' Meeting in Miami
Strang Report

January 6, 2020 Jim Bakker

Televangelist Bakker states on his show that "Trump is a test whether you're even saved. Only saved people can love Trump." After some laughter, Bakker said: "No. You gotta be really saved. You gotta forgive … You forgive when you're saved."

Bakker said Trump is giving the church a window in 2020 and that the church has to "wake up."

[Bakker's remarks occur at about the 40-minute mark.]

January 14, 2020 Stephen Strang

Release of *God, Trump, and the 2020 Election* by Stephen Strang

January 17, 2020 Donald Trump

"Trump 'Fits the Scriptural Definition of a Fool'"
Fred Rand Opinion Piece at *Jackson Free Press*

This is a very long opinion piece by a business leader.

January 23, 2020 Donald Trump

"Evangelicals Love Donald Trump for Many Reasons, But One of Them Is Especially Terrifying"
Stephanie Mencimer at *Mother Jones*

The article highlights the prophetic views of evangelical leaders like Greg Laurie, Don Stewart, John Hagee, Lance Wallnau, Jim Bakker, Paula White-Cain, and Guillermo Maldonado.

"It's not hard to see how apocalyptic evangelicalism might be influencing the Trump administration as it seeks to mobilize the millions of evangelicals reached by televangelists and megachurch pastors preaching the End Times."

January 24, 2020 Donald Trump

Trump speaks at March for Life rally in Washington, becoming the first president to do so.

It is my profound honor to be the first president in history to attend the March for Life. We are here for a very simple reason: to defend the right of every child, born and unborn, to fulfill their God-given potential.

All of us here understand an eternal truth: Every child is a precious and sacred gift from God. Together, we must protect, cherish, and defend the dignity and the sanctity of every human life.

When we see the image of a baby in the womb, we glimpse the majesty of God's creation. When we hold a newborn in our arms, we know the endless love that each child brings to a family. When we watch a child grow, we see the splendor that radiates from each human soul.

January 26, 2020 Donald Trump
"Trump Tied Ukraine Aid to Inquiries He Sought, Bolton Book Says"
Maggie Haberman and Michael S. Schmidt at *New York Times*

January 27, 2020 Donald Trump
Trump denies that he told John Bolton that aid was linked to Ukraine investigations.

January 27, 2020 Paula White
"Paula White Says Video About 'Satanic Pregnancies' Was Taken Out of Context"
Mihir Zaveri and Johnny Diaz at *New York Times*

On January 25, Right Wing Watch posted a video clip of a January 5 sermon by Paula White where she stated, "In the name of Jesus, we command all Satanic pregnancies to miscarry right now. We declare that anything that's been conceived in satanic wombs, that it'll miscarry."

White has said that her words were taken out of context, that she was referencing the spiritual warfare language of Ephesians 6:12, and that her words were meant metaphorically.

January 30, 2020 Peter Wehner
"There Is No Christian Case for Trump"
The Atlantic

Wehner offers a lengthy critique of Trump defender Wayne Grudem and argues that Grudem and other pro-Trump figures are guilty of confirmation bias.

January 31, 2020 Donald Trump
Senate defeats motion to hear witnesses at President Trump's impeachment trial.

February 4, 2020 Shane Idleman
"How can you Follow Jesus and Support Donald Trump?"
Christian Post

"We are not following a man, we are shaping a movement. A better question to be asking, though, is What direction is the country heading? If a leader lacks Christian character but is pointing the nation back to God, is that a bad thing? If they are minimizing murdering babies and maximizing godly values, is that a bad thing? If they are being a terror to terrorists and making America secure, is that a bad thing? If they are honoring hard work and minimizing free handouts, is that a bad thing? God doesn't judge a nation based on the character of one man; He judges it based on the spiritual health of her people. Never forget that."

February 4, 2020 Johnny Enlow
Chiefs Win! A Stunning Prophetic Message
Elijah List

Enlow interprets the victory by the Kansas City Chiefs over San Francisco 49ers in the Super Bowl as having prophetic significance in that "we have entered into a new day for the Kingdom of God and its advancement on planet Earth."

Enlow claims we are entering a "full Jubilee" of blessing. "I have already seen an upcoming 35,000 on the Stock Market at some point, and long-term, the worldwide economic upgrade will be significant. The coming economic shifts will be staggering and unprecedented."

After seeing the number 2 repeatedly in various ordinary ways (a flight number, car rental number), Enlow references Acts 2:2 and Isaiah 22:22

and states that the latter verse connects to Donald Trump. "I am still shocked at the Believers who can't discern that Trump is God-sent. It was understandable at first, as he came in disguised, but now with what his stands and legislation have proven over and over about himself, it is indisputably obvious that Trump is advancing a Kingdom agenda. It is even more obvious that those in high places who oppose him are anti-Kingdom of God. The only reasonable explanation for good people not recognizing President Trump as the most strategic, human kingdom asset in generations is brain washing and mind control."

February 5, 2020 Donald Trump
Trump is acquitted by Senate. The abuse of power charge was defeated 52 to 48 and the obstruction of Congress charge was defeated 53 to 47. Republican Mitt Romney joined Democrats on the first charge.

[Romney received enormous criticism from his Republican colleagues and from the president for his vote in favor of impeachment.]

February 5, 2020 Mitt Romney
"A Profile in Courage"
Peter Wehner at *The Atlantic*

February 5, 2020 Donald Trump
State of the Union address

The president was hailed by Republicans and denounced by Democrats. Trump was criticized for not shaking Pelosi's hand as he rose to the podium. Nancy Pelosi created controversy by not introducing Trump in the traditional manner and publicly tearing up Trump's address after he finished.

President Trump spoke of numerous signs of his administration's success, including economic growth, low unemployment, deregulation, curbing illegal immigration, lowering healthcare costs, affirming right to life, and fighting terrorism.

"This is the time to reignite the American imagination. This is the time to search for the tallest summit and set our sights on the brightest star. This is the time to rekindle the bonds of love and loyalty and memory that link us together as citizens, as neighbors, as patriots. This is our future, our fate, and our choice to make. I am asking you to choose greatness."

February 5, 2020
"Christian Leaders React to Trump's Emphasis on Faith During SOTU"
Caleb Park at *Fox News*

Johnnie Moore called the address a "great American moment." He also stated, "The thread running through every aspect of the president's speech was faith—faith in America because of America's faith in God. He showed again that he is all-in on religious freedom for everyone and absolutely unashamed of America's Judeo-Christian foundation."

February 6, 2020 Donald Trump
Trump attends and speaks at the National Prayer Breakfast.

Weeks ago, and again yesterday, courageous Republican politicians and leaders had the wisdom, the fortitude, and strength to do what everyone knows was right. I don't like people who use their faith as justification for doing what they know is wrong. Nor do I like people who say, "I pray for you," when they know that that's not so.

Religion in this country and religion all over the world — certain religions in particular — are under siege. We won't let that happen. We are going to protect our religions. We are going to protect Christianity. We are going to protect our great ministers and pastors and rabbis and all of the people that we so cherish and that we so respect.

This morning, let us ask Father in Heaven to guide our steps, protect our children, and bless our families. And with all of our heart, let us forever embrace the eternal truth that every child is made equal by the hand of Almighty God.

During his speech, President Trump mentioned the formation of the International Religious Freedom Alliance the previous day.

February 6, 2020 Wanda Alger
Heaven's Response to the Acquittal
https://wandaalger.me

While watching the final vote in the Impeachment trial, the Fear of the Lord came upon me and I heard this message from heaven's court:

"That which was rendered today has been recorded on high. Those who spoke their judgments against My choice have sealed their own fate. Their verbal assent has rendered them guilty of rebellion and insurrection and the consequences will be of their own doing.

Know that in this day, the words you speak carry weight in the spirit and draw their own power. By your judgments you will be writing your own future and determining that which comes to you.

For one who spoke today, the spirit of Saul revealed itself. The man that many believed to be My hopes for this country in 2012 is now seen for his true nature. His verdict against the president of his own party now reveals the bitter root deep within his heart. Though he believes his intentions to be noble, his heart has been misdirected by his own insecurities and false religion. This is why I gave you four more years until I could bring another whose heart was made ready.

Just as David was a man of war set in place to establish My Kingdom reign, so is this one who now sits in the Oval Office. Though his path was rocky and his methods crude, his heart has been formed and his character even now being molded. Battling dark powers far worse than David ever saw, I am teaching him, and you, to rule in the midst of your enemies."

February 12, 2020 Shawn Bolz

"California Pastor who Prophesied Kanye West's Transformation 4 years ago Predicts this About Trump"
Caleb Parke at *Fox News*

Bolz on Trump: "I felt like Trump was going to be president twice and that he would have an encounter in his second term, more of an encounter for God and who he is and for his family, There's going to be more boldness in the second term and it's going to be disruptive, but I think it's helpful because there's so many systems in place that are old and tired, and need to be knocked down."

February 14, 2020 Donald Trump
"Trump Mocks the Faith of Others. His Own Religious Practices Remain Opaque"
Sarah Pulliam Bailey, Julie Zauzmer, and Josh Dawsey at *Washington Post*

The authors provide an overview of Trump's religious history. Critics of Trump are quoted, along with friends. The article ends with noting that Trump accused both Pelosi and Romney of hypocrisy in relation to their faiths.

In a statement to *The Washington Post*, Stephanie Grisham, White House press secretary, stated, "President Trump is a man of God, and faith plays an important role in his life. The President values the close counsel of many in the faith-based community, as well as the daily prayers of the many Americans who pray for him, his family, our country, and our military. I have personally witnessed the President in worship many times and have also seen him use his faith and prayer to privately comfort and console Americans after a tragedy."

February 16, 2020 Holly Watson
This Month Is a Game Changer
Elijah List

"With the 2/2/2020 Super Bowl (54) win of the Kansas City Chiefs, there's much buzz about the 'signs' of the times and this most recent event being a prophetic marker to the billion-soul harvest." Watson sees spiritual awakening coming to the Midwest and there will be "the rise of a new apostolic and prophetic company." She recounts a dream about Bob Jones and claims that the victory by the Chiefs is a game changer spiritually.

"The most recent acquittal of President Donald Trump of all impeachment charges 'changes the game' for many who questioned the hand of God moving sovereignly over the impeachment hearings."

[Note: Since the Chiefs won the Super Bowl, it has been widely reported that Bob Jones (now deceased) prophesied that the victory would signal revival. Mike Bickle, longtime friend of Jones, has gone on record that he has no memory of Jones ever saying that.]

Appendix I:
Lana Vawser and Kevin Vawser
Reply to Questions

One of the more intriguing aspects of prophetic support for Donald Trump is what Lana Vawser, the well-known prophet from Australia, claims happened to her in the fall of 2015 when she had a dream about the future president. Her prophecies are included in this book, and you can see her first account at October 11, 2015. She and her husband, Kevin, are in Christian ministry together, based on the Sunshine Coast in Queensland, Australia. They agreed to answer some questions by email.

1. What did you think when you got the message/vision from God in October 2015 that God was in some sense blessing Trump?

Lana: "I was very shocked. It wasn't something I had expected, in fact it seemed completely opposite to what I had ever thought but the minute I woke up from that dream, everything changed and I had instantly had a heart for Trump and could clearly see how the Lords hand of blessing and favor was upon him."

Kevin: "Like Lana, I was very surprised. I had to use this to weigh up what I had understood at that time against what the bible actually gives us as examples of godly leadership. I learned a lot about where my expectations were compared to what God's are."

2. Did you know much about Trump before the vision?

Lana: "All I knew about Trump was that he was a successful business-man and running for office."

Kevin: "Not much. We have an Australian Apprentice tv show here, so we did not see him on TV much. We knew his reputation as a businessman, businessmen who rise to that level often make decisions based on greed. I would say I considered him as a stereotype. We don't watch much TV and news—we did not have much time to form an opinion on what the news was saying, although I do remember people around us seemed quite upset at him personally."

3. How have you been able to handle the heat/anger you received for your pro-Trump words?

Lana: "To be honest that was extremely difficult. Some of the most vile, poisonous comments were sent to me during that time from believers, but what carried me through was the conviction that I knew that God had spoken to me clearly and it was the word of the Lord. Standing in obedience to His revelation brought the most comfort."

Kevin: "I tried to moderate the FB messages as much as possible. If a comment was attacking personally—I deleted it or banned the user. Getting personal is not productive to anyone and it shuts down conversation before it can begin. If people disagreed, I let them share their point. If there was an obvious flaw in their argument, I may say something, otherwise just let them say their piece."

Appendix II:
Select Prophets and Religious Leaders
Listed in This Book
(*) denotes deceased

Doug Addison (Santa Maria, CA)—http://dougaddison.com/
Che Ahn (Pasadena, CA)—https://cheahn.org/
Joni Ames (Rock Hill, SC)—http://joniames.com/
Wanda Alger (Winchester, VA)—https://wandaalger.me/
Frank Amedia (Canfield, OH)—http://www.touchheaven.com/
Michele Bachmann (Minneapolis, MN)—https://www.facebook.com/
    michelebachmann/
Faith Marie Baczko (Oakville, ON)—https://headstoneministries.com/
Gary Bauer (Merrifield, VA)—https://www.ouramericanvalues.org/
James Beverley (Moncton, NB)—www.jamesbeverley.com
Mike Bickle (Kansas City, MO)—https://mikebickle.org
Shawn Bolz (Studio City, CA)—https://bolzministries.com/
Dean Briggs (Kansas City, MO)—https://deanbriggs.com/
Michael Brown (Concord, NC)—https://askdrbrown.org
Jonathan Cahn (Wayne, NJ)—http://www.hopeoftheworld.org/
Darren Canning (Carlton Place, ON)—https://www.facebook.com/
    darrencanningministries/
Steve Cioccolanti (Melbourne, Australia)—https://newswars.com.au/
Kim Clement (Tulsa, OK)— https://www.houseofdestiny.org/
Don Colbert (Orlando, FL)—https://drcolbert.com
Mary Colbert (Orlando, FL)—https://marycolbert.us/
Kenneth Copeland (Fort Worth, TX)—http://www.kcm.org/
James Dobson (Colorado Springs, CO)—http://www.drjamesdobson.org/
Lou Engle (Pasadena, CA)—http://www.thecall.com
Johnny Enlow (California)— https://www.restore7. org/
Jerry Falwell Jr. (Lynchburg, VA)—www.liberty.edu

Anita Fuentes (Schertz, TX)—http://www.emoaf.org/
Mark Galli (Wheaton, IL)—www.markgalli.com
Jim Garlow (San Diego, CA)—www.jimgarlow.com
Norman Geisler* (Charlotte, NC)—http://normangeisler.com/
Denise and Paul Goulet (Las Vegas, NV)—http://iclv.com
Franklin Graham (Boone, NC)—https://www.samaritanspurse.org/
Jack Graham (Plano, TX)—http://www.jackgraham.org/
Wayne Grudem (Phoenix, AZ)—http://www.waynegrudem.com/
Tania A. Hall (Adelaide, Australia)—https://www.facebook.com/
   taniahallrevivalist/
Jon & Jolene Hamill (Washington, D.C.)—http://jonandjolene.us/
Jane Hamon (Santa Rosa Beach, FL)—https://www.facebook.com/
   ApostleJaneHamon/
Robert Henderson (Waco, TX)—http://www.roberthenderson.org/
Aimee Herd (Albany, OR)—https://twitter.com/aimeejane61
Benny Hinn (Irving, TX)—https://www.bennyhinn.org/
Robert Hotchkin (Maricona, AZ)—http://www.xpministries.com/robert-
   hotchkin/
Rodney Howard-Browne (Tampa, FL)—https://www.revival.com/
Donna Howell (Crane, MO)—https://jimbakkershow.com/guest-bios/
   donna-howell/
Eddie Hyatt (Grapevine, TX)—www.eddiehyatt.com
Shane Idleman (Lancaster, CA)—https://shaneidleman.com/
Cindy Jacobs (Red Oak, TX)—https://www.generals.org/home
Jeff Jansen (Murfreesboro, TN)—http://www.globalfireministries.com/
Robert Jeffress (Dallas, TX)—http://www.firstdallas.org/dr-jeffress/
Lisa Jessie (Texas)—http://www.morningtimelight.com/
Bill Johnson (Redding, CA)—http://bjm.org
Jeremiah Johnson (Lakeland, FL)— https://jeremiahjohnson.tv/about/
Christy Johnston (Gold Coast, Australia)— https://nateandchristy.co/
Bob Jones* (Fort Mill, SC)—http://www.bobjones.org/
T. B. Joshua (Lagos, Nigeria)—http://www.scoan.org
Rick Joyner (Jackson, MS)—https://www.morningstarministries.org
Kat Kerr (Jacksonville, FL)—http://www.katkerr.com
John Kilpatrick (Daphne, AL)—http://www.johnkilpatrick.org/
Alveda King (Atlanta, GA)—https://www.facebook.com/dralvedaking/
Patricia King (Maricopa, AZ)—http://www.xpministries.com

Hank Kunneman (Omaha, NE)— https://hankandbrenda.org/
Richard Land (Charlotte, NC)—http://www.drrichardland.com/
Curt Landry (Fairlake, OK)—https://www.curtlandry.com
Jennifer LeClaire (Hallandale Beach, FL)—https://www.jenniferleclaire.org/
Max Lucado (San Antonio, TX)—https://maxlucado.com/
Johnnie Moore (Glendale, CA)—https://thekcompany.co/
Russell Moore (Nashville, TN)—www.russellmoore.com
Jorge Parrott (Charlotte, NC)— https://cmm.world/about/meet-the-director/
Tony Perkins (Washington, D.C.)—www.frc.org
Ben Peters (Lincoln, CA)—http://www.kingdomsendingcenter.org/
TheresaPhillips(SaintCharles,IL)—https://www.globalpropheticvoice.com/
Chuck Pierce (Corinth, TX)—http://www.gloryofzion.org
John Mark Pool (Biloxy, MS)—http://www.w2wmin.org/
Pope Francis (Vatican City, Vatican)—http://w2. vatican.va/content/vatican/it.html
Steve Porter (Rochester, NY)—http://www.findrefuge.tv/
Stephen Powell (Pineville, NC)—http://www.lionoflight.org/stephen-bio
Prophet Sadhu (Tamilnadu, India)—http://www.jesusministries.org
Ralph Reed (Duluth, GA)—https://www.ffcoalition.com/
Jamie Rohrbaugh (Chattanooga, TN)—http://www.fromhispresence.com/
Sid Roth (Charlotte, NC)—https://sidroth.org/
Martin & Norma Sarvis (Denton, TX)— https://gloryofzion.org/israel-prayer-update/
Darrell Scott (Cleveland Heights, OH)—http://nsrcministries.org/
Charles Shamp (South Africa)—http://www.destinyencounters.com/
Nathan Shaw (New Zealand)—http://www.heartofdavidministries.org/
Dutch Sheets (Colorado Springs, CO)— https://dutchsheets.org/index.php/about/
Steve Shultz (Salem, OR)—www.elijahlist.com
Brian Simmons (New London, CT)— https://passionandfire.com/about/
Jill Steele (Harrison County, WV)—https://steelefaith.com/
Angie Stolba (Washington, IL) —https://angiestolba.com/
Steve Strang (Orlando, FL)—www.charismamag.com
Tony Suarez (Washington, DC)—www.tonysuarez.com
Elaine Tavolacci (Staten Island, NY)—http://awordinseason.info/
Chad Taylor (Georgia)—http://www.consumingfire.com/

Mark Taylor (Orlando, FL)—www.sordrescue.com

Mike Thompson (Las Vegas, NV)—http://www.wordoflifeworldoutreach.org

Pasqual Urrabazo (Las Vegas, NV)—http://iclv.com/resources/thepursuit/
pastor_pasqual_urrabazo/

Kris Vallotton (Redding, CA)—http://krisvallotton.com

Lana Vawser (Springwood, Australia)—https://lanavawser.com

Rich Vera (Orlando, FL)—http://richvera.com

Lance Wallnau (Keller, TX)—http://lancewallnau.com

Kathie Walters (Macon, GA)—https://www.kathiewaltersministry.com

Peter Wehner (McLean, VA)—https://eppc.org/author/peter_wehner/

Jonathan Welton (North Chili, NY)—https://weltonacademy.com

Paula White (Apopka, FL)—https://paulawhite.org/

Bill Yount (Hagerstown, MD)—http://billyount.com

Appendix III:
Further Resources

Trump and Christian Faith

Brody, David, and Scott Lamb. *The Faith of Donald J. Trump: A Spiritual Biography*. New York: HarperCollins, 2018.

Fea, John. *Believe Me: The Evangelical Road to Donald Trump*. Grand Rapids: Eerdmans, 2018.

Haynes, Stephen. *The Battle for Bonhoeffer: Debating Discipleship in the Age of Trump*. Grand Rapids: Eerdmans, 2018.

Henderson, Robert. *Praying for the Prophetic Destiny of the United States and the Presidency of Donald J. Trump*. Shippensburg: Destiny Image, 2020.

Johnson, Jeremiah. *Trump, 2019, and Beyond*. Lakeland: Jeremiah Johnson Ministries, 2019.

_____. *Trump and the Future of America*. Lakeland: Jeremiah Johnson Ministries, 2020.

Labberton, Mark, ed. *Still Evangelical?: Insiders Reconsider Political, Social, and Theological Meaning*. Downers Grove: InterVarsity Press, 2018.

Sparks, Larry, compiler. *Prophetic Words for 2020*. Shippensburg: Destiny Image, 2020. Lake Mary: Frontline, 2018.

Strang, Stephen. *God and Donald Trump*. Lake Mary: Frontline, 2017.

_____. *Trump Aftershock: The President's Seismic Impact on Culture and Faith in America*. Lake Mary: Frontline, 2018.

_____. *God, Trump, and the 2020 Election: Why He Must Win and What's at Stake for Christians if He Loses*. Lake Mary: Frontline, 2020.

Taylor, Mark, and Mary Colbert. *The Trump Prophecies: The Astonishing True Story of the Man Who Saw Tomorrow ... and What He Says Is Coming Next*. Crane: Defender, 2017.

Taylor, Mark, *The Trump Prophecies: The Astonishing True Story of the Man Who Saw Tomorrow ... and What He Says Is Coming Next: Updated and Expanded.* Crane: Defender, 2019.

Wallnau, Lance. *God's Chaos Candidate: Donald J. Trump and the American Unraveling.* Keller: Killer Sheep Media, 2016.

White, Paula. *Something Greater: Finding Triumph Over Trials.* Nashville: Faith Words, 2019.

Political Battles Pro- and Anti-Trump

Anonymous. *A Warning.* New York: Twelve, 2019.

Bongino, Dan. *Exonerated: The Failed Takedown of President Donald Trump by the Swamp.* Nashville: Post Hill Press, 2019.

Comey, James. *A Higher Loyalty: Truth, Lies, and Leadership.* New York: Flatiron, 2018.

Dershowitz, Alan. *The Case Against the Democratic House Impeaching Trump.* New York: Hot Books, 2019.

Hanson, Victor Davis. *The Case for Trump.* New York: Basic Books, 2019.

Hassan, Steven. *The Cult of Trump: A Leading Cult Expert Explains How the President Uses Mind Control.* New York: Free Press, 2019.

Jarrett, Gregg. *Witch Hunt: The Story of the Greatest Mass Delusion in American Political History.* New York: HarperCollins, 2019.

Limbaugh, David. *Guilty by Reason of Insanity: Why The Democrats Must Not Win.* New York: Regnery, 2019.

Newman, Omarosa Manigault. *Unhinged: An Insider's Account of the Trump White House.* New York: Gallery Books, 2018.

Pirro, Jeanine. *Liars, Leakers, and Liberals: The Case Against the Anti-Trump Conspiracy.* New York: Center Street, 2018.

Sims, Cliff. *Team of Vipers: My 500 Extraordinary Days in the Trump White House.* New York: St. Martin's, 2019.

Smith, Lee. *The Plot Against the President: The True Story of How Congressman Devin Nunes Uncovered the Biggest Political Scandal in U.S. History.* New York: Hachette, 2019.

Trump Jr. , Donald. *Triggered: How the Left Thrives on Hate and Wants to Silence Us.* Nashville: Hachette, 2019.

Wehner, Peter. *The Death of Politics: How to Heal Our Frayed Republic After Trump.* New York: HarperCollins, 2019.

Wolff, Michael. *Fear and Fury: Inside the Trump White House.* New York: Henry Holt, 2018.

Woodward, Bob. *Fear: Trump in the White House*. New York: Simon & Schuster, 2018.

Further Resources

If you want to track modern Christian prophecy, subscribe to The Elijah List (www.elijahlist.com). Readers may also subscribe to *Charisma News* (www.charismanews.com), Prophecy News Watch (www. prophecynewswatch.com), and Spirit Fuel (spiritfuel.me). For Christian coverage of Trump, I recommend that readers consult *The Christian Post*, *Christianity Today*, and CBN (Christian Broadcasting Network) and in particular the work of Faith Nation at CBN. This includes the reporting of CBN's David Brody (see Brody file), who works with Jenna Browder, Ben Kennedy, and Amber C. Strong.

For data on Evangelical Protestants and Evangelicalism, go to the analysis at Pew Research Center. To track prophets and religious leaders mentioned in this work, see the comprehensive listing in appendix II. For ongoing pieces about the politics related to Trump, Evangelical Christians, and the American divide over Trump, turn to Real Clear Politics, which provides opinion pieces and news from varied perspectives.

For chronologies of Hillary Clinton's email server controversies, alleged Trump-Russia collusion, alleged spying on the Trump presidency, Trump impeachment, and related issues, visit the following sites. They offer somewhat varied perspectives and enormous detail.

The Trump Russia Timeline—https://www.justsecurity.org/trump-russia-timeline/

The Spygate Project—http://thespygateproject.org/

Muellergate Timeline 2019—https://www.conservapedia.com/Muellergate_timeline_2019

Obama FISA Abuse—https://www.conservapedia.com/index.php?title=Obama_FISA_abuse

A Timeline of Treason (Doug Ross)—http://directorblue.blogspot.com/2017/12/a-timeline-of-treason-how-fbi.html

Impeachment Inquiry Against Donald Trump—https://en.wikipedia.org/wiki/Impeachment_inquiry_against_Donald_Trump

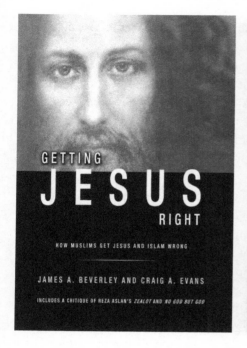
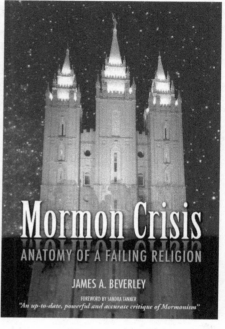

Printed in the USA
CPSIA information can be obtained
at www.ICGtesting.com
CBHW031215040824
12683CB00007B/114